Dear Reader,

I'm thrilled to share with you a charming, revealing, and seductive cultural history of Paris from the Lost Generation to today. Written by Australian expatriate and Paris resident John Baxter, who harbors his own love of food, wine, art, romance, and all things visceral, *We'll Always Have Paris* will have you calling your travel agent as soon as you turn the final decadent page.

In a gossipy blend of hearsay and fact, Baxter takes us behind the scenes of the vibrant, all-night show that is Paris. A visit to the literary cafes of Hemingway, Fitzgerald, and de Beauvoir is quickly followed by an extensive tour through the Parisian underbelly that most guidebooks leave out. The tour includes famous brothels of the '30s such as the Sphinx, patronized by Marlene Dietrich and Duke Ellington, and Le Chabanais, where Salvador Dalí sated his fantasies and Edward VII kept a sumptuous champagne bath for his favorite girls.

Interweaving his own experience of falling in love, Baxter offers us an alternative cultural tour. His unique and idiosyncratic bank of knowledge of films, books, and the visual arts provides a witty and audacious insight into Europe's most romantic capital. As the *London Sunday Times* contends, "His sensitive description of the experiences of others who have fallen for Paris or for Parisians, the feel-good factor associated with his own story, and his nostalgia for a time of love and liberation is considerably more irresistible than many of the performers at Nernadin's Crazy Horse Show."

After reading Baxter's vivid account, you will never see Paris in quite the same way again.

Sincerely,
David Roth-Ey
VP and Editorial Director

© Marie-Dominique Montel

About the Author

JOHN BAXTER is an acclaimed film critic and biographer. His subjects have included Woody Allen, Steven Spielberg, Stanley Kubrick, and Robert De Niro. He is the author of *A Pound of Paper: Confessions of a Book Addict* and is working on a dictionary of modern erotica. He lives in Paris.

Also by John Baxter

A Pound of Paper: Confessions of a Book Addict
Science Fiction in the Cinema
The Cinema of Josef von Sternberg
Luis Buñuel: The Authorised Biography
Fellini
Stanley Kubrick
Steven Spielberg
Woody Allen
George Lucas
Robert De Niro

WE'LL ALWAYS HAVE PARIS

SEX AND LOVE IN THE CITY OF LIGHT

John Baxter

HARPER ● PERENNIAL

NEW YORK ✳ LONDON ✳ TORONTO ✳ SYDNEY

HARPER ⬤ PERENNIAL

HarperCollins books may be purchased for educational, business, or sales promotional use. For information please write: Special Markets Department, HarperCollins Publishers, 10 East 53rd Street, New York, NY 10022.

The pictures in the photo insert are from the author's personal collection.

First published in Great Britain in 2005 by Doubleday, a division of Transworld Publishers.

First Harper Perennial edition published 2006.

Library of Congress Cataloging-in-Publication Data is available upon request.

ISBN-10: 0-06-083288-6
ISBN-13: 978-0-06-083288-9

06 07 08 09 10 ❖/RRD 10 9 8 7 6 5 4 3 2 1

For Marie-Dominique

'... *Taking time. Making sure* ...'

This book contains a cold 'million dollars' worth of sly, peppy, *inside* information that will make your next trip to Paris a whirlwind of Joy. Places – People – Frolics – Stunts – you might not find otherwise.

THE REAL PARIS
Paris, *France*.
Not Paris, *America*.
Paris with the Lid Lifted.
Paris Pipin' Hot.
The peppy, purplish, palpitating Paris that all true 'Joy-seekers' yearn to see.

Bruce Reynolds in *Paris with the Lid Lifted*,
a guidebook published in 1927

CONTENTS

Prelude

ILSA: 'What about us?'
RICK (*tenderly*): 'We'll always have Paris. We didn't have. We'd
. . . we'd lost it until you came to Casablanca. (*Softly*) We got it
back last night.'

Humphrey Bogart and Ingrid Bergman in *Casablanca*; screenplay by
Julius J. and Philip G. Epstein, and Howard Koch, from a play by
Murray Burnett and Joan Alison

JUST AFTER I MOVED TO PARIS IN 1990, THE WOMAN
who inspired this migration, my wife-to-be
Marie-Dominique, took me to a dinner party at
the suburban Paris home of Leo, a journalist
friend.

Though, looking back, I see that evening as a
turning point, it seemed at the time just another rite
of passage in the painful experience of being absorbed

– in more depressed moments I thought 'devoured' – by France.

After a mammoth dinner, and over cognac, coffee and, for the other guests, enough tobacco to asphyxiate an emu, I confided to Leo, a man of about my age, my trepidation at adjusting to a French family.

'John,' he said, 'believe me, I know the difficulties. I too married a foreigner.' He drew on a broomstick-sized Havana. 'She was my first wife. An English girl. Very nice, you know. Well brought up. An English rose. A rose with thorns, as I later discovered, but at the time . . .' He shrugged.

'So . . . I am invited to London to meet the parents. It is nineteen sixty-two, perhaps 'sixty-three. I am . . . what? Twenty-five. Not a boy, but . . . well, a little nervous just the same.

'And it gets worse when I see the family home! A mansion, *mon vieux*! In a *quartier très chic*. And the parents the same. *Haute bourgeoisie*. Not quite the monocle and the military moustache, but you can imagine.

'And here I am, this French upstart, who desires to kidnap their delicate flower. They are not happy.'

So far, I could sympathize. A few weeks before, sitting down to Christmas dinner with the fourteen members of my new French family, I'd felt the same suspicion radiating from them.

'Well, dinner, it is all right,' Leo continued. 'I do not disgrace myself: drink the finger bowl or blow on my soup.

'After the dessert, *maman* and Patricia do what women do, while *papa* and I drink port and smoke a cigar.' He held up his Romeo y Julieta. 'Not so good as this, but I am diplomatic.

'And then . . . time for the bed. Of course, Patricia and I, we are already sleeping together in Paris, but *chez papa et maman* this cannot be. She has her old room, next to her parents', while I am as far away as they can manage – in the attic almost.

'So we go to bed. And I sleep. But almost immediately I wake up. It is deep night. I can't see my watch, but I think it is two, perhaps three in the morning. And I feel terrible. Trapped. Like an animal. I cannot breathe in this place. I must get out. I find my clothes and my car keys, and open the front door.' Leo mimed taking a deep breath. 'And already I feel better. The fresh air, the stars, the trees; London is quite beautiful in some ways, don't you think?'

'Yes. But it's not Paris.'

'Ah, well, no. Nothing is as beautiful as Paris. But it is pleasant anyway, so I decide to take a drive. Into the . . . is it the West End? The centre of London anyway.

'I am alone on the road. Almost no cars. Nobody

3

walking. And it's worse in the city. No cafés, no bars. Everything closed and dark.

'I have almost despaired when I see one lighted doorway. A sign says "Saddle Club", and there are steps leading down to a … how do you say … *une cave?*'

'A cellar?'

'Yes. A cellar. So I park, and I go down the steps.' He smiled at the memory. 'It is a little jazz club, a *boîte de nuit*. The sort I know well from Paris. Like Le Petit Opportun or Le Chat qui pêche. The chairs are up on the tables and the bar is closed, but on the stage are playing some musicians – a guitarist and a *contrebassiste*.

'And I can scarcely believe my eyes! Because the guitarist, it is Brassens!'

For anybody born in France after World War II, Georges Brassens, poet and songwriter, is close to a saint. He died in 1981, but his fame and popularity continue regardless. His warm voice and friendly face with its bushy moustache are icons. His songs have become anthems, known by heart everywhere.

'Incredible,' I said. 'I never knew he played London.'

'I too hardly believe my eyes,' says Leo. 'But yes, it is the voice. And he sings his own song – one of my favourites, *"Ballade des dames du temps jadis."* You know it, from the poem of François Villon? "Where are the girls of yesteryear?" To see Brassens there, in this city so hostile to a young man … this is the answer to a prayer.'

'Did you speak to him?'

'Ah, well, I come to that.'

He carefully ashed his cigar. 'I wondered if I dared. The club is closed. He plays simply for his own pleasure. But as I hesitate, he puts down his guitar, steps from the stage, and walks towards the … *double-vay-cay … le …*'

'The men's room,' I supplied.

'*C'est exact.* And I think: Well, in *les toilettes*, we are all equal, *n'est-ce pas?* Just men. And men may chat.

'So I follow. And there he is. The great Brassens making *pipi*. And so I take the place next to him … And I turn to face him … And I open my mouth to say, "*Bonsoir, Monsieur Brassens*" …'

Leo drew heavily on his cigar, savouring the memory.

'And it is at this moment that I wake up, and find I am urinating in the bed of my future father-in-law.' He expelled the smoke. 'So you see, it is not so bad, my friend. You have not pissed in the bed.'

Even as I agreed, I couldn't help thinking, *It's early days yet*.

1

A Love Story

No amount of fire and freshness can challenge what a man can store up in his ghostly heart.

F. Scott Fitzgerald, *The Great Gatsby*

FOR ME, THE 1920s AND 1930s RADIATE A GLAMOUR they can only possess for someone who didn't live through them.

Shorn of grim features such as the Great Depression, the 1919 influenza epidemic, the Russian revolution and the Holocaust, Europe between the two world wars appears to blaze. Or at least it did to someone growing up in an Australian country town in the 1960s. But like the Hawaiian tsunamis that petered out on Bondi Beach as modest swells, the upheavals that revolutionized art and culture on the other side of the world were ripples by the time they reached us.

I could see the ghost of a new philosphy of design in the streamlining of our Bakelite mantel radio, and recognize Surrealism in the two-dimensional landscape and amputated torsos of a poster for brassières by Hestia (popularly thought to be an acronym for Holds Every Size Tit In Australia), but both looked ill at ease in a country that still based its architecture and its ideas on the English home counties, and where the cutting edge of automobile design was represented by the boxy, underpowered Triumph Mayflower.

Australia, I quickly decided, held nothing for me. Notwithstanding our national song, 'Advance, Australia Fair', the country seemed to be not advancing at all but devolving, the people patiently retracing their steps down the evolutionary line, heading back to the Triassic and a way of life you could *depend* on. In my jaded view, Australians swam like fish and thought like sheep. I wanted out.

My life entered a phase of dual existence. Sitting in the Koala Milk Bar drinking a milkshake, I could squint my eyes and transport myself in imagination to the Café Radio on Place Blanche in Montmartre where, dawdling over a corrosively black *café express*, I watched covertly as a succession of chain-smoking, driven-looking individuals arrived, some with female companions as taut and pale as lilies, to find seats in the huddle that radiated out from a burly man in a green tweed suit, complacently drawing on a pipe – the sage of Surrealism, André Breton, possessor of, it was said in awe, 'the most haunted mind in Europe'.

Another day, while I might be pushing my bicycle along a cracked concrete pavement under the pungent pepper trees of Junee, my world circumscribed by a horizon shimmering in 40-degree heat, in fantasy I stood rapt in the early summer of 1925 under blue skies in a light breeze on Place du Trocadéro. Below me cascaded a hillside of terraces, stylized statuary and spouting fountains, a carpet of white that leapt the Seine to join, under the feet of the Eiffel Tower, the pavilions of the Exposition des Arts Décoratifs. Some of its buildings were sharp and white as sugar cubes, others voluptuously curved, but all dazzlingly announced the arrival of a style so new it had no name. Though the Americans would christen it 'streamlining', to the rest of the world it would always be, in honour of the Exposition, *art déco*.

That I would one day live in Paris, be part of a French family at the very heart of where these great movements were born and flourished; that I would live in the building where the publication of James Joyce's *Ulysses* was planned, and every day climb the stairs up which Scott and Zelda Fitzgerald, Ernest Hemingway, Ezra Pound, James Joyce, Djuna

Barnes, Gertrude Stein and Alice B. Toklas once panted, sprinted or lumbered; this seemed a fantasy close to insanity.

But it doesn't do to minimize the power of love.

All Paris stories are to some extent stories of love – love requited or unrequited, knowing or innocent, spiritual, intellectual, carnal, doomed. The love that brought me to Paris combined a little of them all, as a poorly written movie tries to cram in everything that might draw an audience. My story featured coincidence, the supernatural (or something very like it), Hollywood, and a long-lost love miraculously rekindled, only to be nearly snatched away . . . Cheap romantic nonsense, I would have said had I seen it on screen. But, as Noël Coward remarked in *Private Lives*, 'Extraordinary how potent cheap music is.'

Living in Los Angeles in 1989, on the rebound from a broken marriage, I'd become friendly with Suzy, a woman in mid-level movie management whose long-time lover, an irascible and addictive film-maker, had recently died. Though he'd treated her with casual cruelty, she felt bereft without him, particularly since she'd also lost most of her relatives to Hitler.

'If only I could be sure that we would be reunited someday,' she said tearfully, 'I think I could go on.'

As a practical woman in the movie business, Suzy

put this concept into pre-production. With me as company, she began to audition systems of belief, looking for one that would guarantee reunion with her lover after death. We visited card readers and mediums, and a spiritist church in Encino, where the audience sat enthralled as an elderly lady, seated at a card table with her devoted husband holding her hand, gabbled in what we were told was the voice of the famous medium Edgar Cayce. At one point, the word 'Antichrist' surfaced from the babble. An instant later, a tiny earth tremor shook the hall. We exchanged significant glances with our neighbours. Aaah!

'Fuck this,' Suzy murmured. 'I feel like eating Mexican. How about you?'

The last candidate was a man in the remote suburb of Commerce, who needed subjects to be hypnotized as part of some ill-defined project. Suzy didn't feel like surrendering control of her mind unless somebody she trusted had done so before, so she despatched me into that wilderness of 24-hour poker clubs and used-car lots to check him out.

Joe was a young psychologist who believed that we've all lived before in other bodies. As part of his work at a mental hospital, he used hypnosis a lot, and was convinced that, in a trance, people might reveal that in another life they had met Jesus Christ. I told him frankly that the works of the Blessed Shirley

MacLaine had inoculated me against this concept. Any lingering belief was extinguished by the regiments of cocktail waitresses and bus drivers claiming to be the reincarnations of Napoleon, Cleopatra and the Queen of Sheba.

'Well, OK,' Joe said amiably. 'But as long as you're here, why not give it a try?'

That session and those that followed in Joe's poky little apartment were revelatory. He never pushed me back into any former existence, but along the way I did re-experience some startling events in my own life which I'd presumably suppressed. After half a dozen visits, however, it became clear that any former lives I might have had were so boring that I'd slept through them.

With a sigh, Joe finally accepted defeat. 'But I really appreciate your time, John. And I'd like to give you a gift.'

As I looked around his threadbare home, trying to think of a diplomatic way to refuse, he went on, 'I don't mean money. I mean a post-hypnotic gift. Think of the three things that have given you the greatest pleasure in life. Then, as you name each, I'll squeeze your left wrist. And from now on, every time you squeeze that wrist you'll re-experience the same pleasure.'

My choices, nominated while still in a trance, astonished me. Not great sex, wild music, drug highs or roller-coaster rides – just the solitary pleasures of someone who, though usually surrounded by people, felt himself alone.

The first was the pleasure of getting up before the sun, and sitting down in the pre-dawn silence with a cup of coffee to start writing.

The second was the memory of a song, 'Finishing the Hat', from Stephen Sondheim's *Sunday in the Park with George*, about the painter Georges Seurat. While he paints the great canvas *Sunday on the Island of Grande Jatte*, agonizing about how to render in tiny points of colour the reality of something as prosaic as a hat, his exasperated mistress is lured away to America by a baker who, though no Seurat, can give her the love and attention she needs.

He asked for my third choice. Again, it was connected with Paris.

Years before, I'd been romantically involved with a young French woman named Marie-Dominique. We'd travelled around the world together and had wonderful times, but her life as a radio journalist in Paris and mine as a writer in America or Australia gradually drew us apart.

Now, in a memory so vivid that I felt I'd been physically transported back ten years and across the world, I was standing with her on a winter's day in the huge flea market of Clignancourt, on the outskirts of Paris. We were eating thin *frites* with mustard out of a cone of paper. I could taste the salt and the fat, see the wind ruffling the fur collar of her coat, feel the cold through my feet. Emotions too complex to analyse lifted me like a wave.

Driving back home in a daze, I rang Marie-Do in Paris. Wouldn't she like to visit me in Los Angeles? Not long after, she did.

From the moment she got off the plane, we both sensed a fundamental change in our relationship. Ten years before, I'd been married and she'd been starting her career. Now my marriage was over, and she, still unmarried, was established as one of France's top radio journalists. Like a bottle of wine that only comes into its best after it's had time to breathe, our love was ready to drink.

For the next ten days, we barely spent a minute apart. And in the quiet times, almost without discussing it, we became aware that this part of our lives was coming to a close. We would return to Paris, set up a home, marry, have children.

Within three weeks, to the astonishment of my friends, I'd emptied my apartment, disposed of my possessions, and booked a flight to Paris, a city where I'd never lived, in a country where I knew nobody, and whose language I couldn't speak. I was fifty, Marie-Dominique twelve years younger, and nobody believed it would last a fortnight, if indeed it survived as far as the airport.

They could not have been more wrong. But then, they hadn't reckoned on one thing. They hadn't reckoned on Paris.

2

Home Thoughts from Abroad

A buried memory seems to stab at your consciousness in Paris, and you follow in the steps of an elusive phantom *déjà vu* but never quite catch up. So deeply imbedded in the world's dream of freedom, youth, art and pleasure has this city become that the feeling that the stranger in Paris has is the feeling of *return*.

John Clellon Holmes, *Displaced Person*

WE LANDED IN PARIS JUST BEFORE CHRISTMAS 1989, in a snowfall that sifted down like terminal dandruff. In Los Angeles, sprinklers swished over green lawns and the sun sparkled off Santa Monica Bay. Midwinter Paris, on the other hand, appeared dark and menacing, a city hunched over the Seine like a predatory animal over its prey.

For my first weeks, I woke before dawn and sat by the window of Marie-Dominique's tiny flat – the kind the French call a studio – chilled to the bone.

Had I done the right thing, to uproot myself in three weeks from a city where I had friends, where I was comfortable and where I could earn an easy and pleasant living? I loved the woman who'd inspired this lunacy, longed for us to have children, and to spend the rest of my life with her. But at 4 a.m., in winter chill, good reasons for such a move looked diminishingly small.

But then the sun would come up, and light would fill a sky across which the trails of outbound airliners scrawled broad brush-strokes of dusty pink. The cathedral of Notre Dame emerged from the mist, God's liner, at anchor in a sea of roofs, and the peace that is such a part of Paris would flood into me all over again.

It isn't easy, more than a decade later, to reconstruct the change that I experienced in those first weeks. But occasionally I see it reflected in the eyes of others. Like those of my friend Paulette.

Paulette and I met in the Seventies, when I was teaching at the college in Virginia from which she'd just graduated. Five foot nothing, she sported, then as now, a boy's haircut and a taste for schoolmarm skirts. Her southern accent was rich as molasses, and she really did, without affectation, call everyone 'y'all', but the cornpone was camouflage. A tough, clever mind was evident in her penetrating gaze that recalled Truman Capote's description of himself in his faun-like youth: 'tall as a shotgun, with rather heated eyes'.

A century and a half ago, Paulette, a Colt Dragoon pistol held firmly in both hands, would have stood in a crinoline at the gate of her plantation, ready to defend it from anything Sherman threw at her. But, born too late to sacrifice herself for the Confederacy, she had to be content with a position as vice-president of a major auction house and a world reputation as an expert on rare photographs.

To attend the college where Paulette and I met, you needed only to be two things: a woman, and rich. Among its many agreeable features was its Abroad Program, under which students could study in London or Paris. Reactions to this experience varied radically. The most extreme was illustrated by Lulu, a peppy, short-haired brunette with a few million dollars in her trust fund, who used to enliven classes by turning up in well-filled T-shirt and jeans under a full-length mink. Lulu elected to spend her year abroad in Paris.

At the party to celebrate her group's return, a college trustee, in halting French, enquired if she'd had a good time. Transposing Lulu's response into English of equivalent pungency, what she said, in an accent usually confined to police line-ups, was, 'You *shittin'* me, dude? The food's doggie doo-doo, but the people are muthafuckin' *great*!'

While the trustee was being revived with cognac and cold towels, it emerged that Lulu, like almost all the girls in her group, had found a Paris lover, who'd taught her French by the popular Sexual Injection method. But, in France as everywhere else, the best lovers often come from the worst places.

Unlike Lulu, Paulette chose to study in London, and returned not with a cockney accent but a degree in art history from the Courtauld Institute. Once I moved to Paris, we saw each other too seldom. But twice or three times a year, a breathless email announced that business would bring her to France for a few jam-packed days.

After I'd been in Paris for five years, she arrived on a Friday in autumn, worked through Saturday, but left Sunday free – 'to catch up with y'all', she said, 'and enjoy Paris'.

Thoughts of a leisurely day evaporated, however, when I collected her at 9.30 from her hotel behind the Madeleine. In a ground-sweeping overcoat and scarf long enough to shin down a burning building, she was dressed for a day on the run.

'I've got it all planned!' She waved an itinerary as densely lettered as a railway timetable. 'The Musée d'Orsay opens at ten. There's a show I want to see there. By the time we're done, the European Centre will be open. After that . . .'

'OK. We can discuss it over breakfast.'

'Breakfast?' she snorted. 'I don't eat breakfast.'
You could hear the subtext. *Breakfast is for wimps.*

'Well, I do. The car's out front.'

We drove through a city silent except for the bells of Notre Dame. Solemn and measured, they blanketed the empty streets with leaden sheets of sound. Other cities use these quiet times for street cleaning and road repairs, but so entrenched is the French tradition of the Sunday-morning lie-in that they'd simply never find people to do the work. As a result, Paris on Sunday looks like those cities in science-fiction films, wiped clean of mankind by some cosmic catastrophe.

It was so empty that I easily found a parking spot behind Café des Deux Magots. A few worshippers milled in front of the church of Saint-Germain-des-Prés opposite. On the pavement, lumpy home-made cakes were being sold for charity by no less lumpy students. Otherwise, we were almost alone.

We took a table in the glassed terrace that runs along Boulevard Saint-Germain. The morning sun made it cosy, and, reluctantly, Paulette unwound her scarf. As the waiter approached, she said, 'I'll just have juice.'

'Paulette, this is Les Deux Magots, Paris's most famous café. The cradle of existentialism. That square out there is named for Jean-Paul Sartre and Simone de Beauvoir . . .'

'All right, all right!' she said placatingly. 'Far be it from me to desecrate a cultural monument. A juice *and* a black coffee.'

I told the hovering waiter, '*Deux complets*,' hoping she wouldn't realize this meant two full breakfasts.

We'd hardly begun catching up when he returned with a basket of warm croissants, brioches, and *tartines* – halved lengths of baguette. It was followed by tumblers of fresh orange juice, jam, honey, pats of butter . . .

'John, I'll never eat all this!' But by now she'd discarded the scarf completely, and unbuttoned the front of her coat.

Two pots of coffee and a good deal of backbiting later, the croissants were a scatter of crumbs, as were the reputations of some mutual acquaintances, and Paulette's overcoat and scarf were draped over the back of her chair. But people were filing out of church, and our terrace was starting to fill.

Paulette got up. 'Where's the ladies?'

'Downstairs. Do you have any French money?'

'They're coin-operated?'

'It's for Madame Pipi.'

'*Excuse me?*'

But this wasn't the time to explain about the gorgon who lurked inside most restaurant toilets to levy a fee from every user. She accepted a coin from the small purse we all carry in a country where survival can rest on having *la monnaie*: the right change.

As Paulette disappeared, a girl slouched by outside the glass, hooking my attention as surely as if she'd grabbed my lapels. With her bruised indigo eyes, pale flesh, crumpled jeans and bulky sweater, she might have been the younger sister of the singer Juliette Gréco, existentialism's poster girl, who, ravishing in bare feet, matador pants and a droopy black pullover, posed for a famous photograph forty years ago on the cobbles of the square outside.

This girl's long white fingers clamped the point of a folded pyramid of white paper, inside which, any Parisian could have told you, nestled two warm *croissants au beurre*. They'd have known with equal certainty, from her sullen look and uncombed hair, that she wore neither pants nor bra.

Single-handed, she constituted an entire Parisian story. Prodded out of bed by her lover, she'd have snatched up last night's clothes from the floor and, after a quick pee, pattered, still half asleep, down three or four flights of curving wooden stairs into the chill street, and around the corner to the *boulangerie*. Arms folded, oblivious to the perfume of warm bread, ready to snarl at anyone who looked sideways at her, she'd nonetheless have muttered a dutiful *'Bonjour, madame'* to the baker's wife, slapped down two coins, and carried breakfast back to her companion, who, if he – or she – was any use at all, already had the cafetière bubbling, a pot of strawberry jam on the table, and the radio tuned to France Culture. Into bed afterwards; jammy kisses and a frowsy fuck to the music of some songs by Fauré, then a shower, and lunch with one family or another, and maybe a movie in the afternoon, queueing under the plane trees of the Boulevard Saint-Germain in a haze of autumnal mist and the smoke from a million Gauloises . . .

Paulette returned, and my fantasy – the first passage of a novel? the opening scene of a film? – whisked out of the window, to join the invisible *tourbillon* of ideas and dreams swirling over this most fertile of all intellectual intersections.

'Can we go now?' she said. 'We'll be just in time to beat the first tour buses.'

The old Gare d'Orsay, charmless in its days as a train terminal, became even less welcoming after the railways abandoned it in the Sixties. When I first visited Paris, it was still the desolate and echoing sepulchre used by Orson Welles for his grandiloquent film version of Kafka's *The Trial*. Its main concourse, built to accommodate locomotives and their clouds of steam, smoke and cinders, had dwarfed his stars, a feline, barefoot Romy Schneider and Tony Perkins' window-dummy Joseph K. Only Welles himself, in a cameo as The Advocate, marooned majestically in a giant bed like a hippo with gout, fitted the location.

One could almost believe that Orsay acted as a magnet for eccentricity, like the Roundhouse, in London's suburban Swiss Cottage. Also a converted railway building, the Roundhouse might be filled with chemical fog and cannabis fumes one week for a concert by Pink Floyd, then flooded ankle-deep in water the next for a too-literal production of Strindberg's *The Lady from the Sea*.

For a while, Orsay housed Paris's major auction house, Drouot. Then the theatre company of Jean-Louis Barrault and his wife Madeleine Renaud moved in. Barrault is almost forgotten today, but his pointed, elfin face was a fixture of the pre-war French cinema and theatre. His fame peaked with the role of the gifted but unlucky mime Dubureau in the 1944 film *Les Enfants du paradis*. After that, he concentrated on live theatre for the rest of a long – some might say too long – career.

That Barrault should follow Orson Welles into Orsay exhibited the same inspired lunacy that paired Laurel with Hardy, Abbott with Costello. Though the bloated Welles and the bird-like Barrault were physical opposites, both were ruled by the same kind of manic genius, cursed with similar delusions of grandeur. Kenneth Tynan, the most influential theatre critic of the Fifties, paid ambivalent tribute to Barrault's 'grasshopper mind', but, after watching half an hour of him imitating a horse, wondered if he wasn't 'bent on titillation rather than revelation'. ('They are always mocking my love of pantomime,' whined a wounded Barrault.)

Barrault's exile to the Orsay was his punishment for having disgraced himself while director of the Théâtre de l'Odéon, one of the branches of France's national theatre, the Comédie Française.

Barrault electrified it with a razzle-dazzle circus show called *Rabelais*, which used enormous inflated figures to embody Gargantua and the other larger-than-life creatures invented by the bawdy sixteenth-century writer François Rabelais. In the Sixties, when I was writing the biography of film director Ken Russell, he and his then assistant Derek Jarman hot-footed it to Paris to catch the show, with the idea that they might film it. Derek returned with sketches of wildly ballooning costumes which, though Ken never made *Rabelais*, came in useful when he staged 'Pinball Wizard' in his film of The Who's rock opera *Tommy*. Elton John perched ten feet above the stage on a pair of giant bovver boots is pure Barrault.

'Barrault at his best,' everyone agreed of *Rabelais*. Unfortunately, it was quickly followed by Barrault at his worst, when, in 1968, the rebellious students of the nearby Sorbonne demanded to use the Odéon theatre as a meeting place and he not only let them in, but gave them the run of the costume store. Priceless outfits became fancy-dress overnight. Once the *événements* had run their course and the students were back to their studies, a furious bureaucracy put Barrault and his company on the street.

We could feel all this history swirling around our feet as Paulette and I walked into Orsay that morning. How appropriate, I thought, that, once the station found its vocation as a museum, the artists most at home in its cavernous space should be turn-of-the-century sculptors like Auguste Rodin and Émile-Antoine Bourdelle, masters of knotted muscle, straining sinew and bulging posing pouch. Put overalls on their husky slaves and warriors, and they could be porters heaving steamer trunks into the guard's van. In particular, the festoons of anguished souls in the huge plaster maquette for Rodin's *Gate of Hell* looked just like holiday-makers, desperate to pile their water skis and collapsible kayaks onto the train before the whistle blew.

I turned to share this idea with Paulette, but she'd already pushed through the heavy brass doors and, ignoring the crowds heading for Manet's *Olympia* and the Gauguins, dived into a side gallery.

For the next half-hour I followed her around walls covered with photographs from the early part of the twentieth century, all tinted a deep and – to me – morose cobalt blue. In forests dissolved in a

Debussy-esque gloom, iodized nudes poised on tiptoe as if they'd just stepped from a bath of ink, while nymphs and shepherds cavorted in an Arcadia which, to judge from the tint of their skin, was gripped by an unseasonable cold snap.

As we walked, she lectured me with the passion of a true scholar about the photographer, Paul Burty Haviland (1880–1950). 'The photographs are cyanotypes, a process common especially to amateur photographers at the turn of the century. Haviland was heir to the Haviland china firm in Limoges. Went to Harvard . . . Important associate and patron of Alfred Stieglitz . . . active in the Photo-Secession movement . . . left New York in 1916 to live in France permanently and help out with the china firm. Married Suzanne Lalique (daughter of famous glassmaker René Lalique) in 1917. Eventually became a gentleman farmer . . .'

Well, here was another American who'd succumbed to the lure of France. But then, where else would someone of taste and discrimination have chosen to live between the end of one world war and the beginning of the next? With the franc near-worthless and the dollar on the rise, Paris houses could be rented for the cost of a single room in Manhattan.

Just as I started to get interested in the pictures, it was time to leave. We'd been right to come early. The queue of people waiting to get in stretched out of sight.

'So glad I saw that.' Paulette stuffed the catalogue into her bag with half a dozen hefty photo books she'd bought at the museum shop. 'How do we get to the European Centre for Photography? It's on the other side of the river, isn't it? They've got a show of Richard Avedon portraits.'

'After lunch,' I said.

'I never eat—'

'Well, I *do* eat lunch, Paulette. You'll just have to indulge me.'

Most French diners sit down on Sunday at about 1 p.m., but even at just after noon my favourite brasserie didn't have a spare table.

'But do not *dérange* yourself, monsieur,' Marcel, the owner, assured me, patting my arm. '*Le Beaujolais nouveau est arrivé*. Take a glass at the bar with mademoiselle and we will see what we can do.'

In the end, the Beaujolais was so fresh and fruity that we let two more couples go before us, saving ourselves for a prime table by the window. By the time we sat down, Paulette and I were deep into the sort of confessions that, in less well-ordered countries, emerge only on pillows in the dead of night or in the calm of psychiatrists' offices.

How extraordinary, I thought, this capacity of Paris to free not only the imagination but the inhibitions. For centuries, from all over the world, strangers had straggled into the city, loaded with the lead of their frailties, only to see the alchemy of Paris transform them into gold.

That the Surrealists chose Paris as the theatre for their gorgeous experiments just proved the case. Jean-Claude Carrière, Luis Buñuel's screenwriter and a scholar of Surrealism, thought the magnetism exercised by Paris over the imaginative mind one of the city's greatest mysteries. 'There is absolutely no reason', he told me, 'why Benjamin Péret comes from Toulouse to join the group, why Max Ernst comes from Germany, why and how Man Ray comes from the States and Buñuel from Spain, and they meet at last in Paris.' But something was calling them together. Something they could only experience collectively in Paris.

But the use we make of the revelation depends on the person – something the Surrealists understood. If you invite insight, you'd better know how to deal with it. 'At the touch of human weakness, the gateway to mystery swings open,' warned André Breton's lieutenant Louis Aragon, 'and we have entered the realm of darkness.' Plenty of adoptive Parisians, from Arthur Rimbaud to Jim Morrison, disappeared into that darkness, never to return.

The waiter laid down our starter, a soft goat's cheese on a bed of the curly lettuce the French call *frisée*. Solemnly and in due course, the *gigot* and *gratin dauphinois*, a deliquescent camembert and a wedge of caramelized apple *tarte Tatin* with crème fraiche came and went, as did two bottles of Côte de Beaune and a calvados with the coffee.

By the time I paid the bill, the restaurant was almost empty, and the soft grey and rose evening was descending over Paris. It was the hour Man Ray celebrated in his painting *Les Amoureux: l'heure de l'Observatoire*, with the crimson lips of his treacherous lover Lee Miller floating above the Paris Observatory.

Tipsy, we stood on the corner of Rue Mazarine. Of the Paulette I'd collected at her hotel that morning there was little sign. Then, she'd seemed weighed down by her enormous coat. Now, it was a desiccated cocoon, to be cast off at will, and, with it, everything that tied her to the treadmill of a professional existence. Paris had worked its magic again.

Letting her bag with its heavy books fall to the pavement, she leaned her head against my chest. 'John,' she murmured, 'you saved my life.'

3

Why Paris?

America does more. France *is* more.

French folk wisdom

CURIOUS AS TO HOW I ENDED UP IN PARIS, PEOPLE delve into my past. 'You did French at school, I suppose?'

Not unless you count two terms of ham-handed tuition from the Christian Brothers at Waverley College in Sydney, where any lapse of attention attracted six stinging blows on the palm from a sweat-greased leather strap. All that pain and effort wedged only one nugget of French grammar in my brain – the list of nouns for which one designated the plural with an 'oux' rather than an 's': *bijou, caillou, genou, chou, hibou,* etc. Since these mean 'jewel', 'stone', 'knee', 'cabbage' and 'owl', the information isn't of much practical use if you're asking the way to the Eiffel Tower.

Over the years, this was joined by a ragtag lexicon of film-subtitle French. I knew *'je t'aime'* meant 'I love you' and *'les mains en l'air'* meant 'hands up' – more useful in French daily life, as it happens, but still some thousands of words short of a vocabulary. These phrases crammed a back room of my brain, along with movie titles such as *Les Enfants du paradis* and *La Règle du jeu* – literally 'The Children of Paradise' and 'The Rules of the Game', though I hadn't yet learned that 'the children of paradise' were the punters in the cheap seats at a theatre and that the 'game' of Jean Renoir's film about a house party in a French château on the eve of World War II was more complex than croquet or bridge.

Once people accepted that I didn't speak French when I arrived, they assumed I knew some French people in Australia. Had I perhaps learned about the country from their nostalgic reminiscences?

Sorry, but no. I had one childhood memory of hearing French spoken in an Australian context: a fragment of a Cinesound newsreel, that murky movie precursor of TV news, in which Hubert Opperman, one-time cycling champion turned federal politician, welcomed visiting Frenchmen to Canberra in their own language, presumably learned in his days pushing pedals in Europe. An Aussie talking

French? He'd hardly have astonished me more if he'd turned his back, dropped his pants and exposed a crimson backside, like a baboon.

Meeting someone French in person had to wait until my late twenties. The first I had anything like an adult conversation with was – and I agree this was a wonderful way to start – the beautiful nineteen-year-old actress Claude Jade, who visited Sydney in 1968 to promote François Truffaut's film *Baisers volés*.

Fortunately I rated an invitation to the cocktail party on a ferry gliding around the harbour, and a chance to linger at the rail with her and chat about Paris. She was kindly but abstracted, which I put down to boredom with Australia and Australians.

In fact, she had more personal and pressing reasons to be depressed. As was his habit with his leading ladies, Truffaut had begun sleeping with her during production, but so far broke with tradition as to propose. She wore down her parents' doubts about marriage to a 36-year-old divorcee with two children and, moreover, one with a reputation not only for screwing his actresses but frequenting Paris's better brothels.

The wedding was organized in her native Dijon to follow the release of the film at Cannes in May 1968, the dress bought, the banns posted. But Cannes 1968 was a watershed year for Truffaut. He helped lead the protests against the sacking of film historian

Henri Langlois from the Cinémathèque Française, and was among the film-makers who hung on to the curtain of the main Cannes cinema, delaying the start of the Festival. As their revolt spread through France and the world, igniting what the French circumspectly call *les événements de soixante-huit*, Truffaut shocked Jade by announcing that he'd reassessed his future, and the wedding was off. No wonder she didn't seem to be giving me or Australia her full attention.

No language then, and no French family friends. But surely I'd encountered French culture – the music of Debussy and Satie, the painting of Renoir and Toulouse-Lautrec, the poetry of Baudelaire, the prose of Stendhal, of Balzac, of Proust?

Well, of course. But 'encountering' is one thing, understanding quite another. Any reader, however poorly guided, will sooner or later stumble on *Madame Bovary* or *Remembrance of Things Past*, but decoding their elaborately ironic vision of middle-class French social and sexual habits took more knowledge or persistence than we could spare. Easier by far to read authors like Somerset Maugham, who trimmed back the luxuriant sexual growth of Balzac and Proust to a well-disciplined hedge. The crippled hero in *Of Human Bondage*, besotted with a trashy waitress, was like the Classic Comics version of Proust's Swann in *Remembrance of Things Past*, who could not reconcile his attraction to the delicious but promiscuous Odette de Crécy with his good taste and best judgement. 'To think', he moans, 'that I have wasted years of my life, that I have longed for death, that the greatest love that I have ever known was for a woman who did not appeal to me, who was not my type.'

As with most Anglo-Saxons, my education in the nature of the French wasn't in language, literature, poetry, music or art, but on the level of slang, gossip and myth. And the message we received was very clear: 'French' meant 'sexy'.

With whatever flimsy justification, we believed that the French did nothing that wasn't in pursuit of sensual gratification. After all, the vocabulary and terminology of cultivated appreciation was almost entirely French. Terms such as *connoisseur*, *amateur*, *gourmet* and *bouquet* didn't exist in other languages, at least not with the same precision. 'French' as an adjective implied richness – of detail, of resources, of taste. (It also suggested a tendency to have one's own way; 'taking French leave' meant leaving work without permission.) And the French interest in sex was a given. 'French postcards' were, by definition, erotic. We all knew about a 'French kiss' and 'Frenching', or thought we did. A condom was a 'French letter' – because, in those pre-foil days, they came in little paper envelopes. What a surprise to find that the French call them 'English letters' – just as, in the nineteenth century, syphilis, referred to by everyone else as 'the French disease', was briskly re-exported by the French, who, in an early example of European co-fraternity, repackaged it as *la maladie italienne*.

'French lace', 'French brandy' and 'French cooking' all connoted superiority, not necessarily in effectiveness but in refinement. 'French cuffs', for example, were the fussy sort that had to be turned back on themselves and secured with cuff-links.

To my father, a pastrycook, 'French pastry' defined the lightest and most elegant end of the spectrum, though seldom the most commercial. Occasionally, just for fun, he'd abandon Australian horrors like the Lamington – a cube of stale cake soaked in chocolate syrup and rolled in desiccated coconut – and bake a batch of *cornets* – spiral cones of puff pastry filled with Chantilly – or *profiteroles* – balls of choux pastry, glazed with caramel, oozing chocolate cream – or tarts in which the fruit, bedded on a *couche* of *crème pâtissière*, was coated with apricot jam, then seared in the oven. 'French bread' of course was the classic *baguette*, still in my childhood called 'the husband-beater'. While my father would make a few of these for his own pleasure, or to show that he hadn't lost his touch, they'd generally remain unsold at the end of the day, while his farmhouse loaves, doughy at the heart under a domed crust baked mahogany-dark and porcelain-hard, disappeared by lunchtime.

Gourmets associated 'French cooking' with rich sauces, usually involving wine, but also with adventurousness in the choice of ingredients. One thing everyone knew about the French was that they would eat anything – even, ugh!, snails.

The other thing, equally to do with what one put in one's mouth, was the widely imagined French enthusiasm for oral sex.

'How does a French woman hold her liquor?'
'By his ears.'

This was the first French joke I heard. I was about twelve, and of course didn't understand it, which set the tone of my early relations with France. American terms like 'going down', 'giving head' and 'blow job' hadn't reached Australia, so we still used the antique French sexual lexicon, imported by the few brave travellers who'd visited Paris in the days of Toulouse-Lautrec and Guy de Maupassant. Among the first French phrases adolescents learned was *'soixante-neuf'*, though it took a while to decode this clever little linguistic pictograph for which no other language has ever produced an equivalent. The Australian poet Hal Porter also revived memories when, in his 1963 autobiography *The Watcher on the Cast-Iron Balcony*, he described 'the delight of a *gammarouche*' administered in his adolescence by a precocious schoolboy friend. I remember thinking, when I first heard this term for fellatio, that whatever it involved it must, being French, be both decadent and delicious.

A series of show-business scandals during the Twenties and Thirties embedded oral sex, along with the term 'Frenching', even more deeply in the popular consciousness. One was the release by Mary Astor's irate husband of diaries kept by the actress during her affair with playwright George S. Kaufman. 'It was pretty heavenly', Astor sighed of a dawn drive in a horse-drawn carriage through Central Park, 'to pet and French, right out in the open.'

Charlie Chaplin also revealed, during divorce proceedings, a penchant for 'going down' on his teenage wives, which was widely condemned. This particularly aroused the Surrealists, in whose philosophy sex, as the strongest of irrational urges, held a revered place. To have been making love was the only acceptable excuse for failing to turn up for a Surrealist seance, and Breton once circulated a questionnaire about sexual preferences and practices among members. (Only one revelation truly startled him: a colleague's admission that he sometimes thought of the woman's pleasure before his own. 'Incredible!' said Breton, in genuine astonishment. 'I can hardly believe it.') Though no great admirer of Chaplin, Breton issued a pamphlet defending him and his sexual preference. It was called *Hands Off Love!*

Most national stereotypes rest, however insecurely, on some truth, and it's indisputable that the French pursue pleasure more adventurously and persistently than most. While men and women of all races, like all children, at some time in their lives sniff, lick, poke and put the unfamiliar into their mouths, only the French have consistently fought beyond the 'Urk!' impulse to pause, savour, return for a second taste, then, likely as not, reflect, 'Perhaps with a little parsley and garlic . . .' or 'Maybe if I was on top . . .'

The glamour France held for outsiders in the Fifties and Sixties was in direct proportion to their separation from the reality. What Geoffrey Blainey would isolate as 'the tyranny of distance' maintained Australia in a state of nostalgia for a Europe that, if it had ever existed, now survived mainly in books, films and the memories of the last Australians to visit Europe in any strength, the soldiers who'd fought there in World War I. One of these had been my paternal grandfather. Occasionally my father would drop into the conversation some French phrase, imperfectly learned from his father in childhood. Only years later, when he joked that I should keep an eye out for any men of his age on the streets of Paris who bore a family resemblance to us, did I have any sense that Grandfather Baxter might have experienced France on anything like the level that I was destined to do.

All my latent fascination with France coalesced in 1968 into a short film I wrote and produced with Christopher McGill. *After Proust*, set in Europe in the early twentieth century, followed a man-about-town who, strolling in the park, picks up a girl, takes her back to his room, has sex with her, but feels disgusted with himself afterwards. The unnamed man wasn't Proust – who was homosexual, asthmatic, and went out only at night. But our character's internal monologue showed that the two men shared that jaded sense of time passing, and of houses, trees and avenues being 'as fugitive, alas, as the years'.

Working at the Australian government's documentary-film studios gave Chris and me access to all the equipment we needed. We even unearthed an antique 35-mm camera and a grade of black-and-white film that could reproduce the visual style of early French cinema. Fortunately, the performers, the camera crew, and the composer who wrote and played the Erik Satie-like score welcomed the challenge, and worked for nothing. 'Beats shooting up a fly-blown sheep's arse,' remarked the camera operator, who had just come off a documentary for the Department of Agriculture.

We filmed most of it one morning in Sydney's Centennial Park, a fragment of Edwardian Europe marooned on the wrong side of the world. Kookaburras cackled and blowflies droned as our frock-coated hero and corseted girl went through the frozen-faced evolutions of their encounter.

After Proust bemused the Australian film establishment. Obviously it was about *something* – but what? It was shown at that year's Sydney Film Festival, won some respectful if baffled awards, even had a commercial release, and might have persuaded me to stay in Australia and pursue a film career (as its director did). Instead, within a year I'd sailed for Europe. I told people I wanted to launch myself as a writer, experience new cultures, immerse myself in the European film scene. But to tell the truth, I just couldn't bear listening one more time to someone pronounce 'Proust' as 'Prowst'.

4

A Room on the Island

The sole cause of man's unhappiness is that he does not know how to stay quietly in his room.

Blaise Pascal, *Pensées*, 136

NINETEEN NINETY CRAWLED INTO A CHILLY MID-January. Marie-Do lived on the Île de la Cité, one of the two small islands that, nose to tail, like one dog sniffing another, briefly divide the Seine midway between the Louvre and Notre Dame. For an equivalent location in another capital, you'd need a houseboat next to Westminster Bridge with a private tunnel to Piccadilly Circus, or one moored just off Manhattan, with a permanent walkway to midtown.

That the address was almost embarrassingly fashionable compensated to some extent for the size — a single big room, with tiny bathroom, kitchen and toilet – and the fact that the well-lit floor-to-ceiling windows of our first-floor location placed us centre stage in a never-ending spectacle; an X-rated one, if we happened to come out of the shower when the curtains weren't drawn.

Each morning at 4 a.m. throughout that January, with a kiss tasting of Nescafé, Marie-Do slipped away to her job as news editor of France's biggest commercial radio station, Europe 1. That she had to leave so early was my fault. Having overstayed her leave, she'd agreed to work for a month on the equivalent of the graveyard shift, writing the morning news and delivering it every half-hour between 6 a.m. and 9 a.m.

Thirty minutes later I gave up trying to sleep, brewed a pot of Twining's English Breakfast and, pulling back a corner of the curtain, studied the leafy three-sided space, once the kitchen garden of the nearby royal palace, which Breton had christened 'the pubic triangle of Paris'.

At this hour, it was empty. Even the benches that in warmer weather supported a few sleeping tramps were unoccupied. The watery grey light barely revealed the tiny bookbinding shop opposite, the tea salon next door, even smaller than our apartment – how did they make a living? – and the tailor whose windows displayed bottles of murky liquid with worm-like roots swimming inside: evidence for his claim that he tinted all fabric on the premises with vegetable dyes. Further towards the narrow entrance onto Pont Neuf, I could just see the *papeterie* or stationery store where Colette, author of *Gigi* and *Claudine*, bought her distinctive ice-blue writing paper. They still sold it, from the same wooden pigeonhole, and in the same mode – not in sheets, but by the kilo.

In this oyster light, the square looked unreal, a relic of the Paris of Zola and Proust. But sheltering in a doorway next to the *papeterie* was a representative of modern France – a young cop, muttering into the personal radio clipped to his lapel. Someone was always on duty in Place Dauphine. The big building closing the wide end of the square was the Palais de Justice, France's high court. Next to it, on Quai des Orfèvres – 'the quay of the goldsmiths' – bulked the headquarters of the French police. If I leaned out of the window and looked sideways, I could even glimpse the fifth-floor office nominated as the *bureau* of Inspector Maigret.

Pipe-puffing, plodding Maigret, tracking down killers by day but returning to his wife every night for a nice *pot-au-feu* or *daube*, never fired my imagination, but I was fascinated by his inventor, Georges Simenon. When Denyse, his wife of twenty years, whipped aside the curtain on their private life in 1965, she revealed that the frugal and faithful Maigret had as little in common with his creator as Herman Melville with Moby Dick.

The richest French novelist of his day, Simenon made so much money that the tax people stopped counting, and let him pay what he felt like. Twice a year, he retired to a tower in the garden of his thirty-room home near Lake Geneva, locked the door, and emerged ten days later with a new bestseller. The rest of the time, his wife revealed, was spent in sex. Occasionally his partner was the maid who brought him his meals – each new member of staff was briefed on her employer's ... special requirements – and in his youth he'd dawdled with celebrities, enjoying a lively three months in the 1930s with the black American singer and dancer Josephine Baker. But mostly he preferred prostitutes, ten thousand of whom he confessed to having patronized since the age of fourteen.

At the end of his life, Simenon abandoned his house, put his now extremely rich wife into a clinic for alcoholic millionaires, and went to live with his latest maid in her room in Lausanne. Hard as it was to defend his life on moral grounds, I stood in awe of its Zen-like simplicity, its naked self-interest. Famous, rich, gratified – and all just by staying quietly in his room! Simenon had learned Pascal's lesson almost too well.

Unfortunately, I was no Simenon. All that month,

as a wind blew relentlessly from Russia, I sat in the tiny studio, swaddled in a quilt like Big Chief Rain in the Face, and yearned for the sun, the ease, the comfort and space of Los Angeles, my apartment in Westwood, with its giant living room opening onto a tropical garden, and the best cinemas in the city just a walk away – not to mention the campus of UCLA, to which one could stroll in the evening for a concert by Philip Glass or the Kronos Quartet. What had I done? At times, I felt something like dread. In *Citizen Kane*, Orson Welles warns Joseph Cotten not to go home to Chicago. 'The wind comes howling in off the lake, and the Lord only knows if they've ever heard of Lobster Newburg.' Those mornings, I felt that Chicago chill.

Having been to Paris many times before didn't help. The first time had been in 1970, when, fresh from Australia, I'd arrived for a weekend with a girlfriend. We'd walked hand in hand like young lovers, scuffing the ankle-deep dead leaves of the Tuileries, and stayed in a seedy hotel in the *Quartier Latin*, over a student café that roared with conversation until 3 a.m. Edward Heath had just become Prime Minister of England, and a BBC radio team was interviewing people in the café downstairs. What, they asked, did the French know about the new PM? The students racked their brains.

'*Ah, oui. M'sieur "Eat"! L'épicier, n'est-ce pas?*' said

one, recalling that Heath's nickname was indeed 'the Grocer'.

The other wondered how to phrase his summary of Mr Heath — a lifelong bachelor, musical, a little effeminate in his manner ... 'I sink ...' he said, 'pretty boy?'

So much for the political heritage of the Prime Minister who hoped to be remembered as the man who took Britain into Europe.

On other visits, I'd stand in reverence before Jacques Louis David's painting of Madame Recamier in the Louvre, sit with the world's most famous cinema buff, Henri Langlois, in the film museum he'd created, the Cinémathèque Française, and sigh over Marlene Dietrich in *Blonde Venus*; eat *canard au fil du temps* at Tour d'Argent, and afterwards make love to a girl who, white and scented as a lily in the moonlight, and nude but for a string of pearls, would murmur in my ear sweetly obscene and precise directions for her pleasure.

Later, I too, like those reporters collecting opinions of Ted Heath, would be sent to Paris by the BBC, to make a radio documentary about the revolutionary French cinema of the Sixties, the *nouvelle vague*. I'd spend a week taking tea with Eric Rohmer, chatting backstage with Jeanne Moreau, and, in a fairly surprising encounter, bandying Hollywood gossip with Jean-Luc Godard, who confessed that, while working as a publicist in the offices of an American film company and waiting for his chance to direct, he'd invented the film-star biographies he was told to do. Did anybody *care* where Jayne Mansfield was born or how George Nader got into movies? 'They were my first films,' he said simply of these fanciful profiles.

It was a joy to watch him fencing with journalists, wilfully misunderstanding their questions. Asked 'Would you describe yourself as a revolutionary?' he'd zero in unerringly on the wrong word. 'Would I *describe* myself as a revolutionary? An interesting word, isn't it, *describe*? We say *décrire*. It implies an effort to depict, to, in a sense, deceive . . .' You could feel the journalist wilt.

Anglos got Godard wrong. He wasn't, as Kenneth Tynan would have us believe, a Bogart-esque streetwise Parisian existentialist, eyes slitted, head tilted to avoid the smoke from the unfiltered Gauloise that guttered on his lower lip. In fact, he came from a wealthy Swiss medical family and had more in common socially and culturally with the film-makers of the old school than with his colleagues, the exjuvenile delinquent François Truffaut and one-time pharmacy student Claude Chabrol, who used an inheritance not, as one might have expected, to open his own chemist shop, but to make his first feature film.

True, when it came to aphorisms, Godard was the fastest pun in the west. Film was 'truth twenty-four times a second'. His generation were 'the children of Marx and Coca-Cola'. And he agreed that a story should have a beginning, a middle and an end – 'though not necessarily in that order'. But he delivered these verbal zircons with the dry wit of a man on a Manhattan street corner selling $10 Rolexes. '*I* know they're fake,' he seemed to say, 'and so do you. But fuck them if they can't take a joke.'

On good days during my first weeks in France, I consoled myself with memories of these encounters. On bad days, they simply contributed to my depression. Sitting here, in the chilly present, I was very much afraid that, in Leo's terms, I'd pissed in the bed.

One morning late in January, the doorbell interrupted these rueful reflections. It was barely 7.30. Had Marie-Do come home early? But why ring? She had a key. Pulling on my robe, I opened the door.

The woman was in her late thirties, coltish and smart, with streaked blonde hair, a good tan and a winning smile. Her dress was white, simple and professional, and she was obviously on her way somewhere in a hurry.

'John!' she said, presenting her cheek for a kiss as if we'd known each other since childhood. She smelt of expensive perfume. 'His Claire!'

'Er . . .'

'Now, John,' she went on seriously, in the same clear but odd English. 'Tonight. You and Marie-Do. We 'ave dinner. Hi hinvite you. Downstairs? Hate o'clock?'

'Well, I don't know . . . Marie-Do—'

'You don't worry, John. Hi ring 'er hat her station. *Alors*, now hi must go. Zis morning is *le sporting*.' She mimed vigorous running on the spot – *le sporting* presumably meant the gym – puffed out a breath to indicate the pressure under which she was operating, grinned, offered her cheeks to be kissed – one, two – and clattered down the stairs.

Later, I met the man who'd taught Claire her English; a lugubrious long-term expatriate named Bernard who stayed on in France after the war, eeking out a living with teaching and, on the side, writing what he called 'fuck books' for one of the imitators of Maurice Girodias and his Olympia Press.

'One of the hardest things for the French to learn', he explained, 'is the "h". In French, it's almost always silent, but in English it's the reverse.'

Claire absorbed the lesson too well. Reasoning that if a spoonful is good the whole bottle is better, she scattered 'h's indiscriminately.

When Marie-Do came home, I reported. 'Someone named Claire? She wants us to go to dinner tonight?'

'Claire Claudel. She lives upstairs. She is my best friend.'

'She says eight o'clock at the place downstairs. She invites us.'

'She *invites* us?' Marie-Do gave a *moue* of resignation, then blew out her breath through closed lips. So *that* was what all those French writers meant when they had their characters say '*Pouf!*' 'Then we must go, I suppose.'

'We don't have to. If you're tired.' Anyway, I could think of better ways for us to enjoy ourselves. From her eyes, I saw that she could too.

She gnawed her lower lip. 'Well, but she invites us.'

'Invite' is one of those words the French call 'false friends'. They *look* English, but actually mean something quite different from their English counterparts. 'Guest' in French is *invité*, so a better translation is: 'You will be my guests.' Once invited, you either think of a solid excuse or you go.

'How is the food downstairs anyway?'

'It's not bad.'

I had already inferred this from the rubbish piled by the kitchen staff against the lamp-post three times a week. There was no sign of those restaurant-size cans of ratatouille or couscous, no empty plastic packs of frozen *frites*, none of the boil-in-a-bag entrées that many restaurants routinely employed.

Strawberries were delivered in shallow wooden trays from a farm in Provence. A prosaic four-litre plastic bottle contained cold-pressed olive oil from a small mill near Avignon. Hand-churned butter arrived in slabs from the Atlantic coast in lidded tubs woven from strips of paper-thin white wood. So did oysters from Île d'Oléron. The oysters of my childhood were slimy gobs in narrow glass bottles, like anatomical specimens, swimming in dishcloth-grey water, that stood along the counters of fish shops above the stainless-steel trays piled with fried bream and chips. Others came in a sodden grey burlap bag tied with a bit of string and dumped on the back doorstep by some friend of my father's he'd met in a pub. If I'd seen oysters in these crisp white baskets, it might not have taken me so long to overcome my aversion to the delectable mollusc.

I souvenired a couple of oyster boxes from the restaurant's rubbish and started using one as a waste-paper basket – another amenity the flat didn't possess.

Marie-Do turned it over and read the label stapled to the bottom. 'Oléron. This is near where I have my house,' she said.

It took me a moment to pick up on this. '*Your* house? What house?'

'My summer house. In Charente.'

I knew Charente. It was on the Atlantic coast,

about two-thirds of the way down to Spain.

'How can you have a house in Charente?'

'I inherited it. From my grandparents.'

'You mean the family did.'

'No. Just me. Mother has her own house in the country. At Richebourg.'

'As well as her apartment in Paris?'

'Yes. Why are you surprised?'

'I just never knew a family with more than one house. Most Australians rent. They don't own even one.'

She squeezed my hand. 'That's very sad. Here it is quite usual. Like having more than one pair of shoes. Now I take a shower.'

And by the time she'd emerged, ravishing in a Thierry Mugler jacket, skirt and heels, wafting waves of perfume, there were other problems to be dealt with.

'Where is the blue shirt you wore to Leo's?'

I looked down at the black T-shirt and slacks I was wearing under one of my linen jackets. 'Won't this do?' By Los Angeles standards, I was formal enough for a funeral.

She didn't *say* it wouldn't, but I'd learned to read the signs. I rummaged a white shirt out of my bag, still not entirely unpacked. She looked relieved.

'And let me guess,' I said. 'A tie?' I was rewarded with a smile.

As I followed her down the narrow wooden stairs to the restaurant, I was reminded of something the novelist and screenwriter Frederic Raphael had said to me as we sat by one of the two swimming pools on his Dordogne estate.

We were talking about one of my favourite films, *Two for the Road*, which he wrote, and which, he confessed, was based on his own experience and that of his wife in the days when they divided their time between London and Rome. Driving alone through France offered too many sexual temptations, so they decided they should always travel together – which is what happens to the characters of the film, architect Albert Finney and his wife Audrey Hepburn, whose marriage, over a decade, waxes, wanes and suffers through infidelities on both sides.

'Although Albert was close to Audrey both during and after the movie,' Raphael recalled, 'for the purposes of the movie itself he never understood something of which I've always been deeply conscious because of my own marriage: that you're very lucky to be with a beautiful woman. Perhaps he'd been spoiled in that regard. Audrey understood it, but Albert didn't. And therefore the film was not as much about that marriage as it might have been.'

And that surely was one of the essential facts of my coming to France. I was with a beautiful woman, and in Paris, and about to eat a wonderful meal. Wasn't that enough?

Beside a sunny swimming pool in the Dordogne, it seemed so. In the chill of a narrow staircase in the coldest Parisian January since Napoleon, I wasn't so sure.

5

The Food of Love

You ask why we close the shop for lunch? Because the sky is too high, the ground too low, but the table is just the right height.

French folk wisdom

WHEN YOU DINE WITH THE FRENCH, YOU NEED radically to reorder your vision of what it means to eat.

Ernst Lubitsch's film *Ninotchka*, a celebration of Paris so passionate it could only have been made by Hungarians, Austrians and Germans, contains one of the funniest but, at the same time, truest scenes about eating in Paris.

Greta Garbo, a Russian commissar, enters a café for lunch.

'I think this is the first time you've been in my little place,' says the owner as he ushers her to a table.

'Now, what shall it be?'

Tersely, Garbo orders, 'Raw beets and carrots.'

Instantly there is a chill. 'Madame,' says the owner with simple dignity, 'this is a restaurant, not a meadow.' He hands her the menu. 'Now, here is what we are offering today. Please make your choice. I'm sure you will find something to tempt your appetite.'

I was thinking about all this as we walked into the restaurant.

Lubitsch and his writers were great eaters: at the end of the film, three Soviet apparatchiks who've fled to Paris justify their defection by claiming to be loyal to 'our Russia – the Russia of borscht, the Russia of Boeuf Stroganoff, of blinis and sour cream'. *Ninotchka* acknowledges the most important fact about dining out in Paris: you're not a customer, you're a guest. The restaurant isn't satisfying your need for nourishment but, rather, permitting you to share in its appreciation of good food and wine. The owner is doing you the favour, or at least he is if the place is any good.

The proprietor greeted us at the door, just like in *Ninotchka*. Since Marie-Do and Claire were regulars, there was much embracing – would I ever get used to kissing almost total strangers? – hand-shaking, '*Bonsoir*'-ing, '*Bienvenue*'-ing, and *bavardage*: chat.

I was introduced to, and shook hands with: the owner; his wife; the young man behind the till; *his* wife, who also waited on tables; and two waiters. The whole crowd looked me over. In a few seconds I was assessed, weighed up and given conditional approval. *'Well, at least he's wearing a jacket and tie. And he knows enough to say "Bonsoir" and shake hands all round. He's not some specimen of a tourist.'*

Nothing in France establishes one's credentials as an honorary Frenchman so much as how one deals with food. Jean Renoir's film *The Rules of the Game* anatomizes pre-World War II French society through the metaphor of a country-house party thrown by the Jewish Marquis de la Chesnaye. But Renoir gives the final word not to the aristos and social climbers but to their servants. De la Chesnaye's tacitly anti-Semitic guests tolerate him for his wealth, and out of affection for his witty, well-connected wife. But the chef recognizes his true worth.

'De la Chesnaye may be a foreigner,' he tells the maid, 'but he had me summoned the other day to give me a telling-off about a potato salad. In order that this salad be edible, one must pour the white wine on the potatoes when they are still boiling hot, which Celestin didn't do because he doesn't like burning his fingers. Well, the master sniffed that straight away. You say what you like, but *that* – that's a man of the world!'

France displays the bewildering possibilities of

what can be eaten. There's hardly a bird, beast, fruit, fungus or crustacean the French won't throw a lip over. The ortolan, for instance, a bird so tiny it can only be trapped in a mist net. It's served deep fried, but whole. One devours the entire bird: bones, feet, intestines. And though the gilded horse's head that indicates a *boucherie chevaline* has almost disappeared, sweetish lean horse meat still has a following. The gelatinous worm-like *lamproie*, the old-English lamprey, is a great delicacy in its season: King Henry I of England died from eating a 'surfeit' of them. Cooked in red wine, its aroma is so delicious that each plate is served with a large napkin which the diner drapes over his head so he can sniff up the bouquet before he digs in.

One of the great events in French culinary history took place during the siege of Paris by the Germans in 1870–1. Once every horse, dog, cat and rat had been consumed, the gourmets descended on the zoo and served a banquet of elephant's ears, boiled bison, stewed monkey, macaw with chips, and baboon on a stick.

In the Sixties, a film called *Do You Like Women?* carried *gourmandise* to its ultimate. Members of a French dining club sit down regularly to whole baked girl, with roast potatoes, asparagus and green beans. The least likely thing about such a dish isn't the cannibal element but the serving of any meat dish with vegetables. Not great eaters of greens, the French prefer them as a separate course, the better to concentrate on the pleasure of a good bit of meat with an interesting sauce.

Do You Like Women? wasn't entirely invented. At the International Surrealist Exhibition in 1965, a naked (though live and uncooked) girl was served up in a similar manner as the culmination of the final seance. And in 1930, American journalist Wambly Bald met writer William Seabrook on a Paris street and asked him about the moist-looking parcel under his arm. Seabrook, wild-eyed and heavy drinking, a friend of devil-worshipper and self-styled 'Great Beast' Aleister Crowley, was an authentic madman of the old school. His books included *The Magic Island*, which introduced the words 'voodoo' and 'zombie' into the English language, and *Asylum*, a sensational account of his nine-month self-incarceration for alcoholism.

To Bald, Seabrook explained he was working on a new book, *Jungle Ways*, about his travels in Africa and the Caribbean. While doing so, he'd come to suspect that the Guere tribe in Africa, with whom he'd lived for a time, may have lied when they claimed to have fed him human flesh, and slipped him pork instead. Accordingly, he'd acquired some slices of a recently killed young Frenchman and, in order to make meaningful comparisons with the taste of what the Guere served, was about to have his cook prepare the meat three ways – grilled, fried, and in a *ragoût* with red peppers. Bald saw no reason to disbelieve him and Seabrook duly devoted five pages of *Jungle Ways* to the differences in flavour, texture and smell between human and animal meat.

Nobody offered me baked boy or grilled girl, but some French favourites took a little getting used to. I'd often eaten snails, but *oursin* – sea urchin – is definitely an acquired taste. One cracks the black hairy shell and scrapes out the buds of roe stuck to the inside. It looks like pink shaving cream and tastes a bit like violets, and though I knew that celebrity chefs used it in a sauce for fish, it didn't make it any easier to eat. Nor did I try the recipe suggested by Surrealist painter Salvador Dali. He claimed sea urchins eaten before bedtime induced interesting dreams, particularly if prepared *à la Catalane*, with a sauce based on bitter chocolate.

Lamb's brains, crumbed and fried in butter, or served in white sauce, had been a staple of my childhood cuisine, though when I saw them served Texas-style in the film *Giant*, baked in the calf's head, with the top of the skull sawn off and a large spoon stuck in, my stomach turned over. So I needed a little coaxing to dig into Silkworker's Brains, a dish much favoured in Lyon, once the centre of the silk trade. Made from greyish cottage cheese speckled with chopped herbs, it supposedly resembles the brain of workers suffering from an infection caught from silkworms.

With pork, I thought I was on surer ground. I even occasionally enjoyed the gelatinous delights of the pig's foot, until a friend came unexpectedly into the dining room while I was biting into a plump trotter, and shrieked.

'It was horrible,' she explained later. 'The pig foot was the same colour as your skin. It looked like you were eating your hand.'

After that, I never attacked a *pied de cochon vinaigrette* with the same enthusiasm. Nor did my heart leap at the first sight of Stoker's Apron, another Lyonnaise specialty, made from a slab of some indeterminate part of the pig, breaded and deep fried so as to speckle the surface with ominously carbonized grains.

The rest of the porker was more or less plain sailing. Jellied *tête de porc*, and even *museau*, which is the snout, sliced, were sufficiently like the brawn of my childhood to remain delectable. For the same reason, kidneys and liver were no problem. While I have never managed that other French delicacy, the pig's tail, I have sampled the ear, since an *oreille de cochon*, boiled until soft, then stuffed, deep fried and served with a pickle-based *sauce ravigote*, was a speciality of the Australian chef Gay Bilson, who offered it as an appetizer at her Berowra Waters Inn.

Despite my defeat at the hands of the pig's foot, I felt I was holding my own in the battle of the edible until Claire and Marie-Do took me to the Sunday market on Rue Mouffetard. This narrow street descending steeply from Place Contrescarpe had been Hemingway's old stamping ground. His memoir of those days, *A Moveable Feast*, begins there. George Orwell lived nearby as well, on a characteristically miserable lane called Rue Pot de Fer, when he worked as a dishwasher or *plongeur* – diver – in Paris hotels, gathering material for *Down and Out in Paris and London*, the most depressing book ever written about living in Paris.

On a wet Sunday morning in winter, feet slipping on gritty cobbles, housewives with shopping baskets jostling your elbows, the white light of the stalls cutting through the gloom, and merchants shouting their prices and specialities, it was easy to imagine oneself in the days not of Hemingway but of Émile Zola. The hair on the back of my neck prickled when, at the first intersection, where a narrow lane cut across Mouffetard, two women, mother and daughter, in identical black overcoats and hats, sang in rasping voices to the wheezing of a barrel organ and urged the crowd to suggest the next tune. These weren't songs of today nor even of the Thirties, but of the nineteenth century; songs of the Commune, of the *belle époque*, some of them written by Aristide Bruant, whom Toulouse-Lautrec had drawn in his swirling cape and wide black hat – a hat just like these women wore. I felt a stab of something like recognition. Everyone who comes to Paris to stay realizes that the city has been waiting for them. Even if it takes two hundred years.

A *charcutier* was handing out free samples from a large sausage. We each took a slice.

'His *andouillette*,' Claire said, 'his very good 'ere.'

Most sausages are an agglomeration of meat, fat and rusk jumbled together in a marmoreal mosaic, and baptized with nitrites to a false meaty pink, but this one was grey, and seemed to have been assembled in concentric circles. A slice looked like a section cut through a tree.

'What's it made of?' I asked Claire.

'*Les tripes.*'

Intestines. Hmmm. I nibbled. A bit ... well, musty. And with a curious aftertaste.

The *charcutier* offered another slice, this time with an extended sales pitch.

''E say', explained Claire, 'zat zis is zer real *andouillette*, made *à l'ancienne*. In zer old way. 'E use zer ... *comment on dit?* ... zer *trou du cul.*'

I looked blank.

'What *is* zis?' she said in exasperation. Searching

her English vocabulary for the words, she found them at last. 'Ah yes. Hi ham remembering now. *Trou du cul*. Zer hasshole!'

6

Two Ladies Lunching

Toasted Susie Is My Ice Cream.

Gertrude Stein

YOU CAN FIND A PATTERN IN ANY RANDOM arrangement if you stare at it long enough – and since I had plenty of time to stare during my first weeks in Paris, past events began to reorder themselves in significant ways.

From certain points of view, some of my impetus to live in France could be traced to Gertrude Stein, Alice B. Toklas and Keith Richards... Yes, the Rolling Stones' guitarist. *That* Keith Richards. No, I never met him. But as I thought about it, not even six degrees of separation divided the four of us.

In 1973 I lived in London, on a leafy street in Chelsea called Park Walk. Being the tenant of a sixth-floor walk-up apartment in fashionable SW10 entitled me to wear suede ankle boots, a silk scarf over a T-shirt, and hang out in the cafés along the King's Road, drinking calvados and looking as if I understood more than one word in three of the *Cahiers du Cinéma* I studied with such interest.

My books were doing well, and within a few months I was due to leave for the United States to take up a guest professorship. Everything would have been fine had it not been for my phone.

Once or twice a week, around 3 a.m., it would wake me from a deep sleep and an American voice demand, 'Is Keith there?' Or occasionally, 'Can I speak to Rufus?' or 'Is Anna about?'

On the first few occasions, I just hung up. But a few minutes later, as I was drifting back to sleep, it always rang again.

'We've had a complaint,' said the operator, 'about a call being cut off.'

There was no Keith, Rufus or Anna here, I snarled. Sometimes this sufficed. At other times, they'd call again at 4 a.m. And 5 . . .

The second week, I'd had enough. 'Keith *who*?' I demanded of the next caller.

A long, suspicious pause. 'Who's this?'

I told him.

'Is that . . . ?' He gave my number.

'Yes. But there's no Keith here.'

'But that *is* Keith Richards' house?'

'Keith Richards? Of the Stones? God, no. It's a flat in Chelsea.'

Another long sceptical silence, then a click.

Ten minutes later, the phone rang again. 'I have a person-to-person call from California for Mr Keith Richards ...' droned the operator.

After some furious calls, British Telecom did concede – 'We're admitting nothing, mind you' – that they might, conceivably, have allocated me a number previously used by a Mr K. Richards. But no, they couldn't change it in less than six weeks. And it was *quite* out of the question to give me Richards' current number, since he was ex-directory.

I built up a picture of the Richards ménage. It included a woman named Anna, and actor Rufus Collins, sometime member of Julian Beck's Living Theatre. Various other people came and went. Obviously, Keith changed his phone number often. And, equally obviously, he didn't tell everyone he'd done so.

The following week, another call roused me. 'This is Edward Burns of New York,' announced a cultured American voice. 'I would like to speak to Rufus.'

'So would I, Edward.' I gave him my now well-rehearsed explanation.

'Hmmm,' he said. 'And you are ...?'

I told him.

'Your name's familiar,' he mused.

'I doubt it. I'm not a musician. Or an actor.'

'Nor me. I'm the literary executor of Alice B. Toklas.'

'Really? My publisher is bringing out the Toklas letters . . .'

'. . . which I edited,' said Burns triumphantly. 'So I've seen your name in their catalogue! We must meet. Where are you?'

'Chelsea.'

'No! Really? Anywhere near . . . ?' He read out an address.

'About five minutes' walk. Why?'

'Because I'm going to a party there tonight! I was ringing Rufus to invite him. What a coincidence. Can you come?'

Tall, plump and amiable, Ed Burns dominated the party with his good humour – which was needed, since we were both sorely out of place. Our hostess, a hyper-kinetic French teenager with ambitions to paint, had decorated her tiny apartment in what could only be called 'Moorish whorehouse'. Swags of viridian fabric drooped from the ceiling as in a road-company revival of *The Desert Song*, creating the impression that we were the guests of a very gay bedouin, and giving new meaning to the phrase 'camp as a row of tents'.

Ed was encyclopaedic about Toklas and Stein. One would have liked to quiz him further about this strange couple, but every time I started a sentence like 'About these rumours that Stein collaborated with the Nazis . . .' our hostess would waft by, offer a glimpse down her breathtaking cleavage, and hand us a joint.

I was also increasingly distracted by a woman in black silk who circled the room every ten minutes, sipping a glass of wine and examining the décor with fundamental scepticism.

'You don't seem to be having a good time,' I remarked on the next turn round.

'Are mothers supposed to?' she said. Or rather, 'Are muzzers sue-*po*-zewd to?' French!

'You're someone's *mother*?'

She tilted her head towards our pyrogenic hostess.

'But you're much too young,' I said reflexively.

She didn't greet this cliché with the customary coquettish simper – just looked at me thoughtfully. I sensed an unspoken prompt.

'Your daughter looks like she can take care of herself,' I suggested.

She nodded, as if mulling this over.

'I live quite near,' I went on recklessly.

'Yes?'

'Yes,' I said. 'Shall we go?'

She nodded the way people do when you confirm something they'd thought all along. For the first time,

I realized her turns around the room hadn't been entirely random. 'I find my coat,' she said. At the door, she handed it to me to drape over her shoulders. 'Céline,' she said.

We walked in near silence the few blocks to Park Walk, and climbed the stone steps.

'So bare,' she said, looking around my flat. 'No pictures?'

Bare? I'd thought it attractively austere.

Strolling into the bedroom, she shrugged off her jacket. The slither of silk on silk. 'You do not like a big bed?'

A queen-size had always seemed large enough, but now I wondered.

She unzipped. Lingerie to *die* for. Coffee knickers, with lace along the hems.

'You have some candles? . . . No? . . .'

She draped her scarf over the bedside lamp. Light filtering through what I'd taken for black revealed itself as deep purple. Shadows took on the soft bloom of a bruise.

My first night with a Parisienne – and a Woman of a Certain Age at that – set parameters that remained for life.

'Not so hard . . . Mmmm . . . a little lower . . .' A throaty giggle. '*Coquin!*' (What did that mean?) 'Now the outside . . . yes. Oh, yes, I like that *very* much . . .'

Not orders. Direction ... interpretation ... *craft*.

Toklas, Stein and Ed Burns didn't reappear in my life until I was already living in Paris, but once they did I found them everywhere. Visiting the Père Lachaise cemetery, I found Toklas and Stein's shared grave, with epitaphs on opposite faces of the same stone. If I crossed the Luxembourg Gardens from our apartment, the exit on Rue Guynemer put me at the corner of Rue de Fleurus. Calling at number 27 to collect crime writer Robin Cook from François Guérif, editor of the *Rivages* series of crime novels, I recognized his office as the apartment in which a stolid Stein, surrounded by Cézannes, Braques and Matisses, posed for both Picasso and Man Ray.

Toklas and Stein met in 1907, when Alice started typing manuscripts for Leo, Gertrude's dour and ultimately hostile brother. Diminutive, chain-smoking, fastidious, with an incipient moustache and a penchant for gypsy ear-rings, Alice didn't look like Passion's Plaything, but the bond between her and the lumbering Stein was instant, passionate and enduring.

'Books and food, food and books; both excellent things,' Stein wrote. Since childhood, she'd relished 'the full satisfied sense of being stuffed up with eating'. Alice, an excellent cook, was happy to gratify that urge, as well as the sexual one. The two desires often appeared indivisible. At the table as in bed, 'there should', Toklas wrote, 'be a climax and a culmination. Come to it gently. One will suffice.' They mostly called one another 'Pussy' and 'Lovey', but Gertrude's pet names for Alice included 'Cake' and 'Lobster', while Alice called Gertrude 'Mount Fattie' and 'Fattuski'.

How much sex did the great literary lesbians of Paris really indulge in? As with couples anywhere, it depends. Sylvia Beach and Adrienne Monnier, though companions for decades, may never have been physical lovers. Monnier, who had a beautiful face but a fat, squat body – 'From a distance,' said one friend, 'she looked like a farm labourer standing knee-deep in loam' – was frequently in tears over male writers who didn't return her affection. 'She suffered a lot from having nobody to love her,' recalled her friend Marcelle Auclair. 'She would have liked Jules Romains, [Leon-Paul] Fargue, or Jean Prévost to have been in love with her. But Romains was married, Fargue preferred her sister Rinette, and Jean chased all the pretty clients. "And nothing for *me*!" Adrienne said. That's why I never believed those stories about her romance with Sylvia Beach. I can't imagine her as a lesbian.'

Marguerite Radclyffe Hall, author of *The Well of Loneliness*, also seems to have kept her love life on the intellectual plane. But Nathalie Clifford-Barney, whose salon formed the centre of lesbian life in Paris, was obviously a female Casanova, and the letters of Djuna Barnes are filled with confidences like 'X took Y to Antibes for the weekend, but she wouldn't let her enter her until after the sun went down.' As for Stein and Toklas, their sex life was indisputably carnal. Hemingway, who, though not easily impressed by women, called Alice 'frightening', recalled turning up at their apartment, unannounced, to hear Stein murmuring in the inner room, 'Don't, Pussy! Please, Pussy! Don't . . .'

Gertrude and Alice waited out the war in a village far from Paris, and were never troubled by the occupying Germans or the puppet regime of World War I hero Marshal Pétain. Stein brushed over the period with a single casual sentence, 'And now once more the telephone is working and we can see people and the roads are open and the Germans are gone from the village and everybody is breathing a little more freely, not entirely so but a little so, although some few unpleasant things did happen, oh dear me.' It was rumoured, but not confirmed until 2003, that they owed their safety to Bernard Faÿ, a long-time friend and admirer of Stein who'd written much about her before the war. Appointed head of the Bibliothèque Nationale under Vichy, Fay, a cultured gay, participated vigorously in the hunting down and execution of an estimated five hundred anti-Catholic Freemasons, for whom he had a special hatred. Fortunately for Stein and Toklas, however, Fay wasn't anti-Semitic, and persuaded Vichy and the Germans to ignore their presence. In return, Stein paid lip service to the regime, even writing an introduction to a collection of Pétain's speeches, which her American publisher, fortunately for her reputation, refused to print.

Stein died in 1946. Toklas survived until 1967. Friends persuaded her, in her seventies, to publish her recipes. *The Alice B. Toklas Cookbook* appeared in 1954. Some readers were surprised at the exoticism and obscurity not only of the ingredients but of the titles, which included *Artichokes Stravinsky*, *Gigot de la Clinique* (Hospital leg of lamb), *Green Peas à la Goodwife* and *Poulet Vent Vert* (Green Wind Chicken), though the one Toklas recipe about which everyone knew, even if they had never tried it, was for her famous hash brownies. Did Alice and Gertrude console themselves in rural exile by turning on over coffee and cake? We were never sure, because the recipe didn't appear in modern editions of her cookbook. As with so much else to do with France, we were left with innuendo, myth and expectation.

As with my first meeting with Ed Burns, the next crucial contact with the Toklas/Stein legend was electronic. Only a few years ago, by selling a piece of Toklas memorabilia on the Internet auction site eBay, I got to know Alice's most passionate admirer, a San Francisco investment strategist named Hans Gallas. To celebrate Toklas's 125th birthday, Hans assembled an exhibition at the San Francisco Public Library called 'I Love You, Alice B. Toklas' (after a dreadful 1968 comedy with Peter Sellers, also known as *Kiss My Butterfly*). A local restaurant offered a dinner from the cookbook: squab in Madeira, spring lamb with vegetables, nougat ice cream and, of course, that hashish dessert. Did I know, asked Hans, of anywhere in Paris that might present the show and host a similar dinner? After tortuous negotiations, the American Library agreed to take the show, and Hans arrived to see it installed. Soft-spoken, bespectacled and relentless, he confronted and defeated the intransigent French Customs, which didn't want to relinquish the paintings he'd shipped over. He also chivvied into action the slapdash American Library, and soon had most of the staff working under his direction.

His devotion to the memory of Alice was impressive, his knowledge encyclopaedic. Unpacking an antique kitchen mixer, he told me, 'It's identical to the one Alice had in her kitchen.'

He began unwrapping shards of a shattered green bowl.

'A pity about the bowl,' I remarked.

'No, it's great! Alice broke hers as well. She writes about it in a letter. I found this one on the net. It's exactly the same colour and model. And my bowl got broken too, in the mail!'

He invited us to share the serendipity of it. Some of the helpers exchanged that wide-eyed 'spot the loony' expression, but I understood perfectly. Perhaps only another collector would.

The dinner, however, was another matter entirely. One could rent a restaurant . . . but most were too big. And even then, what French chef would take kindly to being told exactly what to cook? Finally, I made the food myself, brought it to the library and laid out a buffet to follow the talk Hans gave about Alice. Intellectually stimulated, or perhaps just starving, the audience emptied every dish. *Poulet Vent Vert*, with a sauce of fresh tarragon and cognac, went particularly well. Hans explained it was named for the perfume *Vent Vert* developed by couturier Pierre Balmain. 'Alice was *very* close to him. He visited her regularly, and sent cars to pick her up for his fashion shows. She's even buried in a suit by him!'

But one question was asked by all. 'Will there be the famous hash brownies?'

Our generation had grown up with the legend of these hallucinogenic cakes but seldom with any experience of the reality. The few supposed examples I'd eaten at parties never had much effect, other than indigestion. I wasn't surprised, then, to find, when I consulted the unexpurgated *Alice B. Toklas Cookbook*, no brownie recipe.

Alice never prepared this, her most famous dish. Seventy-seven when she compiled her cookbook, she supplemented her failing memory by asking friends to contribute their own recipes. Not all replied in the right spirit. One who saw the chance of a joke was painter and film-maker Bryon Gysin, collaborator with William Burroughs on books such as *The Naked Lunch*, for which Burroughs used Gysin's 'cut-up' method: he threw his notes on the floor, and friends like Allen Ginsberg and Jack Kerouac, usually stoned – as was the author – gathered them up randomly and arranged them in book form.

Gysin (mis-spelt 'Gysen' in the book) mischievously gave Toklas the recipe for his pothead friends' favourite munch. This is the text he sent.

Haschich Fudge (which anyone could whip up on a rainy day). This is the food of paradise – of Baudelaire's Artificial Paradises: it might provide an entertaining refreshment for a Ladies' Bridge Club or a chapter meeting of the DAR [Daughters of the American Revolution, a notoriously conservative association]. In Morocco it is thought to be good for warding off the common cold in damp winter weather and is, indeed, more effective if taken with large quantities of hot mint tea. Euphoria and brilliant storms of laughter; ecstatic reveries and extensions of one's personality on several simultaneous planes are to be complacently expected. Almost anything Saint Theresa did, you can do better if you can bear to be ravished by '*un évanouissement réveillé* [a sense of fainting while awake]'.

Take 1 teaspoon black peppercorns, 1 whole nutmeg, 4 average sticks of cinnamon, 1 teaspoon coriander. These should all be pulverised in a mortar. About a handful each of stoned dates, dried figs, shelled almonds and peanuts: chop these and mix them together. A bunch of canibus [sic] sativa can be pulverised. This along with the spices should be dusted over the mixed fruit and nuts, kneaded together. About a cup of sugar dissolved in a big pat of butter. Rolled into a cake and cut into balls about the size of a walnut, it should be eaten with care. Two pieces are quite sufficient.

There isn't much doubt Gysin meant this as a joke. There are enough nudges and winks in the text, but Alice missed them. Or perhaps she decided it didn't matter.

Even with a food processor, grinding the nuts and fruit was a chore. No wonder people faked it with brownie mix and some Maui Wowie. And what precisely was meant by 'a handful' and 'a big pat'? As for the cannabis, Gysin's 'bunch', depending on the provenance, could represent anything from a mild high for one person to hallucinations for a platoon. Moreover, it would need to be very finely milled indeed to blend with the gooey fudge mix.

Somebody suggested hash – cannabis resin – instead. I consulted our friend Loretta, who, in addition to looking like Catherine Deneuve, was keeping company with a chef; two possibly connected facts. If anybody could lay her hands on some hash, it was she.

'No problem,' she said. 'Any particular kind?'

'There are different kinds?'

'Honey, if you only knew . . .'

A few days later, she delivered a brown turd wrapped in aluminium foil.

'Moroccan. It's the best. But you didn't get it from me, right? What's it for anyway?'

I told her about Alice's recipe.

'"Candy is dandy",' she quoted dreamily, '"but liquor is quicker . . ." Not in this case though, *mon cher*. That stuff will have you climbing the walls.'

At the last moment, I divided the mix, half with hash, half without. The 'B' fudge went on the buffet, but the 'A' mix was offered only to people I thought would appreciate it. They did. And while it didn't, as Loretta said, make one climb the walls, it induced a willingness to try.

Ed Burns, amiable as ever, came to Hans's talk, and

we met again after three decades. I mentioned that early-morning call.

'I'd completely forgotten,' he said. 'I haven't seen Rufus in years.'

But it reminded me that, not long after those events, I chanced to meet Keith Richards' Anna.

We were both guests at a party thrown by the agent of André Previn. Once I realized that this was *the* Anna, I told her about the calls and asked, 'Can I give these people your number?'

She shuddered. 'I'd rather you didn't.'

'OK. Then, could you ring up Keith Richards . . .'

'No!'

I didn't press her for Richards' new number – if indeed she knew it. Though it would have been fun to ring him. At 3 a.m.

7

The Market in Meat

The special quality of pale brilliance of a leg revealed under a
lifted skirt.

Louis Aragon, Paris Peasant

THE CURVE OF THE SEINE PASSING THROUGH PARIS,
kinked as it divides around the Île de la Cité and the
Île Saint-Louis, evokes a woman's face, eyes closed,
upturned as for a kiss. So, at least, believed the RATP,
Paris's bus and Métro administration, which
employed this image as its trademark. It seemed a
charming conceit, appropriate to Paris's commitment
to romance, until a wholesale butcher placed a similar
emblem on his trucks, having discovered that the oval
map of Greater Paris, crossed by the line of the
Seine, with the two islands at the centre, was a
dead ringer for a slice cut through the French

family's favourite Sunday joint, a *gigot* of lamb.

Sex and meat: two matters of deep interest to the French. Paris has always been a place where one could literally buy and sell flesh. Christopher Isherwood, author of the short stories that later inspired the musical *Cabaret*, confessed in his memoir *Christopher and His Kind* that he went to Germany because 'Berlin meant boys'. One could just as well have said of people who came to France in those days that 'Paris meant pussy'.

In London's West End between the wars, one could find a prostitute, male or female, at any time of the day or night. Brothels were less popular, but they flourished in New York, Detroit, Buenos Aires, Sydney, Cape Town. Pornographic films and erotic books were internationally available to anyone with the money to pay. That Paris, in the face of such competition, effortlessly retained the title of world capital of sex had much to do with the French tradition of connoisseurship. Not only was it a matter of pride that anything in Paris should be superior; French whores, gigolos and their clients didn't labour under the same tradition of secrecy as Anglo-Saxon societies. Sex was as casually advertised and discussed as food, politics or the weather. Couples gathered in cafés or clubs where one's simple presence advertised a sexual preference. Lovers kissed on the streets, while men and women made bold eye contact with total strangers. 'That mute invitation used to be known as, "*Suivez-moi, jeune homme*" ["Follow me, young man"],' says the Canadian writer and long-time Paris resident Mavis Gallant. 'It was the prerogative of married women. The unmarried were chaperoned, or didn't dare, or were "semi-professional" – which means to say: just now and then, hoping just for a good dinner in a decent restaurant, a cab home, a bit of cash.'

In 1927, one of the period's best guidebooks, the lively and information-packed *Paris with the Lid Lifted* by Bruce Reynolds, gave practical advice on how to respond to such unspoken overtures.

You are strolling up the Boulevard and you see ze little French Goddess tripping towards you, and she spies you at the same moment and you look ecstatically at her and show your pearly teeth (if you still have them) and she gives you right back that 'come-and-get-me-love-me-carry-me-away wiz you' invitation. You have to make good. Start off right. Tell it to her, in her language . . .

Reynolds suggests a few phrases, as effective now as then: '*Vous êtes ravissante. Je voudrais faire votre connaissance.*' ('You look delightful. I must get to know you') and '*Voulez-vous venir avec moi dans un café?*' ('Will you step into a café with me?')

For the first half of the twentieth century, the flagrancy of Paris made the city a Mecca for both impoverished European aristocrats and nouveau-riche Americans seeking the prestigious marriage they couldn't find in snobbish New York. Edith Wharton anatomized this group in her last, unfinished novel, *The Buccaneers*. Set in 1870s New York and Paris, it showed young American heiresses, pretty and plain, as no less predatory than the men they stalked. They're guided by an ageing expatriate who, at the end of her days as a *grande horizontale*, has become, in effect, a discreet and high-priced pimp.

Wharton's inspiration was the 1895 marriage of American railroad heiress Anna Gould to Count Boniface de Castellane, one of the most handsome men in Paris. The bride, described as 'squat, with crinkly hair, and almost simian in appearance', can't have been in any doubt about her husband's motives, and 'Boni' duly milked her fortune until they divorced.

Film star Gloria Swanson, on location in France in 1925 for *Madame Sans-Gêne*, snagged – or was snagged by – the Marquis Henri de la Falaise de Coudray, a minor aristocrat who, down on his luck, had been hired as her interpreter. Already twice divorced, the petite star with the feral grin and penetrating eyes obviously wanted little more from the Marquis than his title. No doubt glad of a rich wife to restore the family château, he let himself become a trophy, carried back to Hollywood like a Boulle cabinet or a French maid.

The fan magazines did their loyal best to turn him into one of the Real Folks. 'Everybody calls him "Henry",' wrote the editor of *Photoplay* with hearty reassurance. 'Why, even the newspaper reporters have fallen for "Henry". When those hard-boiled birds admit that a chap has come clean, put it down in your little book that he's *there*!'

Henry was certainly 'there' but, as Gertrude Stein said memorably, 'There is no "there" there.' The limp moustache, pained half smile and weary eyes of his publicity pictures make it clear he'd rather be almost anywhere else. Once Swanson wearied of him, her studio, Paramount, made him manager of their Paris subsidiary, Pathé. (This was a popular solution to the problem of inconvenient spouses. Rather than impair Marlene Dietrich's image as a temptress, Paramount found a Paris job for her husband, Rudolf Sieber. Later, she bought him a chicken farm in rural California.)

Swanson soon landed a new lover more her speed — movie financier Joe Kennedy, later US ambassador to London, and the father of JFK. But her marriage to 'Henry' had declared open season on aristocracy. Whole families of handsome young dukes or princes migrated to Paris, their hunt for rich wives cunningly orchestrated by their mothers. One such clan, the

Mdivanis, supposedly part of the Hungarian nobility (or perhaps it was the Ukrainian), did spectacularly well. Hollywood screenwriter Lenore Coffee, whose husband spoke Russian, saw a lot of them, and remembered their rapacity with admiration.

> Serge was extraordinarily handsome, dark, tall and slender, with an almost Mediterranean cast to his features. He performed a wonderful sword dance, the *lesginka*, not unlike the Scottish Highland sword dance. David was blond, a bit plump and easygoing. There was a third son, Alexis. I understand there was a family conclave about who should restore the family fortunes and they all decided that Alexis was the one . . .

Having conceived a plan, the Mdivanis set out their traps at the polo grounds and race tracks of Chantilly, Longchamps and Rambouillet, where the rich gathered, and waited for victims to stumble in. First to arrive were Swanson's movie rivals, Mae Murray and Pola Negri. Snapped up by Serge and David respectively, they returned to Hollywood not mere marquises but actual princesses. Alexis did better still, marrying the millionairess Louise van Alen, and, following their divorce, dime-store heiress Barbara Hutton. (Alexis and Serge Mdivani both died in what might be called 'the line of duty', Alexis decapitated when his car crashed in the south of France, and Serge when a polo pony kicked him in the head.)

Such naked sexual opportunism at the top of society conferred a sort of legitimacy on what was happening lower down in the food chain. By the Twenties, the profession of gigolo was sufficiently well established in Paris to be worth a couple of pages in *Paris with the Lid Lifted*.

> In these Cafés, also see the Male Vamp. He, of the patent-leather hair and dress immaculate. Here to make the night pleasant for the female patrons ... An unaccompanied lady if she cares to dance can summon a Gigolo – take a turn around the floor with him and pay him 10 francs per dance. Moneyed women, however, have been known to 'fall' for their Gigolo – buy him a motor car, send him to the best tailor; even take him back home ...

Some hotels, like the Montparnasse, 'a quiet, ordinary little hotel, abandoned by its old clientele of old English maniacs', as one reporter wrote in 1932, turned themselves into pick-up spots for gigolos. Following a system that had worked in Berlin, the management placed a phone on every table in its large restaurant. At four o'clock each afternoon young men arrived, registered at the door, took a seat alone at a numbered table with a phone, and waited for a call from the women scattered around the room. Ostensibly, they were 'dance partners', but everyone recognized the subterfuge and only a few couples bothered to take the floor.

Until the early 1930s, when Hollywood began to censor itself, movies accepted gigolos as a fact of French life. In the 1934 Warner Brothers musical *Wonder Bar*, written, not surprisingly, by three Hungarians, Ricardo Cortez plays 'Harry the Gigolo', one of many who who hang out in the Paris club run by Al Jolson. In the opening scenes, set on the dance floor, a 'dance partner' sorts through a sheaf of cards with conversational gambits in English, before choosing one that says, 'You are so kind. You remind me of my mother.'

Between the wars, anybody with money, particularly American dollars, could find whatever they wanted in a city that prided itself on putting everything up for sale. *Paris with the Lid Lifted* listed some of the clubs that catered to 'special tastes'.

Le Paradis, Rue Pigalle. Black men dancing with French girls. Black women dancing with white men.

Aux Belles Poulets. The 'waiters' serving the drinks and dancing about the room are young girls without any clothes (not even a bangle on) . . .

La Fétiche. Young ladies dressed as young men. A bar, a cabaret and a restaurant. All manned by women, in men's clothes . . . Be careful of the girl you take with you. Some of these dashing dames of magnetic masculinity may get 'smashes' on her and try to take her away from you . . .

Lesbianism was as public in Paris as its male counterpart in Berlin. At clubs catering exclusively for women, like La Fétiche and Le Monocle, evening gowns and dinner jackets were not only permitted but expected. Elsewhere, female lovers routinely danced together in the jazz bars and *bals musettes* – public dance halls – of Montparnasse. Radclyffe Hall's characters wore male suits and, like English clubmen, addressed one another by surnames. In response, older French lesbians adopted male morning dress: striped trousers, a tailcoat, a waistcoat and, often, a monocle. The artists of satirical weeklies like *Assiette au beurre*, who struggled to find visual shorthand for homosexuals, seized on this uniform and devoted entire issues to *les gouines* – 'dikes'. Most took a typically Parisian *laissez-faire* attitude, often mocking men who didn't realize their wives or fiancées were bisexual. A naked girl phones from the bed of her female lover to explain she'll be staying the night with a girlfriend, or a couple of portly *gouines* watch approvingly as a demure young girl, obviously their protégée, is fitted for a wedding dress.

Male homosexuality was less public. 'Pederasty is not a French vice,' announced Jean Gravigny in his guide *Montparnasse en 1925*. 'All our education, our national literature, our healthy natural dispositions have led us away since antiquity from this sort of sexual practice.' If France was, as people said, 'the woman of Europe', it followed that 'French love' was bracingly heterosexual. Flagellation was 'the English vice' and heterosexual anal sex 'Italian', so male homosexuality or lesbianism had to be 'Greek'. Prominent gays like Marcel Proust, André Gide or Jean Cocteau took no notice of this; nor did France's large and active community of *tapettes*, *pédés* and *petits messieurs*. Even *Paris with the Lid Lifted* couldn't close its eyes to the many gay clubs, though Bruce Reynolds sneered as he listed them.

The Select. Gentlemen with long wavy hair and long, painted fingernails and other gentlemen who, when they walk, walk 'Falsetto', toss their hips and lift their brows . . .

La Petite Chaumière. This is a place where men dress as women. Men of a certain degenerate tendency who infest every large city. If, however, you do want to see these Freaks cavort around and swish their skirts and sing in Falsetto and shout 'Whoops, my dear', this is the place to see them . . .

During the Twenties and Thirties, the concept of Paris as a 'meat market' was often literally true. Since agents and unions didn't exist, workers found that the most traditional of French institutions, the street market, worked just as well for talent as for lettuce and eggs. They simply showed up on a particular street or in a known café, displayed their wares and waited for offers. Typographers gathered on Place Caire, housepainters under the statue of Général Moncey on Place de Clichy, and laundrywomen on the Pont de l'Europe. Actors hoping for a day's work as a *figurant*, or extra, loitered around the studios at Joinville. Artists' models of all ages, male and female, most of them Italian, converged on a lane in Montparnasse.

Musicians went to a café near Porte Saint-Denis, where, to make their skill easily identifiable, woodwind players put a reed in their hatband, string players carried a violin case, bassists a bow, brass players a mouthpiece, and pianists a small satchel of the sort used for sheet music. In the same way, prostitutes, amateur and professional, congregated along certain streets and squares, mostly in areas with plenty of *hôtels de passe*, ready to rent rooms by the hour. A rigorous scale of values operated. Around Pigalle and Barbès, on the *butte* of Montmartre, you'd pay 350 francs for the girl and 250 francs for the room, whereas in the much more chic area of the Madeleine, near the Opéra, the going rate was more like 2,000 francs and a room cost 400 francs.

Girls staked out a territory, often near a public lavatory, where they could make eye contact with potential clients over the metal screen. Those who didn't care to walk the streets made their headquarters at certain cafés, called *brasseries de femmes*. Others haunted what the *Guide Secret des plaisirs parisiens* of 1920 called 'those theatres where one can see audacious pieces dealing with adultery, incestuous love, rape, murder – the whole range of vice and crime'. According to the *Guide*, these theatres were 'frequented by women who, while charming, are wild for such ultra-suggestive shows'.

The best known was the Théâtre du Grand-Guignol, a tiny 290-seat theatre in an old Gothic chapel at the dead end of Montmartre's Rue Chaptal. It staged only one-act plays dealing with mutilation, torture and murder. So expert were the sound and lighting that one could well believe people were being gutted, flayed and seared with acid. Started in 1897 by Oscar Metanier, formerly the Private Secretary of the Paris Police Commissioner, the Grand-Guignol – literally 'Big Puppet Show' – closed in 1962, after having contributed to the language a metaphor for any particularly bloody sight.

That closet sadists made up a large part of the audience was hardly a secret, though almost the only open acknowledgement of the fact was the 1935 film *Mad Love*, produced, surprisingly, in Hollywood. Directed by the great German cameraman Karl Freund, it starred another German, Peter Lorre, as a French surgeon who, obsessed with a beautiful actress, spends every night in his private box, watching with goggling eyes as she's tortured to death.

Girls looking for more conventional partners cruised the lounge or the upper circle at revue theatres like the Folies Bergères and the Casino de Paris, knowing that their semi-nude showgirls, not to mention the uniquely erotic black American star Josephine Baker, would send men in the audience in urgent search of a woman.

Like all colonial powers, the French experienced their subject races as placid and compliant. In the popular imagination, sex with a 'native' was an alien experience, sensual, indolent, exotic and, figuratively if not literally, drugged. Developing a taste for 'black velvet' was considered one of the risks of long service in the tropics, like malaria and a tolerance for spicy food. Casual visitors or tourists to Africa or Asia usually shunned both. The Surrealist Michel Leiris, travelling through Africa in 1932, confessed to his journal, 'One doesn't come close to people by approaching their customs. They remain, after all our enquiries, obstinately closed. I haven't slept with a black woman. That's how European I've remained.'

Josephine Baker's spasmodic near-nude appearances at the Théâtre des Champs-Élysées in 1925 in *La Revue nègre* trampled down the barrier between black and white sex. The following year, she decisively destroyed it when she joined the Folies Bergères for the revue *La Folie du jour* – The Madness of the Day. In yet another mesmerizing appearance, this time wearing only her notorious mini-skirt of sixteen phallic bananas, her acrobatics, set against a décor of picturesque savagery, seemed to import the jungle into the very heart of Paris.

It was ersatz, of course. Africans never danced like this, any more than their music sounded like jazz, but to all but the few French people who might have spent time in Harlem, Baker's performance looked authentic and audiences swallowed the illusion. To see anything like Baker, white Americans would have to wait until the jitterbug fad of the late Thirties. By then, Baker and black sexuality were embedded in French culture.

It took Janet Flanner, the *New Yorker*'s Paris correspondent and a leading light in the lesbian community, half a century to admit what she'd been too weak to say at the time. 'I wrote about it timidly, uncertainly, and like a dullard,' she confessed. Had she been honest, she said, she would have filed a report that betrayed the lust that Baker excited not only in the audience but in her.

She made her entry entirely nude except for a pink flamingo feather between her limbs; she was being carried upside down and doing the splits on the shoulders of a black giant. Midstage he paused and, with his long fingers holding her basket-wise around the waist, swung her in a slow cartwheel to the stage floor, where she stood, like his magnificent discarded burden, in an instant of complete silence. She was an unforgettable female ebony statue. A scream of salutation spread through the theatre. Whatever happened next was unimportant. The two specific elements had been established and were unforgettable – her magnificent dark body, a new model that to the French proved for the first time that black was beautiful, and the acute response of the white masculine public in the capital of hedonism of all Europe – Paris.

Baker's eruption into the public consciousness stimulated outlandish and grotesque fantasies among the French. Inspired by the posters by Paul Colin for *La Revue nègre*, satirical magazines blossomed with pictures of white women in diaphanous gowns sagging in the arms of giant black lovers with exaggerated lips and wild eyes. *Le Guignol* devoted a double-page spread to two images of an overweight middle-aged couple in bed. The man dreams of a near-naked Baker, while his wife fantasizes about a male black dancer in a bulging G-string.

Since 1920, the Russian physiologist Serge Voronoff, as a supposed aid to rejuvenation, had been transplanting monkey organs and glands, particularly testicles, into humans at his private hospital, the Villa Molière in suburban Auteuil. By 1929, he'd treated five hundred men, some of whom claimed miraculous restoration of their virility. Inspired, he experimented with transplanting simian ovaries into women as a 'cure' for the menopause. Following this, he implanted a human ovary in Nora, a monkey, whom he inseminated with human sperm. Not surprisingly, the experiment failed, but it inspired Félicien Champsaur, who specialized in sensational novels about sexual depravity everywhere from ancient Rome to bohemian Montparnasse, to write *Nora, la guenon devenue femme* (*Nora, the Monkey Who Became a Woman*), about what might have happened had the experiment succeeded. His monkey woman becomes a star of the Paris stage with 'her fantastic *ballet nègre*'. Illustrations to the 1929 first printing showed her dancing naked, wearing only a few feathers, or a G-string in the form of a mask – or, prominently featured on the cover, a skirt of bananas. And the novel is dedicated to Voronoff.

8

An Ill Wind

A leaf fluttered in through the window this morning, as if supported by the rays of the sun, a bird settled on the fire escape, joy in the task of coffee, joy accompanied me as I walked.

Anaïs Nin, *Diaries*

ON THE LAST DAY OF JANUARY, I WOKE TO THE rattling of windows. Where we'd left one open, the curtains billowed. It was icy in the room. I shoved the window closed, locked it and looked down into Place Dauphine.

Overnight, the Siberian wind had swept up every leaf and scrap of paper. The man who lived on the ground floor of the building across the park, whom I'd christened M. Gruyère, stuck his head out of a door, hands in the pockets of his coral and lime anorak, Gauloise wedged in the corner of his mouth.

His little dog Snowy peered round his ankles, desperate need warring in his eyes with innate caution. He looked up plaintively at his master, but Gruyère just stared at the slate-coloured sky. Nothing was getting him out in this gale. Eventually Snowy scampered into the park, found a spot in the shelter of a chestnut, performed a sketchy crap and, with only a perfunctory flick of one back foot in the direction of hygiene, fled back to shelter.

'There's a storm,' I told Marie-Do.

'It'll go away,' she said sleepily. 'Come back to bed.'

But when we finally got up at 9 a.m., the wind hadn't gone away. If anything, it blew more strongly. People were propelled across the square like scraps of newspaper, and there was a steady drone over the rooftops.

According to the TV news, a gale had been blowing all night across northern and eastern France. Trees were down and buildings had lost their roofs. Until then, Marie-Do showed little interest, but the mention of roofs had her reaching for the phone.

'I wonder if Mother is at Richebourg.'

She wasn't. Which left nobody to look after her country house, on the other side of Versailles. A quick-fire phone conversation followed, with frequent excursions to the window for a weather check.

'Mother worries that a tree might be blown down on the roof. I said we would go and look.'

'You think it's safe?'

The TV showed a caravan crumpled in a ditch like a sodden cardboard carton. A six-storey building under renovation was coming to pieces, sheets of corrugated iron scaling off like leaves, and industrial-strength PVC ripping like toilet paper.

'No,' she said, 'but let's go anyway. We could stop by the Palace at Versailles. There won't be too many tourists on a day like this.'

Along the *voie express* that bordered the Seine, we felt the full force of the storm. Trees thrashed, and torn twigs littered the road. The wind had jammed pleasure boats against the stone abutments, and down by the Pont d'Iéna men were struggling to close the big plastic windows of the *bateaux-mouches* – the tour boats – before the wind blew them out.

Once over the Seine and on the heights at Saint-Cloud, the wind got worse. Trees had been levered from the ground like rotten teeth. The roads were almost empty, and any drivers we did see clutched their wheels and stared ahead with an attention one never expected to see in a Frenchman.

We took the Versailles exit alone and skirted the huge park. Inside the spiked railings, amid lawns, forests and boating lakes, private theatres, fountains, pavilions and wooded avenues out of paintings by Poussin and Claude Lorrain, Louis XVI and his

Austrian wife Marie-Antoinette had lived as if this was the only reality.

Nobody manned the main gate today, but we found the *gardien* about fifty metres down the wide avenue. He'd taken shelter in a plastic box the size of a telephone booth, from which he stared in astonishment – whether at the chaos or at two people crazy enough to be out in it, one couldn't tell.

From the woods we heard a rushing crack.

'The trees are falling!' he yelled over the noise, with a sort of glee. 'Marie-Antoinette couldn't do it. Louis *Seize* couldn't do it. But they're coming down now!'

At the foot of the drive, the road ended at the edge of the lake. The gale rushed across the grounds like the revolution that had blown Louis, Marie-Antoinette and their court to decapitation on the Place de la Concorde. Under the scudding clouds we were alone but exhilarated, infected by the same madness.

Beyond Versailles, a giant beech had hammered a car flat. A cop, amazed to see anyone about on a day like this, directed us round the wreck. At Richebourg, one of the poplars was down and the garden was littered with shredded twigs, but the house was safe. Not even bothering to take down the heavy wooden shutters, we hid inside while the wind buffeted the house. Twenty-eight people died in France that weekend, and many more in the rest of Europe. That night, in a wide bed tucked into an alcove overshadowed by walls of bookshelves, while the wind slammed against the shutters, our daughter Louise Virginie Caroline was conceived.

We drove back to Paris on Monday at around lunchtime, chastened by the ruin inflicted on the country – on the whole of Europe – while we'd clung together in the dark. Twigs ripped from the plane and poplar trees, and sometimes whole branches, littered the road. Bits of buildings were tangled in hedges fifty metres away.

Houses had survived better, particularly the twentieth-century ones. Clearly built by the smartest of the three partners in *Trois petits cochons et compagnie*, most were brick, but in a style as robust as it was unlovely. Some were faced with irregular slabs of stone fitted together, 'crazy paving' style, each piece edged with a raised rim of cement. Others had the warty finish the English call 'pebble-dash' – tiny stones pressed into wet plaster – or the even less attractive 'Kentish rag', which replaces pebbles with knobs of flint. All featured a stubby brick chimney belted in rusted steel. Lumpy balconies of two-by-four, bolted together and thickly painted in green or brown, were fastened to the walls with brackets that would have done credit to a dreadnought. At the approach of the storm, heavy wooden or, occasionally, pierced steel shutters had been swung in over the windows and secured with iron bars. Ugly as they were, these houses succeeded in the one category where architecture counted for anything with the French: endurance. Not even a hurricane could dent them, or their owners.

Half the country seemed to be out in its garden that morning, examining the damage and telling storm stories. Most looked like close relatives of our neighbour M. Gruyère. That fat old man with the white walrus moustache, standing in moleskins, wellies and a lime green *pull*, and pointing his walking stick in satisfaction at his unscathed house, was probably Gruyère's dad, a retired butcher. The teenager with him must be his nephew, Jean-Loup. To judge from his baggy two-tone orange and chocolate sweater, worn over yellow lycra running pants, and the gigantic Great Dane pissing like a fire hose against the nearby tree, he'd inherited the family's taste in clothes and animals.

'*Regardez, mon fiston*,' his grandfather would be saying. 'This house will still be here when I'm in the ground. Not like . . .' He waved his cane at the carpet saleroom opposite, a flat-roofed box with all-round windows and a rooftop billboard like the dorsal fin of Bruce, the shark in *Jaws*. Today, the billboard with its offers of '*Promotion! Occasion! Entrée libre*' was a hundred metres away, jammed halfway up a power pylon, and a tree branch had reduced half the windows to glittering drifts on the frosty grass.

Even there, however, good nature flourished. As men shovelled glass into a skip, a girl pulled aside one of the yellow tarpaulins hung to protect the stock and stepped into the winter sunlight. She was carrying mugs, and coffee in a vacuum flask as big as a fire extinguisher. From the appreciation with which the workers slurped, it was evidently *augmenté et fortifié*, probably with *marc*, that gullet-scarifying brandy distilled from the skins and pips left after the grapes are pressed for wine. In times of trouble, the rural French turn to *marc* as religiously as the British to a cuppa and the Australians to a beer.

The men raised steaming mugs in our direction. The French have their character faults, but self-pity isn't one of them. The Four Horsemen of the Apocalypse were, if not their old friends, then at least familiar enemies. In 1940, German panzers thundered down this road, en route to occupy Paris. Over the next few years, bands of Maquis partisans operated in these fields and hedges, harrying their supply route. A few kilometres away, a low roadside memorial, its discolouring bronze letters bolted into cement gone near-black and slimy with lichen, commemorated four partisans executed on the spot in

August 1944. Their only epitaph is the terse *'Souvenez-vous'*. Remember.

While some French fought the Germans, most, like M. Gruyère the elder, dug in and waited out the storm, carrying on business as usual. Disaster was to be endured, maybe even profited from. It was an Englishman, George Herbert, who said, 'Living well is the best revenge,' but the French who put it into practice. Despite the Nazis seizing almost all of France's food for shipping to Germany, along with most of its healthy young men, cafés and restaurants managed to stay open, and to offer at least a shadow of their former menus. Even the Resistance patronized them. André Malraux, later de Gaulle's Minister of Culture, commanded a batallion of the underground army all week in Alsace, then hopped a ride into Paris on Friday afternoon and spent the weekend with his mistress Louise de Vilmorin. On Saturday night they'd go to Fouquet's, still today the smartest restaurant on the Champs-Élysées, and enjoy a leisurely supper while Nazi officers dined at nearby tables.

Brothels, segregated into 'Officers' and 'Other Ranks', were busier than ever. Arletty, star of films like *Les Enfants du paradis* and *Hôtel du Nord*, a sometime artist's model and probably a prostitute herself at one time, brushed aside post-war accusations that she'd betrayed her country with a series of German lovers. 'My heart is French,' she said, 'but my ass belongs to the world.' If France needed a national motto, that would be it.

Nothing had changed in half a century. As we drove past Versailles, forestry experts were already noting with guarded approval that most of the 250 trees torn down in the storm were old, and would have needed to be felled anyway. A year later, the gardens, thinned out, neatened up and replanted, would reopen with a fanfare. Everyone would agree they were a vast improvement. The owners of the carpet company would be sitting round a bottle of cognac and scheming how to make the insurance cover some new air conditioning. The men cleaning up the broken glass and shattered trees were looking forward to a nice bonus.

In the same way, Paris in June 1940 needed a couple of days to absorb the reality of occupation, but by the following week panic had subsided, refugees were trickling back to their homes, and bar-owners, watching the *Wehrmacht* stroll in their thick grey uniforms, thought, *Mon dieu*, they must be thirsty, and called over their shoulder, 'Gaston, put another keg on ice.' By September, Garnier Frères, one of France's oldest publishers, already had a handy pocket-sized German–French dictionary on the market.

'People's tension slackening', Sylvia Beach's companion Adrienne Monnier noted in her diary two days after Paris was declared an Open City. '[They think] "What if the Germans are here, there will at least be order".' On her way to take tea with a friend at Le Dôme, she saw German soldiers buying jewellery at the Samaritain department store. The other great café on Boulevard Montparnasse, the Rotonde, had also reopened, so that afternoon the bookshop, Shakespeare and Company, opened its doors too. Three subscribers to the lending library came by, and Adrienne even sold a book, the first to cross the counter under Nazi occupation. Not inappropriately, it was *Gone with the Wind*.

It remained open until 1941, when, at least according to legend, a German officer tried to buy a copy of *Finnegans Wake*, and Sylvia refused to sell it. Whatever the reason, the shop was ordered closed and the books seized. Although most of her clients had fled from Paris, enough remained so that, in two hours, the stock had been moved to the apartment above the shop and the famous sign painted over. When the Germans returned, it was as if the most familiar landmark of expatriate literary Paris had never existed.

9

The Freedom of the City

'Bombs will fall, civilization will crumble. But not yet, please.
What's the hurry? Give us our moment.'

Ninotchka; script by Charles Brackett, Billy Wilder and Walter Reisch,
based on an original story by Melchior Lengyel

WHAT HAPPENED TO US IN FEBRUARY WAS EVERYTHING,
and all of it at the same time. First, and most
important, we found that Marie-Do was pregnant.

Over the next year, this fact would dominate our
lives. When, calling up the ghostly black-and-white
interior of Marie-Dominique's abdomen on her
screen, the *échographiste* laid an electronic pointer on
a peanut with a flickering pulse at its heart, I would
stare in awe, instantly converted to a pro-Lifer. Kill
my baby? Over my dead body!

I found myself thinking about *West Block*, a novel

by Sara Dowse, an American writer transplanted to Australia. One of her characters, the house-proud Jonathan, resists fathering a child for fear of the mess it will make of his ordered life. A year later, we rediscover him as a deliriously happy father, minding the new baby in his now-ravaged flat:

> The catch on the gold cigarette case had long since ceased to function. Surrendering, Jonathan consigned that, too, to the box where he kept the baby's toys. The baby loved to chew it, hard and cold on the gums. As he loved the top of his father's coffee percolator, [...] a small travel clock ripped from its case, and the key to the liquor cabinet. These were the prizes that nestled among rattles, squeeze toys and building blocks [...] and collected at Jonathan's feet like shoals of fish in a lagoon.

Taking the baby for a walk, he notices the birds, which have always seemed to him symbols of freedom. For the first time, however, it registers with him that most birds fly in pairs.

Did we want to know its sex, the *échographiste* asked.

Yes. Absolutely. Though in our hearts we knew that already.

'It's a little girl.'

Marie-Do and I became the most absorbed of expectant parents. We christened the baby 'Louise' and talked about her for hours as we lay on the bed at Place Dauphine. Occasionally we looked round the tiny studio and wondered where on earth we were going to put her.

We devoured everything we could find on childbirth. One book explained what to do if, in an emergency, we were forced to deliver the baby ourselves. 'The umbilical cord should not be cut until it has ceased pulsing.' *Pulsing*!? All had brief but reassuring chapters about what might go wrong during the pregnancy, rather than at the last minute. We didn't take much notice of them. Marie-Do was healthy. We were well insured. What could happen? A great deal, as it turned out, and none of it good. But that was all to come.

Incipient fatherhood made it even more crucial that I legalize my presence in France. The Consulate in Los Angeles had given me a visa that demanded I leave the country every three months and stay out of it entirely for six months of any year. We'd already taken a quick weekend in England to get the visa renewed, but the end of my first half-year loomed.

Most mornings, after Marie-Do left for work, I sat over a coffee and thought about the alternatives. I could, of course, just go into smoke. Australian friends had lived like that for years in Britain, rats in the walls of the welfare state. But while this might work for them, or for an illegal cleaning pools in

Sherman Oaks, I could hardly take research trips by smuggling myself in and out of France in a load of pineapples. And not many publishers were ready to commission books by meeting me on a street corner at midnight with a brown-paper sack of used notes.

Also, France was ferociously policed. There seemed to be a *flic* on every corner. Each carried an automatic pistol attached to his or her belt by a curly white plastic lanyard, like a telephone cord. In the narrow streets around Rue de Grenelle, where some of the ministries were located, a couple of navy-blue Berthier buses, their windows reinforced with wire mesh, always lurked. Inside sat grim men in military fatigues, wearing the shield-shaped patch of the CRS militia whose activities in the *événements* of 1968 had led students to claim 'CRS' stood, not for *Compagnies Républicaines de Securité*, but '*Connards, racistes et salopards*' – assholes, racists and bastards.

In New York or London, the homeless can sleep for years in the tunnels of the IRT or a cardboard box under the bridge arches of the Thames Embankment and never be rousted, but in Paris ten minutes can scarcely pass before a cop strolls up, pokes them in the ribs or taps the sole of their shoe with his *matraque*, or truncheon, and enquires, 'You are waiting for a bus, *m'sieur?*' They won't be arrested or even moved on, but if they have any sense they'll be gone when the cop returns.

Every night, in the small hours, a bus circulates through Paris, picking up the *clochards* and anyone else sleeping rough. Politely but firmly, they are taken to Nanterre, an unlovely satellite of Paris, all concrete and mercury vapour street-lamps, and there washed, given medical treatment, a meal and, if they want it, a bed. By dawn most are back on the streets, but that is their choice.

The French are used to being regulated. Every citizen carries an identity card, and all resident aliens a *carte de séjour*, which has to be produced on demand. Not that middle-aged ladies in Saint Laurent knock-offs, en route to morning *chocolat* with their friends at Angelina on Rue de Rivoli, run much risk of being patted down and told to 'Assume the position'. To see the system in action, you had to descend into the labyrinthine shopping complex under Les Halles, a popular hangout at weekends for Africans and Caribbean people who clustered just out of sight of the cruising cops, their fear as pungent as if they'd trodden in dog shit.

I explained my concerns to Marie-Do.

She didn't even contemplate such a *bétise*. 'We will fix it.'

'Won't that be difficult? I mean, if it's in my passport . . .'

She shrugged off this detail. 'I will talk to some people.'

All over Europe, any action, from renting an apartment to declaring war, is virtually impossible without 'knowing someone'. Through the capillaries of an intricately connected social system, news of our problem percolated to every corner of France. And since Marie-Do's uncle went to school with somebody's lawyer who was sleeping with the sister of a *juge d'instruction*, within a few days we had the name of a Madame Latour and a rendezvous at the Préfecture of Police.

The Préfecture of the 1st *arrondissement* massively occupies an entire block. Almost next to Notre Dame, it's a cathedral in its own way as well – not to God but to the social order for which the Revolution was fought. Over the years, its vast halls and arched gates have been modified to accommodate cars, mobs, terrorists, air conditioning and a flood of emigrants. As a result, the building is as riddled with holes as a Gruyère cheese, and only to be entered, as we discovered after applying at the two entrances which looked out on the river, through a tiny door on the landward side.

We were directed to a room with a ceiling at least eight metres high. A block of chairs in the centre offered ease to a shifting population of supplicants, to whom, in glassed-in cubicles around the edge of the room, unsmiling men and women were giving a variety of hard times. The majority were Asian and

African, most of whom kept wiping their foreheads with handkerchiefs. Some were in tears. My heart sank.

Madame Latour's office, on a dais at the other end of the room, made it clear that she was senior to the torturers in the cubicles. A lady in her early forties, she seemed marginally less steely than some of the others. But maybe she just kept her sadistic impulses better reined in.

For my benefit, the conversation was conducted in English.

'I have a letter agreeing to take responsibility for Monsieur Baxter,' Marie-Do said. 'Legal and financial.' She handed over the document, cooked up with her lawyer the previous week.

'Hmmm.' Madame put it aside without reading it. 'Your passport?' she said to me.

I gave it to her.

'Ah,' she said, leafing through it. 'You like France?'

'Of course. Who could not?'

This was clearly the correct response. Finding my visa, she turned it on its side to read it.

'They explained in Los Angeles', I began, 'that I could stay for only six months . . .'

'Yes.' She handed the open passport back to me, and asked pleasantly, 'Where does it say that?'

I read the visa from beginning to end — something

I'd never bothered to do before. To my astonishment, there was no reference to a six-month limit. Apparently, providing I left France once a year and got my passport stamped on my return, I could stay here for five years.

I flashed back to that day in the French Consulate some months before, and the bored visa clerk.

'What is your purpose in visiting France?' he'd asked.

'I'm working on a book.'

It wasn't *entirely* a lie. My laptop contained one third of *Bondi Blues*, a crime novel. But the story was set almost entirely in Australia, with some digressions into southern California, and, as I'd been living in Los Angeles for more than a year, those were now thoroughly researched. The writing could as easily be completed in Palm Springs as Paris.

'You understand you will not be permitted to take paid employment in France?'

'I don't intend to.'

He pondered this answer. 'You're resident here, Mr Baxter?'

I took out my Green Card, entitling me to live anywhere in the USA and accept paid employment. For the first time, he looked impressed. It was hard to get these things.

'Hmmm.' He glanced over my shoulder at the backpackers gathering in the corridor beyond the glass door, all eager for tourist visas. 'There's only one kind of visa I can issue you,' he said, reaching for the rubber stamp. 'It is for six months . . .'

Then why had he not put the six-month limit on my passport? I thought I understood. How many other eager men and women, with the same gleam in their eye as myself, had he seen belly up to his counter? Hundreds, no doubt – and all of them, like myself, sick with love for some visiting French person, and desperate to follow him or her back to Paris. And how many had returned within a few months, depressed, disappointed and alone? Almost the same number.

An Australian? A film writer? With a Green Card? How long before the sex ceased to obscure the challenges and complexities of living in Paris? I'd be back; he was sure of it. And to his belief in my inability to survive there, I owed his casual conferring of the freedom of France.

'So . . . what do I do now?' I asked Madame Latour.

I must have registered how delighted I felt. She smiled. It made her look almost beautiful.

She handed back my passport. 'You just need a new stamp,' she said. 'I would slip over to Brussels and buy your lady a box of chocolates.'

10

Stealing Soup

EMPLOYEE ON HONEYMOON CABLING BOSS: 'Request extra week. It's wonderful here.'

BOSS IN REPLY: 'Get back to work. It's wonderful anywhere.'

IS PREGNANCY APHRODISIAC? IN MY CASE, THAT WAS its effect. Or perhaps Paris's romantic influence just became stronger this close to the source. Whatever the reason, I couldn't go far from the apartment without being seized, sometimes in an embarrassingly revealing manner, with the urge to hurry back to my delightful companion.

But in the languor following one particularly uninhibited morning, a nagging thought insinuated itself. 'Now that I can stay indefinitely in France, I should think about earning a living.'

The head on the pillow next to me gave its muffled agreement.

In Los Angeles, I'd thrived as a screenwriter and film journalist. The appetite of Australian and British magazines for articles about California's wilder side was insatiable, and I'd become a prime supplier.

In that respect, however, Paris was a closed shop, as I found when I approached those British and Australian editors who'd been my best clients. 'Sorry, mate. Old Charlie Farley's been our Paris man for years. Lives in some rat hole in Montmartre and relies on us for his rent. I wouldn't have the heart to cut him off.'

It was same story everywhere. Once established in Paris, freelance correspondents clung to their spot until the grave, relinquishing it on their deathbed, and then only to some equally tenacious friend.

The ruling literary limpet was Janet Flanner, who provided the *New Yorker* with Paris reports from 1925 to just before her death in 1978. She was such a typical expat that I chose her *nom de plume* 'Genet' as my email address. Most people think she adopted 'Genet' as a compliment to the writer Jean Genet, though it preceded him by decades. According to legend, the *New Yorker*'s unlettered founder Harold Ross suggested it, assuming, wrongly, that 'Genet' was how the French spelt 'Janet'.

Though, like many other freelancers in Paris, Flanner was homosexual, she was exceptional in having a number of partners, even raising a son with one of them. Most, however, lived alone, and in considerable frugality. A French press card got them invited to press receptions – which, this being Paris, were generously catered. But while a few of those each week, added to a knowledge of the city's cheaper restaurants, shrank their food budget considerably, existence remained hand-to-mouth.

Some developed ingenious ways of milking the system. Early in my time in Paris, one of the English-language giveaway magazines that pop up like mushrooms, and last about as long, published a glowing restaurant review. Marie-Do and I tried the place that night. Halfway through a respectable, if not inspired, meal, a man arrived, to be greeted effusively by the owner. Wine was opened, a table prepared, a lavish complimentary dinner served. From much flourishing of the magazine we'd read, we concluded he was the reviewer.

One film critic – call him Simon Sponge – registered an imposing magazine title of the order *French Film News*, and, for the record, cranked out an occasional single-page collection of reviews under that name. But the title alone, listed among English-language publications, was enough to get him on the guest list of every film producer, publisher, couturier, restaurant owner and public-relations company in Paris. Soon you couldn't open a manhole without

Simon's presence. Colleagues leaving a press conference would find him already at the buffet, stuffing himself and stashing sandwiches in his briefcase for later. 'The little bastard even has rubber-lined pockets,' snarled one critic, 'so he can steal soup.'

Sponge overplayed his hand when an unsophisticated but wealthy film festival in the Far East included him, to his gratified astonishment, among the European journalists flown in for the event. Back in Paris, correspondents for respectable national papers let it be known they didn't care to be lumped in with Simon, and he was blacklisted. Defiantly, he arrived, uninvited, at the next film preview, but was turned away. Half an hour later, during a quiet moment in the film, shouts were heard from the men's room. Ushers discovered Simon stuck in the window through which he'd been trying to crawl.

Marie-Do also got her share of invitations through her radio station, so we frequently found ourselves nibbling wafer-thin *foie gras* sandwiches and drinking Moët with the best. A high point was the reopening at the Opéra Garnier of its beautiful little library of theatre and ballet materials, restored through the munificence of LVMH, owners of Vuitton, Dior, Moët et Chandon and Hennessy. They also funded the lavish opening-night reception, held in the ballroom-sized main foyer of that gaudy chunk of baroque at the heart of the snobbish Right Bank. Trumpeters in mirror-bright silver breastplates lined the wide marble stairs, at the foot of which young women in tailored mini-skirts, and with perfect legs, handed out hard-bound catalogues to the library's inaugural exhibition, of designs from Diaghilev's Ballets Russes. On the first landing, guests were greeted by Culture Minister Jack Lang, who, with characteristic good taste and style, had chosen as his fellow host not a bureaucrat from the Élysée but the historian LeRoy Ladurie.

The crowd was too well bred to cluster round the buffet of tiny sandwiches, thin as razor blades, and jewel-like petits fours, which, in any event, were so beautiful that one felt more like admiring than eating. As we sipped our champagne and celebrity-spotted, a gaunt figure emerged from the back of the building and skulked round the fringes of the crowd. He wore a lopsided black beret, and his wrinkled cords and old sweater swam on his thin body, but the face, though shockingly wasted from Aids, was recognizably that of Rudolf Nureyev, just fired from his job as boss of the Paris ballet, whose headquarters this was. Unnoticed by almost everyone, he hovered until he caught the eye of friends, then plunged into the crowd towards them. Within a year he was dead, and the gorgeous contents of his mansion on the banks of the Seine auctioned off. When Paris creates legends, it exacts a price.

Other invitations were less painful. Through another friend of Marie-Do's, an American journalist, we were invited to dinner at the PM's official residence, the Hôtel Matignon. Not *with* the Prime Minister, true, but with one of his cabinet, to whom our friend was married. Someone must always stay by the Red Telephone, so members of the inner circle take turns sleeping at Matignon. They aren't expected to doss down on a camp bed – this *is* Paris, after all. A comfortable apartment is provided, with a view over the Prime Minister's private garden. Their wife or *petite amie* can stay too, and they can invite up to four guests a night to dinner, catered from the Prime Minister's kitchen.

Our arrival was suitably cloak-and-daggery. A tiny unmarked door in a quiet side street opened onto a classic eighteenth-century hallway, but jammed with twenty-first-century scanning technology. After being X-rayed to our underwear, we were led up a flight of marble stairs by liveried servants, and into the guest apartment – to be greeted by a barrage of barking from two large black poodles. Even though the fate of the world might rest on that night's decisions, our friends couldn't bear to spend one minute away from their dogs.

France has eight million dogs and nearly nine

million cats, but since 550,000 of the dogs are in the Paris area the city seethes with canines. Scotties on leads, dachshunds and kelpies scampering underfoot, boxers and Dobermans pushing imperiously through the crowd, St Bernards and Great Danes lumbering along, confident nobody will get in their way.

Few places exclude them. Some supermarkets try, though with classically French diplomacy: instead of 'Dogs Not Allowed', the signs say 'We Ask Our Four-Legged Friends to Remain Outside'. But everywhere else, barriers have long since collapsed. Doggy eyes peep from shopping bags and inside overcoats. What appears to be a duster on that woman's office desk is more likely her little *toutou*. And it's nothing to look under the table at a restaurant and see a Jack Russell or Yorkshire Terrier lounging at its mistress's feet, nibbling on scraps – if the restaurateur hasn't provided a bowl for the little rascal.

But there is a downside to all this togetherness. Paris spends more money per head on sanitation and street cleaning than any city in the world. High-pressure hoses sluice every pavement at least once a week and, three times a week, water floods the gutters. The reason is obvious. Pooches extrude an estimated ton of droppings onto its streets each day.

One develops a kind of subliminal radar to warn of the slimy heaps and smears, but since tourists are less skilled in the Doggie DooDoo Two-Step, successive city governments have introduced encouragements for dog owners at least to keep the crap off the pavement. One administration glued green plastic dachshunds to the kerb, with arrows pointing suggestively at the gutter. People simply ignored them, as did their dogs. Ronald Searle, inventor of the demon girls of St Trinian's (and a long-time French resident), was commissioned to draw a series of cartoons on the theme. They had no effect. Then there was a poster campaign featuring stark examples of the inconvenience and downright danger inflicted on the handicapped by dog dirt. It showed how wheelchair wheels and white canes become slathered in ordure, and how readily old people slip and fall. In the most self-absorbed city on earth, the posters barely caused a ripple.

The same could be said of the motor bikes fitted with built-in vacuum cleaners which used to cruise the streets, their white-suited riders sucking up the offending heaps. Parisians sarcastically dubbed them '*la moto-crotte*' or '*la crottinette*': puns on MotoCross and *trottinette*, or scooter ('*crotte*' meaning 'dropping'). One pitied the riders. Occasionally you'd meet the eye of some doleful school leaver hosing out his box. It was a long way from Marlon Brando and *The Wild One*.

In 2002, the sanitary adviser to Paris's new mayor

decided to get tough. Dog toilets were set up in the larger parks. If owners didn't use them, they were expected to clean up what was deposited elsewhere, even in the gutters, under pain of fines ranging from 180 to 450. Once again, the response was a hoot of derision. Only one proposed deterrent looked even moderately promising, and so far no city administration has had the *culot* to introduce it. It's simple enough. Just choose seven dog owners at random each week, and deposit a ton of ordure on the doorstep of each.

Rather than end up like Simon Sponge, I never looked for work as a full-time journalist in Paris, which turned out to be the right move, since, once editors decided I was no risk to their resident person, they gave me the jobs that the regulars couldn't or wouldn't do.

Mostly these involved attending one of France's innumerable festivals. Festivals are a major industry in Europe. Their product is tourist revenue, their by-product prestige, their raw material journalists. The government invests generously in festivals, a fact which city governments exploit by spending as little as they can on the programme and as much as possible on administration. Some festivals present films, plays or exhibitions, but many don't bother. Instead, they offer plenty of bunting, some fireworks, tastings of local delicacies in the town square, a *brocante* or antiques fair, performances by folk musicians from the area, a show of livestock, a parade – in short, anything that people are likely to do for free.

A fraternity of mid-level administrators exists to think up festivals and find local councils to fund them. Rumpelstiltskins all, accomplished in spinning gold from straw, they are fun to talk to. One such was the man appointed as director of a festival in a left-wing, mostly immigrant, satellite community of Paris. A veteran of the funding wars, he had survival down to a fine art. His festival poster showed a sparrow on a branch, double exposed, so that it appeared to be looking in two directions at once.

'Does it symbolize something?' I asked.

'*Tout à fait*,' he said, obviously improvising. 'We are a bird with two songs: our classical repertoire and the music programmes for the ordinary working people of our district.'

'But sparrows can't sing,' I pointed out.

'Ah, then it is a symbol of our vision: we look both to the past and to the future.'

'It isn't meant to indicate', I suggested, 'that, while the festival has flourished under the Socialists, it's prepared to look in a different direction under the new right-wing administration?'

He grinned, enjoying the game. 'No – but it may

mean that the sparrow, the poor bird of the people, and of art, may fly away if we do not feed him the crumbs . . .'

He had an answer to everything – but then he played cultural ping-pong for a living. I was just an amateur.

One year, BBC radio sent me to Avignon, in the south of France, to cover the annual drama festival – a far more artistically serious event, though just as commercial at the heart, since it's the main trade fair for France's numerous freelance theatre companies. For ten days in the hottest part of July, every public square, restaurant, cinema, scout hall, garage and building site in the medieval city on the Rhône becomes a theatre as they jostle to attract the attention of regional managers who come there to book next year's programme for their civic entertainment centres, the maisons de la Culture.

Borrowing an idea from the film critic Gideon Bachmann, who did all the interviews for his Cannes Festival reports on the dance floor at the ball on the last night, I set up in one of the large open-air cafés on the Place de l'Horloge, the piazza at the centre of town, and grabbed people as they passed. On a typical afternoon, they included New York playwright Israel Horowitz, author of *Park Your Car in Harvard Yard* and *The Indian Wants the Bronx*, who was being honoured with a retrospective. Only Molière had more plays being performed that year, I pointed out. 'He has more relatives in France,' Horowitz said drily. Next was Nikki Fink, a voluptuous young woman in an abbreviated vampire costume, who dropped off a tape of her show, a musical version of *Dracula* being performed on the barge in which her company had sailed here from Paris. Then a girl who distributed festival publicity, a producer from French TV, and finally Marie-Dominique with two couples, the five of them sun-tanned and wind-blown after a hard day round the pool.

As it turned out, an interesting dynamic, worthy of a film by Claude Chabrol, was at work between Couple A (upwardly mobile TV executive and his anorexic alcoholic ex-actress wife) and Couple B (the TV man's middle-aged financier and his slim, carnal, barely-out-of-teens wife). Over the next few months, husband A and wife B would start an affair, culminating in a confrontation with elements of high comedy, in which the deceived husband stormed into the office of his nervous rival. 'I have spent all night struggling between jealousy and friendship,' he announced, 'and . . .' holding out his hand '. . . friendship wins, so she's yours.'

Maybe the heavy Avignon air was charged with this melodrama, because an American lady came over to our table. 'I don't know who you are,' she said plaintively, 'but you seem to know *everyone*. Can you recommend a show tonight that a couple of people from New Jersey might enjoy?'

We handed her over to Nikki, the Dracula lady, and they went off happily, while we fortified ourselves for the night's big event.

This always took place in the roofless shell of the medieval Palace of the Popes. Starting at about 10 p.m., when the sun had disappeared behind the ruined walls, it sometimes didn't finish until the sun rose again. People who'd paid a fortune for their seats approached the performances with reverence, but those of us with press passes often found it hard to keep a straight face.

In an open-air playing space of that size, performers were at the mercy of the elements. Bats swooped through conversations that were supposedly taking place in eighteenth-century drawing rooms and which continued even when it began to rain. Sometimes an evening breeze blew up, so stiff that actresses in their fussy gowns had to tack to their places like yachts in an ocean race. For one epic by the near-forgotten Spanish playwright Valle-Inclan, the lights came up on a large bed spotlighted in the middle of the paddock-like playing area. A moment later, a nude girl sprinted out of the darkness. Assumed to be a streaker, she was greeted with hoots and whistles until we realized she was just an actress making her entrance.

For every experience like Avignon, however, there were a dozen where editors only wanted a sarcastic five hundred words on the comic French, or a thirty-second summary of a subject that really needed half an hour. Though this didn't entirely sour me on journalism, it reminded me of the pleasure of independence. Never a team player, I felt even less like one in a city to which so many writers had come to stretch their literary legs and write what they pleased.

'I'm thinking of writing a book,' I said one icy morning in my first Paris winter. 'A biography.'

'About whom?' Marie-Do asked.

It turned out to be Federico Fellini – followed in quick succession by Luis Buñuel, Steven Spielberg, Woody Allen, Stanley Kubrick, George Lucas and Robert De Niro. Having carelessly uprooted myself from California, I seemed, miraculously, to have found even more congenial soil in Paris.

11

Monsieur Right

MRS MACMILLAN, wife of the then Prime Minister of England: 'And you, Madame de Gaulle, what do you wish for most in life?'

MME DE GAULLE: 'A penis.'

GENERAL DE GAULLE (*hurriedly*): 'I believe that is pronounced "happiness", my dear.'

MARIE-DO AND I FELL INTO A ROUTINE. BY THE TIME she came home late in the morning, I'd have written my daily quota, so we'd shop, visit a gallery or catch a film. More frequently, however, as the pregnancy progressed, she preferred to sleep after lunch, so I'd go out on my own, often looking for books, or places where books had been inspired.

Far from being suppressed by the strangeness of Paris, my interest in books became more acute in a city where literature seemed to flow from the pavements. One couldn't pass a corner where Scott Fitzgerald and Hemingway or Gertrude Stein and Alice B. Toklas had not once sat, argued, drunk, passed out, or sometimes all four.

I tracked down the Dingo Bar – now an Italian restaurant – on Rue Delambre where Fitzgerald and Hemingway first met. I also located the café on Rue Jacob, site of their lunch during which, as Hemingway describes in *A Moveable Feast*, a profoundly depressed Fitzgerald revealed that Zelda had told him he could never satisfy any woman sexually.

'It's a matter of measurements,' she'd said.

Reluctantly, Hemingway agreed to go with Fitzgerald to the men's room for what the army called 'a short-arm parade'.

'You're OK,' he reassured him afterwards. 'Nothing to worry about.'

When Fitzgerald still seemed uncertain, they walked over to the Louvre, where Hemingway pointed out the modest dimension of the penises on the Greek and Roman statues. In Fitzgerald's place, this would have made me feel worse. Traditional art never emphasizes genitals; where are the Greek and Roman statues with dicks one can hang one's hat on? And is 'nothing to worry about' the phrase one would chose to stiffen someone's confidence?

When *A Moveable Feast* was published, Arnold

Gingrich of *Esquire* magazine, in which many of Fitzgerald's stories appeared (and Hemingway's too), was moved to write an editorial. In the Thirties, he said, he'd often visited a less-than-sober Scott in his New York hotel. Once, the writer answered the door in his dressing gown, which hung open, revealing the organ of which Zelda complained. Gingrich was thus, he explained, almost uniquely qualified to refute her slur. He was not, he told readers, about to go into details but would follow the Rolls-Royce company, which, when asked about the horsepower of its cars, simply replied, 'Adequate.' Scott's bedroom equipment was, he assured everybody, 'adequate'.

It was just as well Fitzgerald wasn't alive to read this. If 'OK' and 'nothing to worry about' didn't do the job, Gingrich's chilly adjective would have shrivelled his organ to the size of an olive. One way or another, history will record that the author of *The Great Gatsby* was hung like a hamster.

My walks also took me to Paris's few second-hand English-language bookshops, where I'd comb the shelves, partly for material on Fellini, but mainly for rarities, either for my own collection (still stored in Australia) or to sell.

A few of these shops have always limped along in Paris's secluded corners. Cannibal Pierce's, down an alley in the suburb of Saint-Denis, even specialized in

Australiana. Named for an escaped convict who eeked out his life in Tasmania by eating whatever – or whoever – he could catch, the shop was closed both times I made it out there. The owners were a raffish couple named June Shenfield and Ken Shepherd, he a poet and graffiti artist, she an unpublished novelist (who told an interviewer she was writing about 'female crosslegged masturbation – the last taboo'). As cultural ambassadors for Australia, they didn't inspire confidence: asked why they had settled in Paris, Shepherd said, 'We'd rather be in the heart of the world than the arse.' So it's perhaps just as well that Cannibal Pierce's closed down soon after I arrived.

I also liked to stop by a place I'll call The Dog-Eared Diner, a combination bookshop and tea-room tucked up a narrow street on the unfashionable side of Boulevard Montparnasse. Because you could have coffee and a brownie there as well as buy books, it attracted Americans with time on their hands. One day, I eavesdropped on two women as they inspected the battered stock. It didn't take long to figure out they worked at the Embassy.

'I went to a dinner party last night,' one said. 'I met this guy who's Desk Officer for Germany. It was real interesting.'

'Was he cute?' asked her friend, dipping into a well-worn Barbara Taylor Bradford.

'Well, sure. I guess. But I never knew that Desk Officers—'

Her friend dropped the Bradford back in its box. 'He married?'

'No, I don't think so. But apparently Desk Officers—'

She picked up an Anne Tyler. 'You gonna see him again?'

Paris, City of Love.

The Diner belonged to Sandy, a rangy blonde from Iowa, married, unhappily, to a Frenchman who, perhaps because the marriage was so dismal, always seemed to be out of the country.

Fossicking in her overflowing shelves became a high point of my walks, particularly after I discovered first editions of William Burroughs' *The Naked Lunch* and *The Ticket That Exploded*, published in the Fifties by Maurice Girodias's Olympia Press. Sandy priced all her paperbacks at 25 francs, even these rarities which, particularly as they were in their dustwrappers (discarded by most buyers at the time, since the plain green card covers were less likely to attract the attention of Customs), were already, even then, worth $300, and today more like $1,200.

I persuaded Sandy that, rather than buy items piecemeal, I should go through her stock, wherever she had it stored. This turned out to be at her home, a deeply authentic and unrestored mid-nineteenth-century house in Versailles, all creaking parquet, over-varnished landscapes, and mottled antique mirrors framed in dusty gilt. Racks of rifles gleamed in locked glass cases. Stuffed heads of wildebeeste and warthog grimaced from the walls. We walked on zebra skins. 'My husband's a hunter,' she said unnecessarily.

She led me to a garage piled with books – containing, as it turned out, first editions of Gertrude Stein, Walt Whitman and James Joyce. Over the next year, I depleted this accumulation at roughly the same rate as Sandy's marriage declined. Her 'buying trips' to the US became longer, the references to the absent hunter husband more acid, until one day she introduced me to the new owner, a recent divorcee with – metaphorically at least – a tear-sodden hanky still in her handbag, and the Midwest swallowed Sandy up.

She would have been better off staying. For a woman, Paris is a good city in which to be alone. Since almost everyone lives in an apartment, there are always pleasant studios for rent where the view or the location make up for the lack of space. Most of the expatriate women writers who, since the turn of the nineteenth century, created our image of the city – Edith Wharton, Jean Rhys, Janet Flanner, Nancy Mitford, Mavis Gallant, Diane Johnson – were laureates of loneliness who, even though sometimes married, preferred to live and work by themselves.

Marie-Dominique had been one of these lone – which is not to say lonely – women. The best evidence of the life she led before I arrived was her kitchen. I found a case and a half of 1986 Bordeaux, a magnum of Bollinger champagne, and half a dozen bottles of whisky and brandy, still in boxes from Fauchon, the equivalent of Fortnum & Mason; in Paris, as everywhere, media personalities didn't lack for Christmas gifts from hopeful or grateful PR firms. Otherwise, it was well stocked with wineglasses, ice-cube trays, toothpicks, and dishes to hold a dozen olives or a few handfuls of smoked almonds. That was mostly it, except for a nest of steel saucepans and a frying pan, all so little used that they still bore labels from the department store Samaritaine.

'Didn't you ever eat here?' I called.

'Of course. I even had dinner parties.'

'What with?' I surveyed the provisions cupboard. 'Potato crisps, powdered mash, noodles and...' I rattled a glassine bag of desiccated shreds the colour of dried blood. '... seaweed?'

She came into the kitchen and looked over my shoulder. 'That's herb tea. I brought it back from Egypt.'

'Noodles and Egyptian herb tea? That's a dinner? Where's *haute cuisine*? *Cordon bleu*?'

'Who has time to cook? I go to the *traiteur*.'

The nearest Australian or American equivalent to the *traiteur* is the deli, though the resemblance is remote. Ask for a ham on rye with a pickle at Fauchon and you'll be shown the door. But if you want an entire gourmet meal for ten, they can furnish it, from *vols-au-vents au caviar* and *boeuf poêlé à la Matignon* to four kinds of cheese, *tarte aux fraises*, *crème fraiche*, and wafer-thin after-dinner mints, all packed in sealed plastic dishes. You warm what needs warming, decant it into your own china, add sprigs of parsley or mint (these you have to buy yourself), and serve it as if you just whipped it up. True, such a meal costs the equivalent of Zaire's national debt, but that wasn't the point.

Sex, companionship and affection are also available to the single woman, if she cares to pay the price. The transaction is seldom as vulgar as putting an ad in the *petites annonces* – the French equivalent of 'the personals' – or trolling on the Minitel Rose, the anonymous meat rack that operates through the French telephone system, but just as much of a trade-off is involved between the need for love and the demands of career and independence.

In *Tender Is the Night*, Fitzgerald wrote approvingly of Parisiennes who, unlike their American sisters, 'were happy to exist in a man's world. They preserved their individuality through men and not by opposition to them.' For most women in Paris, these are the ground rules in a nutshell. Men generally regard marriage and children as too high a price to pay for a relationship, and women learn to live as much within their emotional budget as their economic one.

Unlike the Manhattan singles of *Sex and the City*, who gather to talk dirty and compare dimensions, the women of Paris maintain a feline reticence and a similarly cat-like disinclination to compete – or at least be seen to do so. For her novel *Le Divorce*, Diane Johnson created an archetypal expat woman. Isabelle comes to Paris to help her sister through a pregnancy and divorce, only to start an affair with a distinguished seventy-year-old Frenchman. Both her own family and her French in-laws, scandalized, conspire to break it up, but Isabelle is unconcerned. Paris has given her a postgraduate course in the skills of a *grande horizontale*: the correct way to conduct oneself in a smart restaurant, the appropriate sexy lingerie – 'the artillery of the night' – to wear for later, and even such exotic information as the fact that drinking fruit-scented *tisane* will perfume her sexual juices. As the book ends, Isabelle, unsuspected by anybody, even the man in question, is assessing the Deputy Minister for Culture as her next lover.

Last summer I had lunch with my friend Jacqueline, a vivacious American lawyer, who, when her French husband died, remained in France, adopted a child and raised her alone.

'It's Wimbledon this week,' she said dreamily. 'I always used to go.'

'You like tennis?'

'Not a lot. But I had two lovers who were Italian tennis journalists, and they invited me.'

'Lovers at different times, I assume.'

'Oh, no. The same time.'

'They weren't jealous?'

She grinned mischievously. 'Oh, no.'

I opened my mouth to ask if 'at the same time' meant what I thought it did, then closed it again. If the policy of 'don't ask, don't tell' began anywhere, it was here in Paris.

All these thoughts converged when we were invited to dinner by Oliver, the lover of Marie-Do's friend Claire. A divorced businessman with adult children, he lived in the building directly behind ours, but facing the river. The narrow walkway between the buildings was Claire and Oliver's almost private corridor, but though they sometimes went on holidays together, and, one assumed, enjoyed the normal amount of sex, in ten years they'd never shared an apartment. At the point where, in Anglo-Saxon culture, intimacy segued into cohabitation, even marriage, the relationship came to a halt.

Sixty-ish, with sleek grey hair and a commanding

manner, Oliver ushered us into a living room with a spectacular view of the Seine. As if at his signal, a *bateau-mouche* crept by outside, its searchlights sweeping the riverside façades, and, for a moment, brightness glided around the room. It glowed on the medieval hand-hewn chestnut beams of his ceiling, his cabinets of family silver and porcelain, his mural, a Poussin pastiche of nymphs and shepherds, but also on Claire – *his* hostess, who chatted lightly at the other end of his table, and summoned the maid to fill our glasses.

The maid was, I knew, hired for the night. And from the *oeuf en gelée* moulded in the distinctive style of Coesnon, the best local *traiteur*, I knew the food too was catered, right down to the *salade verte*. It was like a stage set, with all of us performing under Oliver's direction. Which, obviously, was the way he preferred to live; and so, it seemed, did Claire. When dinner was over – the guests gone, the dishes washed, the maid paid off – and when Claire, presumably after an hour of discreet passion, had slipped back across the walkway to her own bed, there'd be nothing to show that the dinner party had taken place.

It was an elegant, understated evening, peculiarly French. The American poet Marianne Moore, who herself spent some time in Paris – inevitably alone – might have been thinking of Claire, Jacqueline, Isabelle and all the other smart, quiet but, in essence,

141

deprived *Parisiennes* when she wrote somewhat frostily about 'superior people' in the poem 'Silence'.

> the deepest feeling always shows itself in silence;
> Not in silence, but restraint.

12

Failures

Each one of us, in his timidity, has a limit beyond which he is outraged.

Man Ray

IN 1999, GEORGE WHITMAN ASKED ME TO GIVE A reading at his bookshop Shakespeare and Company on the banks of the Seine opposite Notre Dame. It was a warm evening, so we did it outside. George even disinterred a bottle of champagne which, from the frost on it, had been buried in the bottom of a deep freeze since the Second Empire.

As I stood up, a girl who'd been idling at the rear of the crowd with a neutral-looking young man walked purposefully over and stood next to me. The moment I began to speak, she struck a pose and froze in it, like a fashion model on a photo shoot.

I stopped reading and asked, 'What's going on?'

She didn't reply. Her eyes were fixed on the middle distance. I looked towards the young man, but he just stared over my head.

I shrugged, and began to read again. The poses continued – chin lifted; arms above her head; toes pointed.

A moment later, Karl, the manager, shot out from the back of the shop, shooed her away and glared at the young man. Unperturbed, she snatched the bottle of champagne and walked around the crowd, offering it to them silently to drink. Pretty as she was, most shrank from her. This was obviously nothing new, since, just about the time Karl returned inside to call the police, her silent friend took her by the arm and firmly led her away.

'She's American,' Karl told me later. 'Very rich, but completely crazy. Her parents sent her here. Her boyfriend sees she takes her medication and doesn't get into any trouble.'

Expatriate Paris has plenty of people like her: the losers, the lost, the remittance men and women; the mad, the bad, the dangerous to know. Traditionally they've clustered round the American Library, the American Church and the American Centre – institutions on which the long-time exiles who manage them often impose their own eccentricities.

Readings like those at Shakespeare and Company bring out the idiot fringe along with the literary enthusiasts, so it's not surprising that I met Frances after another such event. An Australian in her early thirties, she'd just arrived, she explained, spoke good French, had spent time as aide to an Australian politico, and wanted research work.

It was all downhill thereafter. In quick succession, she ran out of money to pay the rent, overstayed her tourist visa, and was hounded out of her apartment by a Russian madman she'd invited in off the street for coffee and who had turned up again with a knife, displayed a body covered in self-inflicted scars and proposed to carve her the same way. She found a sub-lessor for the apartment and ended up sleeping in our guestroom for a week. While doing so, she screwed up my computer so thoroughly that it took two long calls to the London Microsoft hotline to sort it out. 'How did you come to do this?' the engineer asked, impressed by the scale of my incompetence.

Even when she fled back to Australia, her presence lingered. Cryptic young men kept calling, and her sub-lessor rang forlornly from the apartment, where she was sitting in the dark, since Frances had failed to pay the electricity bill. The tapes of two important interviews went with her. It took a number of calls to Sydney to retrieve them, the first to her parents.

'I'm trying to contact Frances . . .' I began.

'She's not here!' a man said hysterically and slammed down the phone. I sympathized.

Paris is a victim of its mythology. *If Picasso and Joyce and Stravinsky flourished there*, muse the hopefuls, *why not me? Perhaps it's something in the air, or the water, or the wine* ... And to live there is one ambition that doesn't require years of study to satisfy, nor proof of talent, nor even a single written word – just a one-way ticket.

For these innocents, finding that even in the City of Light you have to pay the electricty bill can be a traumatic experience. Most flee. Some stay, but never recover. Even people of talent aren't immune. The poet Nancy Keesing endowed a Paris studio for use by Australian writers. They can stay for up to a year, but one playwright fled after a week, spooked by the strangeness. The painter father of actor Robert De Niro – also called Robert – revered Picasso and particularly Matisse, and believed he would only truly develop his talent in Paris. Friends clubbed together to send him there, and he sailed from New York in April 1961. After three lean years wandering in rural France, he was rescued by his son. 'It was an absolute nightmare,' comments the actor tersely.

Since Paris is the national capital of culture, of finance, of politics, of art, it's understandable that French art, literature and film show it as the Great Good Place. Superficially, American books and films appear to share this appreciation, but the mythology of *An American in Paris*, *Funny Face*, *Daddy Long Legs* and *The Last Time I Saw Paris*, not to mention the work of Twenties and Thirties expatriates, is ambiguous. At least one character in any American film or book set in Paris is a failed novelist drinking away his talent, an ageing actor, an eternal student, or a poet well past his or her sell-by date. To go to Paris, the received wisdom has it, feeds the soul; to stay there rots it.

In *Paris Blues*, jazz musician Sidney Poitier is persuaded by a radical girlfriend to leave the ease of Paris and join the Struggle back home. Painter Gene Kelly in *An American in Paris* acknowledges his mediocrity and resists wealthy dilettante Nina Foch when she tries to take him up. In *Funny Face*, Audrey Hepburn, a bookseller from Greenwich Village, is bullied into becoming a model, but accepts because it will take her to Paris and a meeting with the philosopher she admires. When he tries to seduce her and the fashion show is a disaster, she ends up with photographer Fred Astaire, who presumably takes her back to America.

It's no different in real life. Numerous expatriates who showed promise in their home countries produced little or nothing in Paris, succumbing to the bottle, the lassitude of café society, or, in the case of men like Harold Stearns, Hemingway's model for a number of such characters, to the lure of the racetrack. Stearns spent numerous long afternoons at Longchamps and Auteuil, occasionally placing a bet, but mostly soaking up the atmosphere. Harry Crosby, co-founder with his wife Caresse of the Black Sun Press, the earliest publisher of Hemingway, shared his enthusiasm for the track, and his *anomie*. An inscription by Crosby in a collection of essays about *Finnegans Wake* encapsulates the intellectual lassitude that enveloped some Americans in Paris. 'Here is the book I mentioned', he wrote. 'Terribly sorry we can't come for cocktails on Wednesday as we are leaving tomorrow (Tuesday) for the Moulin [their country house]. Hope you didn't play our grubstake yesterday at Chantilly . . .' Only James Joyce and Samuel Beckett can be said unequivocally to have done their best work in Paris.

Whether or not you learned from Paris, or even enjoyed the experience, has little to do with material success. George Orwell spent months of misery as a dishwasher, had little good to say about the city, but produced the enduring *Down and Out in Paris and London*. At thirty-one, Harry Crosby left the city and killed himself and his mistress in a New York hotel. Often, the experience only comes into focus when one looks back on it. No country more effectively inspires the sweet pain of nostalgia. Almost the first reference to France I remember reading is the comment by the Water Rat in *The Wind in the Willows*, 'Sometimes I dream of the seafood of Marseilles and wake up crying.' Might Frances's lacerated lodger and bizarre behaviour turn up later in a novel or film? Even the mad girl at my reading could, at this very moment, be creating an account of her madness as painfully readable as Sylvia Plath's description of her own breakdown, *The Bell Jar*.

Since nobody knows in advance whether Paris will inspire or dismay them, going there can seem as random and desperate an act as making a pilgrimage to Lourdes. Thousands arrive in hope at the shrine, all take the waters, but, aside from the occasional cure, the vast majority leave as ill as before, if marginally consoled. Why are those few cured but so many sent away unhealed? Did they pray harder, carry a greater cargo of saintliness or need? Or maybe there's a trick to it. How ironic if miracles depended not on goodness or prayer but were invested in one particular cup, a certain conjunction of the stars, a precise form of words, or pure chance.

Success in Paris sometimes takes no more than the right meeting. When Dali arrived in 1925, he carried letters of introduction to the many Spanish expatriate artists. But he only wanted to meet Pablo Picasso.

The painter Manuel Angeles Ortiz took him to Picasso's studio.

'I have come to see you before visiting the Louvre,' Dali said.

'Quite right,' responded Picasso complacently.

He examined without comment the small painting Dali had brought as a gift, then led him round his studio, in silence, displaying example after example of his recent work. At the end of the tour, he gave Dali a searching look, as if to say, 'You get the idea?' Dali's responding glance said all that needed to be said. Paris had given him what he wanted from it. He could leave the city, knowing that his future as an artist was assured.

13

Odéon

Every man has his natural place. Neither pride nor price determines its altitude: childhood decides it. Mine is a Parisian sixth floor with a view over the roofs.

Jean-Paul Sartre, *Les Mots*

I CAME BACK FROM A REVIVAL OF *FREUD: THE SECRET Passion* one Saturday afternoon to find Marie-Do and her mother in serious conversation. An empty teapot and the remains of a box of macaroons suggested it had been going on for some time.

'Mother thinks we should move,' Marie-Do said. 'Before Louise is born.'

'Great idea. But where? And how?' Whatever Marie-Do and I earned, it didn't run to heavy investment in property.

'We think', Marie-Do said, 'that we might exchange apartments.'

Claudine Montel lived on the sixth floor of a building in the 6th *arrondissement* that dated back to the 1700s. Though only about ten minutes' walk from Place Dauphine, it was another world in comparison with the tiny studio. Every time we visited her, I couldn't hide my admiration of the big bedrooms, the large kitchen and bathroom, but mostly the long living and dining room, which opened onto a terrace with a spectacular view of Notre Dame.

It was a gesture of extraordinary generosity, no less so for making sense. Marie-Do's studio was fine for a woman living alone who liked to eat out, but no place for a couple with a child. On the other hand, the big apartment on Rue de l'Odéon was ideal for a family. Claudine had raised two daughters there herself. And increasingly, she spent much of her time in her country house.

Still, one had doubts, and it was to neutralize them that we went round there the next week to look things over.

The area from Boulevard Montparnasse down past the Luxembourg Gardens to Boulevard Saint-Germain is like a museum of expatriate literature. Gertrude Stein and Alice B. Toklas lived on Rue de Fleurus, Scott Fitzgerald and Zelda on Rue Madame. Man Ray had his last studio just around the corner from the Odéon, on Rue Ferou. African-American expatriates like James Baldwin, Richard Wright and Chester Himes used the Café Tournon, at the top of Rue Tournon, as their informal club.

Further up the hill, beyond the Luxembourg, along Boulevard Montparnasse, you can hardly sit down at a café or restaurant that someone hasn't immortalized. Salvador Dali hawked paintings at La Coupole to other Surrealists like Robert Desnos, and met Louis Aragon and Man Ray in the bar. Miguel de Unamuno convened his afternoon *pena* at the Dôme while, at another table, Catalan exiles plotted revolution. At the Bal Bullier dance hall, Luis Buñuel danced *le fox*, his sexual tastes satisfied by casual frottage with his anonymous partners, while opposite, at the Closerie des Lilas, a brass plate marks the table at – and sometimes under – which the hard-drinking Ernest Hemingway could often be found. Rue de l'Odéon itself had two plaques indicating houses of special artistic interest. At number 16, Tom Paine wrote *The Rights of Man*. And at number 12, Sylvia Beach founded Shakespeare and Company.

The daughter of an Episcopalian minister, Beach served as an agricultural volunteer in World War I, digging potatoes in Serbia. In Paris, she met the vivacious Parisienne bookseller Adrienne Monnier, who had a shop on Rue de l'Odéon called Les Amis des Livres. Beach bought the shop opposite and turned it into Shakespeare and Company, the centre of expatriate literary life in Paris between the wars. Its lending library helped Hemingway, Fitzgerald and James Joyce keep up with new American literature. She hosted soirées and signing sessions, held mail for visiting writers, and, when Joyce couldn't find a publisher, issued the first edition of *Ulysses*. During World War II, Samuel Beckett lived in the apartment on the first floor, hiding from the Germans.

Beach and Monnier took another flat just up the street, at number 18 – the building where Claudine lived. I never climbed the winding spiral staircase without a sense that every step was sacred. Though the green and gold carpet with the motif of Napoleon III looked frayed enough, it hadn't been trodden by Scott and Hem, but the worn mahogany balustrade had certainly sustained them as they staggered down from the fourth floor where Sylvia and Adrienne lived.

A few months after we moved in, the octogenarian Mme Dechaux on the first floor described to me over tea how Monsieur 'Emingway had arrived in June 1944 to liberate the building. While his men drove snipers from the rooftops opposite, Hemingway took Adrienne aside and demanded her assurance that, under the Nazis, Sylvia had never collaborated. After that, he and his gang roared to the Ritz Hotel for a historic meeting with André Malraux, another writer who'd run a private army during the Resistance. He and Hemingway locked horns over who'd commanded the most troops and taken the greatest risks. When it looked like Hemingway would lose, one of his men beckoned him into the bathroom and murmured, 'Hey, papa, want me to shoot this asshole?' Fortunately, Hemingway acknowledged defeat. Malraux lived to become not only De Gaulle's Minister of Culture but also a major figure in post-war French literature.

At the top of the Odéon staircase, breathless, we stepped into the hall of Claudine's apartment. On this spring day, it seemed overheated. And were the ceilings really that low? Nor did I care for the furniture, a lifetime's collection of massive *armoires* and heavy dark chinoiserie cabinets in carved mahogany. But it took only one glance at that view and at Marie-Do's look of beatific contentment to make me realize that, furniture, ceilings, heating and the lack of a lift notwithstanding, we wouldn't be going back down in a hurry.

I'd found my Paris home.

14

Invaders

There was movement at the station, for the word had passed
around . . .

Andrew Barton 'Banjo' Paterson, The Man from Snowy River

IN AUSTRALIA, THE FIRST HEAT OF SUMMER BRINGS
blowflies. In Paris, it brought Australians.

'Had any visitors yet?' Cindy asked one day.

An American who'd come to France on the
rebound from unhappy experiences as a
congressional aide in Washington, Cindy settled
down with her husband Tom, a freelance journalist
and hopeful novelist, to a few years of Doing Paris.
She helped out at the American Library, one of the
floating population of young married women not
content with sitting at home, changing the cat litter
and watching CNN. After six months of aimless

library activity and, in Tom's case, unsuccessful attempts to sell his novel, they'd begun – in yet another well-established tradition – to compile a guidebook.

'Visitors?' I said. 'We've only just moved in. And nobody knows I'm here.'

'Is that right?' Tom said with that 'you'll see' inflection.

'Natalie, the woman we rented our apartment from,' Cindy said, 'told us that one summer she had someone staying here every day from the middle of May to halfway through September . . .'

'Sometimes two lots at the same time . . .' Tom added.

'. . . and more calling up every week.'

'I don't know that many people,' I said desperately.

'John, until you've got an apartment in Paris,' said Cindy, 'you don't know *who* you know.'

'And anyway,' added Tom, 'you don't even need to know them. It's enough that they know about *you*.'

They sent me a clipping from the *New York Times* in which its correspondent Alice Furlard described her experiences: the calls from the airport by stranded backpackers, the midnight arrivals of people she scarcely remembered. She cracked when a New Yorker ringing from the Gare du Nord, just off the train from London and demanding to spend a few nights – 'on the couch is fine' – turned out to be the daughter of her ex-husband's ex-girlfriend. She said 'No', but 'for several days thereafter,' wrote Furlard, 'young men telephoned from the United States at hours like 4 a.m. asking for the girl'.

It's easier if you can get to them first, says Art Buchwald, long-time Paris resident and *Herald Tribune* columnist. He offered a stock letter guaranteed to freeze off unwanted visitors. Highlights included:

> Herbert and you can stay in Marilyn's room. Of course it's a single bed . . .
>
> We had to take an apartment without a bathtub and we all go round the corner once a week to take our baths . . .
>
> John is fine, but business hasn't been very good. As a matter of fact, he mentioned something about asking Herbert for a loan . . .

In the case of friends of friends asking to stay, he suggests replying that *your* friends, the Duponts, are about to visit New York and would appreciate the same hospitality. Unfortunately they speak no English, have three children and are broke, but are keen to visit all the best restaurants, not to mention Radio City Music Hall, the Bronx Zoo and Chinatown. Monsieur Dupont manages a slaughterhouse and hopes his hosts can arrange a tour of an equivalent American establishment . . .

Marie-Do and I read these horror stories and laughed – until Bert and Marlene arrived.

I had only myself to blame. In the first flush of acquiring a spare room, I'd responded expansively when Bert, a remote acquaintance from Adelaide, told me he'd be passing through Paris with his partner Marlene en route to a conference in Stockholm.

'It would really be nice', he wrote, 'to spend a few days in Gay Paree and catch up.'

I told them we'd be delighted. In the Australia of my childhood, doors were seldom locked, and people routinely dropped by unannounced. To refuse hospitality was as heinous a sin as watering beer.

Some weeks later, a typed itinerary arrived, covering every stop on a twelve-week trip across Europe and the United States. By far the longest visit was with us. We were allocated ten days.

'They don't mean it,' Marie-Do said, half in amusement, half in apprehension.

'I'm sure not.'

Bert, whose academic speciality was institutional food – he was a world authority on lard, and knew more uses for soya protein than any man alive – was on a fact-finding tour of catering facilities. I seized on this.

'They'll be travelling. They probably just want a place to leave their bags.'

Later, toting up the transgressions of Bert and Marlene, we couldn't think of one they'd missed.

First, they didn't turn up on the day they were expected. We hung about the apartment until sunset. Next morning, the phone rang. 'It's us!' said a jovial Australian voice.

'Oh?' I pecked away at the final sentence on my computer, suspecting they'd be the last words I'd write that day. If I'd known it would be more like a fortnight, I'd have hung up right away. 'Where are you?'

'Paris,' Bert said.

'Yes, but *where* in Paris?'

'Ah.' I sensed a hurried conference. 'Don't know.'

'Well, are you at Roissy? I mean, the airport?'

'No. We got a train. *Terrible* food on the plane. But we ate some good tucker in Kuala Lumpur. Did we tell you we stopped off for an extra day in Malaysia?'

'No, you didn't. Where did you get off the train?'

'This morning, you mean? Oh, Paris.'

It was all getting out of hand.

'What *station*?'

'Oh.' Another muffled conference. 'Saint something.'

Of the scores of Saint-something stations, I took a punt on the most obvious. 'Saint-Michel?'

'Yair. That's the bugger. Saint Mitchell. Oh, right. There's a sign.'

'Which entrance?'

'Um . . . how d'ya mean?'

'Are you on the Place Saint-Michel side or over by the river? Can you see any kind of landmark?'

A long pause. 'There's a big church.'

'Two towers?'

'Yair.'

'That's Notre Dame.'

'Oh, right.' I heard him explain, 'He says that's Notre Dame.' Back to me, he said, 'Marlene wants to know if they've got a dunny in there. She's busting.'

'I shouldn't think so. Try a café.' I had a sudden vision of hunting them through the hundred cafés of the Latin Quarter, and, worse still, their loos. 'On second thoughts, don't move. I'll come and get you.'

They weren't hard to find. They'd created a two-person barrier to pedestrian access by piling their numerous suitcases in the middle of the narrow footpath. Marlene was half slumped on top. Bert had wandered off to browse the stall of the nearest *bouquiniste*. Never the best-tempered of men, this one was muttering audibly and glaring at the luggage blocking his clientele. Bert regarded him amiably, nodding every few seconds and smiling.

Seeing me, he wrung my hand. 'G'day, mate. How ya goin'?' He nodded towards the *bouquiniste*, whose face by now was almost aubergine. 'Why's Lucky Pierre got his balls over his shoulder? I don't know a word of the lingo.'

I hurriedly steered him back to the bags. 'We'd better get these to the flat. How are you, Marlene?'

Marlene grimaced wearily from her semi-recumbent position. A lanky woman with red hair, freckles, pipe-stem legs and horn-rimmed bottle-bottom glasses, she could hardly have been more of a contrast to Bert, who was just over five feet four, with a ponytail, a reminder of his hippie student past. Both wore anoraks, roll-neck jumpers and crumpled cords that would have seen them through an Albanian winter.

We manhandled the luggage into a taxi for the five-minute trip to Rue de l'Odéon. With no way of getting their bags upstairs short of a block and tackle, we stuffed what we could into a tiny space under the stairs and ascended with one bag apiece.

They didn't think much of our spare room. A view of Notre Dame came a poor second to an en-suite bathroom. While Bert subsided on the Napoleon III bed Marie-Do had inherited from her grandmother, his crepe-soled Earth Shoes propped on the scrolled woodwork at the foot, Marlene described the turquoise- and gold-fleck simulated Travertine jacuzzi they'd just installed in their Adelaide home.

'If they have all this money, why don't they stay in

a hotel?' Marie-Do asked as we left them to 'freshen up and take a rest', hopefully for the remainder of the morning.

I tried to explain about the tradition of Australian hospitality. I didn't get far before they burst into the living room.

'So what's the schedule?' Bert asked brightly.

It started badly and got worse. Rue de l'Odéon didn't impress them. They'd never heard of Shakespeare and Company, Samuel Beckett or Scott Fitzgerald, though Marlene thought she'd seen a movie from a Hemingway story once. Something about a fish . . .

'Hey,' Bert said, nudging me. 'You hear the one about the bloke who had the fish tattooed on the knob of his old feller?'

With sinking heart, I half-listened to this chestnut as we trudged towards the Luxembourg.

Bert dismissed an exhibition of Limoges from the national collection ('I see enough crockery on the job'). The lofty, shadowed space of the Orangerie didn't detain them either ('Where's the bloody oranges?'). Grudgingly, they agreed that the formal gardens laid out by Catherine de Médicis and generations of royal tenants weren't bad ('Nice show of petunias') but as a topic of conversation they paled beside the fact that Bert, using the public lavatory, had been asked to pay for the privilege.

'There's this sheila in there,' he explained indignantly, 'and when I tried to leave she yelled at me and pointed to this saucer full of money.'

'It's only a franc,' I said.

'That's . . .' he made a mental calculation 'twenty-five cents! Just to drain me dragon! Back home—'

Before he could explain that in South Australia he peed for free – or perhaps had his eliminations subsidized by the Australia Council – I hurriedly said, 'What about some lunch? There's a nice little restaurant . . .'

I might as well have proposed chartering a Learjet to St Tropez for caviar and champagne.

'We're on a tight budget, mate,' Bert began.

I gritted my teeth. 'My shout.'

Au Bon St Pourcain is one of the joys of Parisian eating. A simple one-room restaurant on a narrow back street behind the church of Saint-Sulpice, it keeps alive the tradition of Auvergnat country cooking. The menu is chalked up on a board: half a dozen starters, five main dishes, followed by either a slice of gâteau or a bowl of apple compote, the latter made to the recipe of the chef's grandmother. The wine list is even simpler.

It was usually full for lunch but, since we were early, François, who ran the place, squeezed us in. A minute after we sat down, he was back with three glasses of Sancerre, compliments of the house.

Marlene tasted it and made a face. 'Urk! It's bitter.'

'They do some really great whites in the Barossa,' Bert said. 'We should have brought some.'

'The snails here are wonderful,' I said. 'They cook them with butter and Pernod . . .'

'Snails!' Marlene shuddered.

'. . . Or there's the cold sausage. It's wind-dried and sliced very thin.'

'We don't eat meat, John,' Marlene said gently, with the tone of an explorer explaining to a cannibal that they'd skip the boiled missionary.

'But you're in catering . . .'

'Well, yeah,' said Bert, 'but that's just what I teach. Doesn't mean I have to *eat* the stuff.'

'Well . . . what *do* you eat?'

There was a long, considered pause. 'I could murder a Vegemite sandwich,' Bert said.

François was looking at me with genuine pity. I could almost see what he was thinking. *Now do you see why we hate tourists?*

June came to an end, but Bert and Marlene remained. By day, they lay side by side on the bed, steadily consuming my collection of science fiction. At dusk, like bats, they ventured out to find fruit, which they took to their room and ate alone.

Desperately, I consulted their itinerary, then waylaid Bert the next morning as he dived into the bathroom. 'Aren't you supposed to be visiting the Air Force catering corps today?'

'Aw, yair,' he said reflectively, 'that's right. Blokes in Canberra set it up.' He looked out of the window at what smelled, from the mixture of flower fragrance and hot croissants, like a beautiful early-summer day. 'But it looks like it's going to be another scorcher,' he continued. 'Marlene's crook too. Something wrong with her legs. Listen, mate, do us a good turn and ring them, will you? Tell 'em I'm giving it a miss.'

There was no trouble getting onto the catering corps, though the woman on the switchboard sniffed when I asked for Monsieur Vermoux, listed on the itinerary as Bert's contact. '*Général* Vermoux?' she said frostily.

'*Bien sûr*,' I said, trying to sound as if I'd known all along that I was dealing with the *gratin*, the big cheese himself.

The conversation with *M. le Général* was brief and heated. What did I mean, the monsieur was not coming? This visit had been arranged at the highest level, government to government. There were protocols to be observed. He'd made special arrangements. Executives were holding themselves at his disposal. M. Desmoulins, his *adjoint*, had cancelled a visit to Martinique in order to be present. There was to be a lunch. The chef was even now preparing his speciality: quail stuffed with black grapes. The general himself had brought from his own cellar some bottles of excellent Saint-Estèphe '88.

I stumbled through as plausible an excuse as I could muster. Monsieur was desolated, but Madame was ill ... the strain of travel ... her legs ... But I could tell he wasn't fooled, and the conversation ended tersely. Hanging up, I consoled myself that we were saving the general, not to mention Bert and Marlene, from far worse. Told that their guests would be happier with Vegemite sandwiches and Coca-Cola, the outraged executives would probably have choked on their quail and Bordeaux.

In a billow of steam that indicated he'd used all the hot water, Bert emerged from the bathroom, drying his hair with my towel. Washing his mousy mane took more time and hot water than shampooing a St Bernard. 'All fixed up?' he said. 'Listen, mate. You got any more shampoo? This one's empty.'

He upended the bottle in his hand. He'd used Marie-Do's special conditioner, a few bottles of which a friend in the firm's press office gave her every Christmas. It cost about the same as *foie gras*.

A few minutes later, Marlene ambled out. Below the hem of her pink chenille dressing gown, her unlovely calves were the colour of strawberry yogurt. She scratched surreptitiously. 'I think I got a bit burnt,' she said, disappearing into the bathroom.

But later that morning, it looked as if they might

finally have got the message. Over breakfast – croissants and coffee for us; bran, bananas and herbal tea for them – Marlene said, 'We're thinking of taking a little trip.'

'Wonderful!' we chorused. 'Where to?'

'Might take that fast train – TGV? – someplace,' Bert said. 'Bordeaux maybe.'

'Good idea,' I said, adding reflexively, 'It's "Bor-doe", by the way. You don't pronounce the x.'

'Bordeaux's a wonderful old city,' Marie-Do nudged. 'Some beautiful buildings.'

'Well, we thought we'd go tomorrow,' Marlene said.

Twenty minutes sorting out their train reservations was a small price to have them out of our hair. 'Want me to book a hotel?' I asked.

They exchanged a worried look. One could see the pictures flitting through their heads, of marbled halls, and flunkeys demanding tips that, back home, would keep them in Vegemite for a month.

'Maybe there are youth hostels,' I said hurriedly. 'They'll know at the Bordeaux station.'

At 8 a.m. the next morning, I escorted them to the Métro and gave them a slip of paper with all the directions they'd need to get to Gare Montparnasse. Coming back, I was walking on air. Free!

For the first time in a week, Marie-Do and I went for a stroll in the Luxembourg. Then we ate at the Au

Bon St Pourcain, where François was so relieved to see us alone that he gave us two glasses of Sancerre each. After lunch, we saw the new Woody Allen film. We climbed the stairs to the apartment, luxuriating in the thought of a whole evening, perhaps even a day or two, of privacy . . .

The first sound as we opened the door was the TV. Marlene and Bert were in front of it, watching the BBC news. Marlene's feet were propped up on one of our best armchairs, her calves lathered in what looked like zinc cream.

Amazed, I said, 'What happened about Bordeaux?'

'It was all right,' Bert said.

'But . . . it's a five-hour trip.'

'About that,' he agreed.

'We walked around the station a bit,' Marlene said. 'Took a look at the buffet.'

'Then you just got on the train again?' Marie-Do said in disbelief.

'That's all we were *really* interested in,' Marlene said. 'That, and the sandwiches.' She reached towards her legs, intending to scratch, then pulled her hand away. 'Have you got any sunburn cream? I think I got burned again.'

By the next day, Marlene's legs looked as if she was wearing pink woollen stockings. In Britain, the United States, even Australia, your only chance of getting a doctor to your house on Sunday morning is at gunpoint. In France, however, we just rang the medical emergency service and within an hour a competent young MD was knocking on the door.

Marlene lay on our bed, moaning softly.

'So what is it? The legs?' The doctor glanced at the offending appendages. '*Mon dieu!*' he muttered, making the *pouf* noise, whether at their condition or their shape it was hard to say.

Dabbing away some of the cream with a sterile dressing, he peered at the inflamed skin. Over the next ten minutes, he discarded sunburn and excessive walking as possible causes, excluded the more familiar allergies, and was working his way towards certain tropical skin conditions mainly known through anecdotal accounts of nineteenth-century explorers. Marie-Do's English was strained to the limit. We had to consult the four-volume Harrap French–English dictionary for some of them. As I was wondering when he'd get to leprosy, elephantiasis and King's Evil, he asked, 'Has madame . . . er, *done* anything to her legs recently?'

Marlene looked embarrassed. 'Well,' she admitted, shamed by this confession of personal vanity, 'I did have them waxed.'

Light dawned. The waxing, excessively vigorous, had exposed the open follicles to infection. As he wrote out some prescriptions, the doctor was shaking his head in disbelief. 'I'll give madame a *piqûre*,' he said, 'but this medicament is best administered as a *suppo*.'

'What did he say?' Marlene asked.

'Um, well . . .'

It's a standing joke in Europe that French medicine is either *piqûre ou suppo*: injection or suppository. To Marlene's dawning horror, I explained she would have to have the medication . . . well, inserted in . . . um . . .

What broad hints, high prices and a lack of Vegemite had not been able to achieve, the spectre of the suppository did. By the next day the swelling had begun to disappear, and so had Bert and Marlene. At noon their bags were packed; at two, both wearing sunglasses and with white smears on their faces that looked like the industrial-strength sunblock normally utilized only by Saharan explorers, they were poised on the doormat.

'We'd love to stay . . .' Marlene began.

'But with her legs . . .' Bert added.

'Our friends in London know an Australian doctor . . .'

'You're absolutely right,' we said in unison.

'And if you're ever passing through Paris again . . .' Marie-Do added as they descended out of sight.

'. . . we're leaving town,' I muttered as I closed the door.

15

The Sexual Restaurant

I live in a narrow street on the Left Bank, in Paris, closer to Montparnasse than Saint-Germain-des-Prés. We all look into the rooms of near neighbors, know the programs they watch, the musical instruments the children play, but we never acknowledge one another in the street. We do, however, nod and smile (but never speak) if an encounter takes place at Le Midi, the café-bistrot at the corner, on the rue du Cherche-Midi. So much for local customs.

Mavis Gallant

IN 1929, THE YOUNG ARTIST SALVADOR DALI, THE gifted but naïve son of a wealthy Spanish landowner and a classic product of Spain's repressive Catholicism, arrived in Paris to help his friend Luis Buñuel shoot a Surrealist scenario they had written together. True to the spirit of Surrealism, which professed to find eccentricity and fantasy in the everyday, the film title parodied the warning sign that appeared in all railway carriages: *Dangereux de se pencher en dedans*, 'Dangerous to lean *inside*'. Halfway through shooting, however, Buñuel would cross out this title in thick blue pencil on the cover of his script and write in a new one: *Un Chien andalou* – 'An Andalusian Dog'.

At the Gare de Lyon, Dali ordered the taxi driver to take him directly to a brothel. The cabby delivered him to the most famous in Paris, 12 Rue Chabanais. Here, demonstrating expertise and tact, the manageress – under French law, only women could run a bordello, though men invariably owned the business – conducted the virginal Dali to a room furnished with peepholes. One of these, provided for clients who preferred to choose a girl in privacy, looked into the lounge. The other showed one of the house's most popular bedrooms. A stupefied Dali left some hours later, with, he said, 'enough to last me for the rest of my life in the way of accessories to furnish, in less than a minute, no matter what erotic reverie, even the most exacting'.

Ironically, while Dali preferred to observe, Buñuel, just as wounded psychologically by a guilt-drenched upbringing, harboured a pathological fear of being watched. He even thrust hatpins through keyholes to blind imagined voyeurs, a fetish he attached to the insane hero of one of his strangest films, *The Criminal Life of Archibaldo de la Cruz*. If other people were in the house when he and his wife Jeanne made love, he'd push furniture against the doors. He felt safe from scrutiny only in the bathroom, and Jeanne confided that both their sons were 'water children', conceived under the shower.

Despite a long courtship, he and Jeanne never slept together until they were married. Like most Spanish men, including his compatriot Picasso, Buñuel grew up believing he could find sex only in marriage or the brothel. To both men, Paris and its casual attitude to sex were revelations. Picasso found partners among his numerous admirers, though he'd quite flagrantly pick up women in the street. 'I want to draw you,' he told seventeen-year-old shop assistant Marie-Thérèse Walter, eventually his mistress and mother of his child. 'I'm a painter. I'm quite famous.'

Buñuel, with none of Picasso's brass, gravitated to the *bals musettes* or public dance halls. His favourite was the Bal Bullier, at the intersection of Boulevard Montparnasse and Boulevard Saint-Michel, opposite Hemingway's favourite restaurant, the Closerie des Lilas. It attracted many of the Spanish crowd who hung out at Le Dôme, a few blocks down Boulevard Montparnasse, but Buñuel would have been happy anywhere that the curious etiquette of the *bal musette* applied, near enough to that of the brothel to make him feel comfortable. Any man wanting to dance with a girl simply walked to her table as the band struck up the next tango or a jig-like *java*. If she agreed, they walked onto the floor, grabbed one another in a crushing grip and danced in complete silence. A man who wanted to become better acquainted might offer her a drink later, but to talk during the dance or even exchange names was decidedly *de trop*. This suited Buñuel, since a night of rubbing his body against a succession of anonymous young women gave him as much satisfaction as Dali gained for a couple of hours glued to the peepholes at Le Chabanais.

Voyeurism, one of the gentlest of sex acts, has always been popular with artists. Not surprising, then, that it should flourish in France's exhibitionistic culture. Parisians dress – and, often, undress – in the expectation of being seen. Even to visit the baker, a man will put on a jacket, a woman a skirt and high heels. At the Monoprix supermarket on Rue de Rennes, girls in black cocktail dresses and ankle-strap stilettos stroll the aisles like gazelles, reviewing with a pout of disbelief the creamy avalanche of the yogurt shelves, or musing on the merits of *beurre doux* as against *demi-sel*.

Thanks to advertising, the French are confronted at every turn with rounded bums and pert breasts, grappling couples and sexual innuendo – all to sell mineral water, car insurance, even the TGV. Most nights, they can catch an X-rated movie on TV. The five free-access networks stick to soft-core, but some cable channels, even the prestigious Canal+, broadcast a Saturday-night slab of '*le hard*'. Every four weeks, Canal+ also airs *Le Journal du hard*, in which an earnest young reporter in a dark suit insinuates his mike into a mess of *hardeurs* to enquire what impact revised EU tariffs on DVDs will have on the business.

Sex is simply too large a segment of the French national culture to leave room for Victorian *pudeur*, adolescent ignorance, Hollywood sentimentality, or PC complaints about 'commodifying the body'. In a country where people prefer to look and evaluate rather than listen and learn, sex comes under the same tireless scrutiny.

A few years ago, a Parisian couple tried explaining procreation to their pre-teen son and daughter. After a few minutes, the twelve-year-old boy stopped them. 'Look, it's all too complicated,' he said. 'Next time you do it, just call to us. We'll come and watch.'

The vanguard of French sexual exhibitionism, both from the point of view of the watcher and the watched, is the Crazy Horse Saloon, the world's most opulent strip club.

In the 1965 film *What's New Pussycat*, Woody

Allen, playing a horny writer in Paris, tells his friend Peter O'Toole he's found work at the Crazy Horse. 'I help the girls dress and undress,' he explains. 'It's twenty francs a week.'

'Not much,' sympathizes O'Toole.

Allen shrugs. 'It's all I can afford.'

Alain Bernardin, the Crazy Horse's founder, was a painter and art dealer who fell for American culture after World War II, though not always with great discrimination. He first opened the saloon as a square-dance club; hence its incongruous name. Friends like Bing Crosby and humorist Art Buchwald warned him it was doomed, but when it did go bust, Bernardin relaunched it as a cabaret with strippers – one of them his wife.

Small, balding and fatherly, Bernardin, a Madame Tellier of the club scene, didn't fit the show-business stereotype, which undoubtedly helped. So did the site of his basement theatre, not in a raunchy district like Pigalle or Saint-Denis but just off the Champs-Élysées, only a hundred metres from one of Paris's most prestigious hotels, the George V, and directly opposite couturier Yves Saint Laurent.

From the start, he envisaged a show so stylish that the President of the Republic could watch it without squirming or compromising his reputation – and, moreover, one he could safely bring his wife to the next week. No girls strut on the bar while drunken punters stuff ten-euro notes into their G-strings. Instead, audiences sit in darkness in a raked auditorium, sipping champagne and watching a show so elaborate in its use of tinted and patterned lights that one can barely tell if the dancers are naked or not. There's little actual stripping. Instead, singly or in groups, the girls, dressed in a few grams of summerweight thistledown, prowl the stage, or simply pose motionless, breathing heavily as they glower out into the darkness. The effect on watchers ranges from hypnosis to frenzy. One tourist, accustomed to overtly raunchy clubs, so far forgot himself as to yell 'Get 'em off!' He was shushed by icily disapproving neighbours. 'It was like we were listening to one of Beethoven's late quartets,' he said indignantly.

'Bernardin was involved with every detail,' recalled one of his dancers. 'He created the concept of the show. He created its famous lighting. He chose the music, even wrote some lyrics. He drew sketches for costumes. He designed the theatre. He didn't choreograph the numbers, but since he was a painter he saw each dance number as if it were a painting.'

Shrewdly, he showcased the work of painters and fashion designers, particularly Paco Rabanne, whose gowns of plastic and metal discs fitted the Crazy Horse style. One can still check off the influences in a Bernardin show: young limbs moving in soft golden light like a photograph by David Hamilton; girls in black chiffon striding among dead trees in a high wind, an effect lifted from Surrealist Paul Delvaux; a dancer crawling over Dali's red velvet couch designed in the shape of Mae West's lips. (Not surprisingly, Salvador loved '*Le Crazy*'. He saw the shows often, and was invited to sketch rehearsals.)

Man Ray once suggested to the madame of his favourite whorehouse that she clean the stained-glass windows that looked onto the street, and even install lights to show them off. She declined. Whatever might be taking place inside shouldn't be advertised too boldly. At most, a simple red light would suffice.

In the same way, Bernardin retained a doorman dressed absurdly but unthreateningly as a Canadian mountie, and a low-lit plush foyer that recalled some exclusive theatre.

'We had a private exit so no one would see us leaving without our make-up on,' said one dancer. '[Bernardin] didn't allow us to meet men from the audience or date anyone who worked there. He didn't allow us to talk to stagehands. Our boyfriends could not pick us up in front of the building – always around the block.' Rock star Prince was one of many celebrities who angled for a 'private meeting', but was refused by Bernardin. 'We were his girls,' said the dancer, 'almost like his daughters. He was very possessive of us. So, any man that wanted to just hang around with us after the show was not welcome. We were special to him, you see?'

Further to protect their anonymity, Bernardin gave all his dancers stage names. There was a tradition of this, from American strippers like Stormy Tempest to an English performer who called herself, imaginatively, Cha Landres, but Bernardin carried it into realms of caricature. An imperious Dutch dancer re-emerged as Akky Masterpiece. The smallest girl in that year's cast was Tiny Semaphore. Others became Paula Flashback, Queeny Blackpool, Zia Paparazzi and Volga Moskovskaya. The names implied that the girls came from all over the world, but, while the troupe always included a few Britons, Canadians and the occasional Australian, Bernardin's taste for short blondes with feral smiles, medium breasts and generous bottoms meant that Eastern Europe predominated. The current line-up mixes French girls with some from Poland and the old Soviet Union, but one of the stars, a demure brunette with a page-boy haircut who's called 'Roxy Tornado' – real name a secret, like those of all the girls – comes from Palmerston North in New Zealand.

What's New Pussycat introduced the Crazy Horse to the movies, and vice versa. During the production, Woody Allen, then a little-known stand-up comic who'd never written a film, lived at the George V, and, under the pretext of research, gravitated towards the club. 'I spent quite an hour and a half in there,' he wrote to a friend, 'chatting with them. The fact that I didn't understand a word of it didn't matter. I just nodded my head, smiled, and kept looking.' His script made Paula Prentiss a dancer at the club, giving her the stage name 'Liz Bien'. A photographer shot Woody lurking backstage, peeking at the girls, and *Playboy* set up a photo shoot in which some of them, bare-breasted, played football with Woody, likewise stripped to the waist, though with less erotic effect.

Bernardin also sent the girls 'on holiday' to the Cannes Film Festival in 1977, where they were photographed cavorting on the beach with the little-known Arnold Schwarzenegger, who even then was beginning to justify his description by critic Clive James: 'like a brown condom stuffed with walnuts'. By then, the Crazy Horse had become the acceptable face of French eroticism, imitated all over the world. Bernardin even fought a court case over the use of the name by a Las Vegas show, and when l'Abbé Pierre, France's Mother Theresa, pleaded for help to feed the homeless during the bitter winter of 1974 Bernardin put the revue at his disposal.

Such gestures made it permissible, even fashionable, to be seen there. Liza Minnelli and Prince Albert of Monaco came. So did Madonna – three times. Bernardin held up the show for almost an hour when Sammy Davis Jr announced he was on his way. And Jimmy Connors consoled himself there after losing the French Open to Michael Chang. It became such an institution that, when France's largest TV channel wanted a big event to celebrate New Year 1991, they presented Bernardin's current show, uncut and certainly undressed.

Bernardin didn't live to see his creation enter its second half-century. In the mid-Seventies, a new dancer joined the troupe, a blonde from rural France with the imperious stare of a Valkyrie. He christened her 'Lova Moor', and promptly fell in love with his creation, whom he married. Then he took her out of the show and tried to launch her as an actress. A small role in a 1979 Italian film suggested she had little talent, so she tried singing, pacing statuesquely about the stage, miming to some forgettable Europop. When that failed, so did the marriage. In 1994, amid rumours of an imminent break-up, Bernardin, aged seventy-eight, committed suicide.

There's little a Parisian won't do in public. Eating, smoking, delivering lectures, playing music, carrying on business or a conversation, making love or making *pipi*: it's all the same. Privacy is an accessory. One dons it much like a woman puts on clothes, to draw attention to what's underneath. When Umberto Eco first came to Paris in the Sixties, two things impressed him: the way everyone on the Métro seemed to be reading a book rather than a newspaper or magazine, and the casualness with which lovers embraced on the banks and balustrades of the Seine.

The same casualness extends to relieving themselves. France has a long tradition of public defecation. The word 'loo' is a corruption of *'Regardez l'eau'* – 'Watch out for the water' – which the French of the eighteenth century used to shout before they emptied chamber-pots into the street. Despite Mel Brooks's theory in his film *The History of the World Part One* that the approved method of relieving yourself at the court of the Sun King was calling for a flunkey with a pail, most courtiers, and even kings, simply went behind a tree – or, in extremis, dispensed with the tree. King Henry III was assassinated by a monk whom he'd invited in for an audience while he took a shit. At Versailles, servants strewed straw along the corridors at night and the grandees just opened the door and let fly. Early each morning, the straw was scooped up and scattered around the royal strawberries.

True Parisians lament the passing of the public urinals or *vespasiennes*, named after the first Roman emperor to tax them. Introduced to Paris around 1900, thirteen hundred of them once decorated its street corners, advertising their presence a block away by their ammoniac pong. With a fretted metal shield that started above the knee and ended below the shoulder, the *pissoir* made minimum concessions to propriety. To see some tourist doing his damndest to look nonchalant as he stared out at the crowded pavement and urged his frozen bladder into action was to see misery at its most acute.

Feminism saw the end of *pissoirs*. (A single museum piece survives on Boulevard Arago, below the walls of the Santé prison; obviously nobody was likely to spend much time loitering *there*.) Grudgingly, cafés, museums and department stores installed proper toilets.

Soon the '*Madame Pipi*' who guarded them became as much a Parisian stereotype as the indifferent *flic* and the snooty *vendeuse*. These women continue to exercise an absolute tyranny. Get on the wrong side of them and you could wet your pants for all they cared. And as for expecting them to work on public holidays, or in the month of August, forget it. An Edwardian postcard shows a Madame Pipi, complacent and beaming in the doorway of her closed *cabinets*, reading her paper while gentlemen cross their legs, clutch their bowels, a woman has a quick pee into a grating around a tree, and even a cat craps on the pavement.

Presumably some remote shop in the outer suburbs of Paris stocks racks of the Mesdames Pipi uniform, an off-white wrap-around overall, shiny with starch and worn threadbare at the hems. Maybe it even holds classes in the standard Madame Pipi tone of nasal disdain. In 1966, Jonathan Routh, compiling his *Guide Porcelaine to the Loos of Paris*, summarized a typical exchange.

When a tourist asks, 'Do you think I might wash my hands?' Madame replies, '*Mais certainement*, monsieur. To facilitate this procedure, here is a cake of paraffin wax and a table napkin. Behind you, on the floor, is a sink ... That will be two thousand francs, including service. Should you require water, I can, for an additional three thousand five hundred francs, procure it in a vitreous enamel jug from the tank on the roof of the sleeping-car attendants' hut.'

Routh's 'Useful Phrases for the Toileteer in Paris' includes '*Comme c'est gentil, madame, comme c'est généreux de me montrer les pages du journal d'hier, mais je les ai déjà lues*' ('Very kind of you, madam, to offer me these pieces of old newspaper but I read them yesterday'), but also the heartfelt '*Vous êtes une misérable, une vieille, une fille de cocotier; pas de carte du Diners Club pour vous*.' ('You are a miserable old crone and I would not even waste the effort to show you my Diners Club card.')

The old and elegant, if malodorous, *pissoir* of my first visits to Paris has been supplanted by a new high-tech version. Fluted metal cabinets with sliding doors that respond to a coin, they are engineered to resist the most virulent microbe and determined graffiti tagger. Disinfected water floods the interior after every use. Grimly unisex, they cost a euro to use, need as much electronic equipment as a BMW, and malfunction as often as a public telephone. Most Parisians still prefer to buy an unwanted *café express* and use the toilet in a café, but they appeal to tourists and to the hookers around Rue Saint-Denis, who find them useful to turn a quick trick.

Our local supermarket installed one, about the size of a lift, but in stainless steel. A sign warned about the automatic dousing and explained that you *must* wait for the cycle to end, but who reads? I'd just stepped out when a man brushed past me and nipped round the door as it snicked shut. There was no time to warn him. Already, overhead, I could hear relays closing, motors whirring. I visualized him unzipping his fly, perhaps glancing at the ceiling, frowning at the noise of the pumps as they prepared to douse him with gallons of disinfected water . . . Some scenes are better enjoyed in imagination. I left him to a fate that I like to think was something like the man in Peter Arno's cartoon who, trapped in a glass shower stall flooded to the ceiling, is gesturing desperately for someone to open the jammed door.

With the apartment on Rue de l'Odéon now ours, I relished the new perspective it gave me. Watching the play of light in the eastern sky and the way it altered the landscape of metal roofs and art-deco chimney stacks gave me a new appreciation of the architecture of the city. But it was almost as entertaining to watch what went on in the apartments across the street.

Directly opposite, on most mornings, a slim teenager with teacup breasts and dark hair halfway down her back drifted across a window below me wearing only a pair of black briefs. Her father followed, in shorts, and her mother in just a long skirt, also naked to the waist. They subsided onto the couch with their coffee and turned on France 3 to watch the morning news. Two windows along, a man and woman periodically enjoyed vigorous sex on the carpet, unconcerned – but surely not unaware – that they could be seen from half a dozen other apartments. I didn't feel like a snooper, because they obviously didn't mind being watched. I'd been wrong about all those French films in which adolescents stare dry-mouthed across the street at the girl undressing, or middle-aged recluses become obsessed with the day-to-day life of the lonely girl opposite. What seemed like voyeuristic fantasy was documentary realism.

I could even understand for the first time Barbet Schroeder's startling film *Maîtresse*. A young Gérard Depardieu and his buddy burgle apartments locked up and left for the holidays. One of them, however, turns out to be not empty at all but the workplace of dominatrix Bulle Ogier, who lives upstairs (while keeping one of her high-paying clients caged in its bathroom). Descending on a steel staircase in needle stilettos, with a Doberman on a leash, she scares off the pal but keeps Depardieu as a pet and helper.

Seeing *Maîtresse* in London, the premise seemed far-fetched. Now I wasn't so sure. Schroeder boasted that the people seen chained, flogged and pinioned in the film were all clients of the dominatrix who acted as his technical adviser. After all, as I knew from Philip Soupault's *Last Nights in Paris*, so forensically translated by the American poet (and doctor) William Carlos Williams, the railings of the Luxembourg Gardens, just round the corner from us, had been the preferred meeting place in the Twenties for Paris's sado-masochists. How did I know that someone like the man in the film, naked but for a leather mask, wasn't, somewhere in Paris, even now strapped into the same sort of dentist's chair, with, as in the film, his scrotum spread out and thumb-tacked onto a plank, like a bat awaiting dissection?

16

Sacred Monsters

To show my arse and to see my face. There are few pleasures to equal this double polarisation.

Catherine Millet, *The Sexual Life of Catherine M.*

THERE IS ALWAYS AN ELEMENT OF THE UNREAL IN touring a battlefield. No amount of vivid description can dispel a sense of the ridiculous. Ten thousand men died just to capture this grassy slope? How could all that energy, let alone a human life, have been expended to gain an advantage so trivial, so transient?

Chronicles of the Sixties' sexual revolution collide with the same absurdity barrier. Why the fuss over Kenneth Tynan saying 'fuck' on the BBC, or *Playboy* permitting its pin-ups to display pubic hair, or *Avant Garde* magazine showing nude photos of a mixed-race couple? As for the British legal Establishment grudgingly permitting the publication of *Lady Chatterley's Lover*, the query of prosecuting counsel Mervyn Griffiths-Jones, 'Would you want your wife or servants to read this book?' seems more appropriate to a Victorian stage melodrama than to our world.

I could hardly believe Stanley Kubrick's partner James Harris when he explained how they won agreement to film Nabokov's *Lolita* from the Legion of Decency – could that *really* have been the name of the Hollywood self-censorship authority? – by promising not to deal with sex at all. Instead, their theme would be 'the humour that arose from the problems of a mature man married to a gum-chewing teenager'. To neutralize any lingering curse on the relationship of Humbert and Lo, they would 'treat the novel so that the man was married to the girl in some state like Kentucky or Tennessee where such is legal'.

In retrospect, we can recognize these skirmishes not as battles but rearguard actions. The Establishment knew the war was already lost. By 1968, the sexual genie was out of its bottle. Contraceptive pills and antibiotics offered protection from the worst risks of promiscuity. The days when pornography circulated mainly among the rich in elegantly bound limited editions were gone for good. Cheap printing opened up the market for erotic books, magazines and films. From now on, the world belonged to *Playboy*, *Screw* and *Suck*, and to the sage-green paperbacks of Maurice Girodias's Traveler's Companion series.

Between the invention of the pill and the arrival of Aids, sex became for the middle class what it had always been for the poor, the best fun going for the least expense. America blossomed with 'clothes-optional adult leisure centres' like Sandstone in California, presided over by the author of runaway bestseller *The Joy of Sex*, an ageing minor English poet and critic named Alex Comfort, who could scarcely credit his luck as legions of lithe young women embraced him as their guru.

New York's Continental Baths, the notorious gay pick-up spot where Bette Midler began her career (with young Barry Manilow as her accompanist), relaunched itself into heterosexuality as Plato's Retreat, offering carpeted, mirror-walled rooms with piped music, discreet lighting and a well-stocked bar. Leaving one's clothes at the door, one could cruise the talent of both sexes, goggle at a few low-rent celebrities such as Sammy Davis Jr and Margaux Hemingway, slip into one of the alcoves for a semi-private orgy, loll in the tiled steam room with its suggestive copies of Greek statues, or catch the action in the mat rooms, where couples fornicated in crepuscular proximity on pads laid out on the floor of a gym-like space.

The more inhibited could attend a live sex revue like *The Dirtiest Show in Town* or the more sophisticated *Oh! Calcutta!*, conceived by Kenneth Tynan, with sketches by Samuel Beckett and John Lennon, and a title lifted from a painting by the French Surrealist Clovis Trouille of a ripe female bottom; 'Oh Calcutta!' is the phonetic of '*Oh quel cul t'as!*', 'Oh, what an ass you have!'

In this revolution as in many others, Paris was a powerhouse. It had exported political change in 1789 and again under the Commune in 1870 – the setting for the stage version of *Les Misérables*. Later in the nineteenth century, Impressionist painters made the city a magnet for artists from around the world, just as its welcoming social and economic climate attracted American writers after World War I.

As the world capital of sensuality, Paris had a reputation to uphold. In 1973, the French government effectively removed film censorship. Within a few months, France had a healthy erotic film industry which flourished until 1975, when public pressure forced the reimposition of controls. By then, French sex films had thrown up such articulate and confident stars as Brigitte Lahaie and Claudine Beccarie, who, unlike their American counterparts Linda Lovelace and Marilyn Chambers, were able and more than willing to defend their work in public. When Lahaie, a slim, haughty blonde who could have modelled for the art-deco nudes that decorated the pavilions at the 1926 Exposition des Arts Décoratifs, wrote a memoir describing her upbringing on a farm and resulting love of animals, a TV programme tried to ambush her by confronting her with a cow in the studio. Unfazed, Lahaie brought along an enormous Alsatian for company and, on being shown the cow, sat down and started milking it.

In 1975, director Jean-François Davy devoted a feature documentary, *Exhibition*, to Claudine Beccarie, in the course of which he took the peppy little brunette to a Paris cinema playing one of her films. In *Exhibition*'s funniest scene, she introduced herself to nervous and occasionally incredulous patrons as they left. At least one didn't recognize her at all.

'Don't I look like the one in the movie?' demanded a miffed Beccarie.

'Well, I don't know,' said the man doubtfully. 'I'm not sure one looks very much at the faces.'

Of another, she demanded, 'If I asked you to make a movie with me, would you do it? You think you could go all the way in front of the cameras?'

When the punter responded gamely, 'Well, why not? It would be very nice,' Beccarie rounded on him indignantly, her professional pride offended.

'Well, you have never thought about it. I can tell you it's very difficult!'

Echangiste clubs blossomed; here participants could arrive with one partner and leave with another. It was also an open secret that, if one such drove to the roundabout at Porte Maillot, on the other side of the Arc de Triomphe, put on the left-turn indicator and cruised slowly for a few minutes, other cars would tag on until, a good number having been reached, the first car would peel off and lead the rest to a suitable location for the orgy.

This period of French sexual history has its Samuel Pepys in Catherine Millet, a respected art historian, editor of the monthly *Art Press* but, in her leisure hours, an addict of promiscuous sex. In her 2000 memoir, *La Vie sexuelle de Catherine M.*, she revealed a thirty-year addiction to what the French call *la partouze*.

Group sex, Millet explains, entered her life only a few weeks after she lost her virginity at eighteen in the late Sixties. With three men and another girl, she explored its permutations beside a sunlit swimming pool near Lyon, and enjoyed them all. Thereafter, most of her spare time was spent in this agreeable pursuit. Her book omitted no detail of the people, the activities or the ritual. Describing one soirée in an imaginatively landscaped garden, she wrote, 'Eric installed me on one of the beds or couches placed in one of the alcoves, and, following the etiquette of these events, took the initiative in undressing and exposing me. He would start to caress and kiss me, and the relay was immediately taken up by others.'

Sometimes the encounters were less formal. She had sex with her dentist and his nurse in the chair, and with removal men in their van as they shifted paintings from airport to gallery, while the driver watched in the rear-view mirror. Her descriptions captured the tunnel vision of the true obsessive.

At the time Catherine M. was indulging herself so freely, nobody but the small circle of fellow enthusiasts knew anything about it. Her sense of exclusivity, of being part of 'my little community', obviously contributed to her pleasure, but it also reflected a traditional separation in French culture between public and private life.

French law offers ferocious protection against even the most trivial invasion of privacy. Magazines can be forced to print apologies equal in size to the offending photograph or article, and fined as well. Unlike American courts, those in France don't recognize a 'public right to know'. When the doctor of François Mitterrand revealed, after Mitterrand's death, that the late President, after having solemnly campaigned on a promise to provide annual reports on his health, had lied for years about his fatal disease in order to prolong his time in power, Mitterrand's widow and illegitimate daughter sued and won, even though his book had little to say about either of them. Writer and publisher were crushingly penalized.

Yet, furious as they are when someone steals their privacy, the French, under the right circumstances, will give it away eagerly. (When Jane Fonda lived with film director Roger Vadim, the wall between their bedroom and bathroom was made of glass – a useful metaphor when dealing with French celebrity.) Anything you say or do may be taken down and later sold to *Hello!* magazine, whether you like it or not, as American novelist Nelson Algren discovered when Simone de Beauvoir wrote about their affair in detail, even quoting his love letters. The author of *The Man with the Golden Arm* and *A Walk on the Wild Side*, not noted for shyness, balked at this assault on his privacy. 'I don't have any malice against her, but I think it was an appalling thing to do,' he said. 'I've been in whorehouses all over the world and the woman there always closes the door, whether it's in Korea or India. But this woman flung the door open and called in the public and the press . . . That's a Continental view of how to do things, I suppose.'

Often, it's money that persuades the French to drop the veil. Television news readers and fading novelists connive at 'indiscreet' pictures of themselves lounging half-naked on the beach with their latest lover or cuddling an illegitimate child. By contract with the Rainier dynasty of Monaco, the popular picture magazine *Paris Match* has exclusive rights to every royal indiscretion, scandal and divorce.

But some confessions, like those of Catherine Millet, are made just for the pleasure of it. The volume of French tell-all literature is enormous, from Jean-Jacques Rousseau's *Confessions*, the homosexual memoirs of André Gide, Jean Genet and the diplomat Roger Peyrefitte, to Jean Cocteau's account of his opium addiction and its various unsuccessful cures. Some find it cathartic to spill the beans. Others luxuriate in exhibitionistic pleasure at the outraged fascination they evoke. A few even become the kind of extravagant celebrity, notorious for self-indulgence, that Jean Cocteau – who knew the type well, being one himself – christened '*monstres sacrés*': literally, sacred monsters.

Monstres sacrés bloom in limelight and feed on publicity. Anglo-Saxon culture has its share of them, from Andy Warhol and Truman Capote to Liza Minnelli and Elizabeth Taylor, but as usual the French do this sort of thing far better. One can't, for instance, imagine any other country providing the rich medium in which might flourish the friendship of fetishist photographer Pierre Molinier and confessional memoirist Emmanuelle Arsan. Each in his and her way unique, they created together the kind of relationship to which only grand opera can do justice.

Diminutive, almost elfin, Molinier was born in 1900, in Bordeaux, and started his creative life in the 1920s as a painter of Cézanne-like landscapes. But a narcissistic fascination with his own body nudged him into dressing in women's lingerie and imagining how it might be to have sex with a man – or, to be precise, with himself.

This fantasy invaded his life. Though he produced a daughter and a son, his only real love object was himself. For decades, always working alone, he painted and photographed himself, often masked, in black stockings, long gloves, suspenders and stiletto heels, sometimes with shop mannequins similarly dressed, and often with the addition of an arsenal of dildoes. Gluing, overpainting and rephotographing these images, he wove intricate photomontages, seldom more than a few inches across, in which a dozen shapely stockinged legs radiated from a single body, or were centered on an anus from which poked a rose.

Like the plant that blooms alone in some remote crevice, reseeding and refertilizing itself each season, to be reborn in an increasingly freakish shape, Molinier's fantasies became more vivid and rank with each generation. His lean body scarcely aged, but as his face began to show the years he replaced it in his collages with one snipped from an identification card carried when he was twenty.

In the 1930s, André Breton, eager for converts, welcomed Molinier briefly into the Surrealists and sponsored his first major exhibition in 1955, but work like his had no business going on public display. He might have lived and died alone, locked within his obsession like the legendary Man in the Iron Mask, had he not encountered a woman who, in her way, was almost as rabid a fabulist herself.

Every season brings its sexual page-turner in France, but few had the impact and enduring popularity of a pale-green-covered paperback, issued by minor Paris publisher Eric Losfeld in the spring of 1959, called simply *Emmanuelle*.

It purported to be the memoirs of Emmanuelle Arsan, a twenty-year-old French innocent who follows Jean, her older and more sexually experienced diplomat husband, to Bangkok. Airborne sex with two strangers on the plane to Thailand opens her eyes to the new sexual climate she's entering, and she isn't entirely surprised to find that years in the more complaisant East have made Jean indifferent to European sexual habits. When she asks how she should occupy herself during his long absences, he says, 'You may play tennis, golf, explore the canals, and you can make love.' A willing experimenter, Emmanuelle dabbles in lesbianism, voyeurism, mutual masturbation and, finally, group sex with some Thais, supervised by Mario, an older and wearier local, who finds his satisfaction in initiating innocents into sexual hedonism.

Even more exciting to readers than the Thai setting of *Emmanuelle*, with its echoes of France's lost colonial empire, was the revelation that the pseudonym 'Emmanuelle Arsan' disguised the real wife of a French diplomat and that the whole story was quite true. The de Gaulle government promptly banned it as yet another slur on its foreign service, already battered by books like Roger Peyrefitte's gay indiscretions in *Les Ambassades*. Although Grove Press's American edition made the novel an international bestseller, it remained on the official French banned list until 1992.

Publisher Losfeld was careful to keep the writer's true name and appearance a mystery. He knew that readers who visualized her as the pale white northern European ingénue, embodied so successfully in the 1974 film by Dutch model Sylvia Kristel, might have been put off by the real 'Emmanuelle', who, while no less sexy than her film incarnation, was not young, innocent or white.

'Emmanuelle Arsan' was actually Maryat Rollet-Andriane, a full-blooded Thai, born Maryat Bibidh, the daughter of Thai politician and diplomat Knun

Bibidh Viregggaka. Depending on which birth date you believed, she was twenty-four, twenty-one, eighteen or sixteen when she married UNESCO administrator Louis-Jacques Rollet-Andriane in 1956.

As a diplomatic wife, Maryat hosted receptions for visiting dignitaries to Bangkok and modelled in the informal fashion parades run by Queen Sirikit. There's no way of telling if she also indulged in a voyage of sexual discovery instigated and choreographed by her husband, though a hint was given by Sylvia Kristel. In 1975, Maryat wrote and starred in *Laure*, a movie intended as a comeback for Linda Lovelace until the *Deep Throat* star backed out. When the press asked Kristel if she'd been invited to play in *Laure*, she replied sniffily, 'No, because that's her drug. For her – though finally more for the fantasies of her husband, I believe.'

Surprisingly, one of Arsan's most fervid fans was the reclusive Pierre Molinier. He read the book eagerly, and was turned on by the sexual reminiscences of a woman who seemed able to gratify her sexual desires with the confidence and independence of a man. In May 1964, having discovered her identity and address, he sent her a portfolio of his photographs. Shortly after, she received envelopes from him that contained only blank sheets of paper. Taking the hint, she wrote him a letter, describing the sexual delirium evoked by his images in terms which he could only have found completely seductive:

> I love them. I melt in her. I *am* her. I am both women, and the third as well, and those who are embracing, caressing, penetrating, who split and open themselves. I am their eyes, their lips, their breasts and their sexes. And I am also she whom they love, whom they love to have watch them, at the same time as she loves to show herself and to be seen. Thus I am at the same time myself and you, without knowing who you are.

Molinier invited Maryat to contribute a text to a film being made about him by Raymond Borde, and when she came to Paris in 1964 he travelled from Bordeaux to see her. 'I met Emmanuelle in person,' he told a friend. 'She is a fascinating woman, and far more beautiful than the photographs she sent me. I am madly in love.' In Paris, and with the approval of Louis-Jacques, he photographed Maryat crouched naked in front of one of his paintings. Before he left, he presented the couple with two of his canvases, and a selection of dildoes for their personal pleasure.

Back home, Pierre worked obsessively on the images of Maryat, painting in a veil, stockings and a cape, incorporating her into his private universe. They continued to exchange letters and cards, the texts of which seemed, to Louis-Jacques, closer to the semi-fiction of *Emmanuelle* than to real life. 'It was like a drug of which he had to have more and more. He didn't mind repeating things he had said before. He would exclaim, "But surely you've tried that," and then Emmanuelle would respond, "Oh, yes. That's right. I did as well ..." They excited one another in their minds.'

In May 1967, it went beyond the mind when the Andrianes visited Molinier in Bordeaux. They stayed only one day, during which the sixty-seven-year-old Pierre, in the words of the presumably complaisant Louis-Jacques, 'did what he had already done hundreds of time in imagination: that is, he made love with her. But what he called "making love" wasn't limited by traditional attitudes. There were all sorts of kisses, caresses and words. For him, sex didn't take place in silence; words played a principal role and gestures a supplementary part. He thought of himself as the lover of Emmanuelle long before he met her in the flesh. So this physical coupling was almost a secondary incident in their love story.'

Pierre and Maryat kept up their correspondence for some years, but never met again in the flesh. The relationship with Molinier remained, however, one of the most significant in her life. Louis-Jacques felt that the encounter had taught her something important about herself – that, whatever her absorption in her sensual life, she would always understand the difference between the two parts of her character, Maryat and Emmanuelle, while, for Molinier, no such division existed; he *was* his fantasy. As if to confirm this, Pierre remained alive only as long as failing flesh could sustain his narcissistic imaginings. In 1976, he shot himself, having, precise to the last, left the following note on his door:

Died 19.30
For the keys, see:
Claude Fonsale, Notaire,
11 Cours de Verdun BX 33
Tel. (56) 44 23 48.

17

The Man Who Knew

Do not go with a so-called 'guide'. These 'guides' infest the boulevards from the Rue Royale to the Opéra. They sneak up to you, want to sell you NAUGHTY postcards, take you to naughty cinemas, to 'houses' and 'exhibitions'. *Walk away from them*.

Bruce Reynolds, *Paris with the Lid Lifted*

TO PEOPLE VISITING PARIS, BOOKS LIKE *LA VIE sexuelle de Catherine M.* give a tantalizing glimpse of the world of vice for which the city has become famous over the last two hundred years, but a glimpse is all it is. Foreigners who try to dig deeper often go hilariously wrong.

A few years ago, BBC radio sent a team to make a programme on guidebooks and the degree to which they reflect the reality of any city – in Paris's case, as the capital of romance.

George, the presenter, adopted the character of an innocent looking for love, or at least signs of it, with the help of Baedeker, Michelin and Fodor. On the Bir-Hakeim bridge, across which Maria Schneider and Marlon Brando in *Last Tango in Paris* walked to their fateful appointment with a pat of butter, he interviewed me about the romantic image of Paris as seen in films.

After that, he roamed Paris – starting, by coincidence, with a street in our neighbourhood. Unfortunately, he chose to ask about candlelit dinners at a noisy bistro specializing in business lunches. The maître d' politely denied that it attracted many clandestine couples, so George wandered out, commenting, 'Well, another illusion shattered . . .' Further up the same street, he asked at a bookshop for a copy of *France coquine* – literally, 'Naughty France' – listing *partouze* clubs, bondage shows and gay bars. Its staff, scandalized, showed him the door – and no wonder. The shop was *Le Moniteur*, specializing exclusively in high-priced architectural books.

So where *was* lovers' Paris? *France coquine* contained some interesting indications, and books of the Twenties often referred to brothels, homosexual clubs and opium dens, but when it came to specifics I was as much in the dark as George.

All that, however, was about to change.

* * *

From the late nineteenth century to just after World War II, anybody looking for lovers' Paris would have tripped over it at every corner. No tourist could spend more than a few minutes gawping before someone sidled up to offer sexy postcards or a guided tour, to any degree of depravity they cared to name. Numerous *Guides roses* listed bordellos, sex shows and sometimes individual prostitutes. Dozens of publishers issued erotica, from cheaply produced paperbacks to elaborately bound and illustrated books that would find a home in serious libraries all over the world. Erotic magazines flourished, many filled with pin-ups and cartoons, but all subsisting on their small classified ads: the *petites annonces*.

Until they were outlawed in 1946 after a crusade led by World War I heroine Marthe Richard, bordellos flourished in every French town. They ranged from a couple of weary working women in a rented room, to four-storey establishments with their own bars and restaurants, furnished with antiques and stocked with dozens of girls catering to every sexual taste. Though every country had brothels, France was rare in permitting them to operate openly. Called *maisons de tolérance* (tolerated houses), *maisons closes* (closed houses) or occasionally *maisons de fantasie* (houses of illusion), they enjoyed their privileged status because wealthy men in an ostensibly Catholic country wanted a place to relax. Whereas Americans went to the Elks, the Kiwanis or the Shriners, and Englishmen to the Masonic lodge or a pub, Frenchmen visited the whorehouse, where they ate, drank, played cards, gossiped and, from time to time, had sex. When brothels were forced to close, the author Pierre Mac Orlan wailed, 'The foundation of a thousand-year-old civilization is collapsing!'

How fundamentally French society accepted and indeed relied on brothels was satirized by the author Guy de Maupassant. His story 'La maison Tellier' begins with a description of how a brothel fitted into provincial life.

> They went there every evening at about eleven o'clock, just as they would go to the club. Six or eight of them; always the same set, not fast men, but respectable tradesmen, and young men in government or some other employ, and they would drink their Chartreuse, and laugh with the girls, or else talk seriously with Madame Tellier, whom everybody respected, and then they would go home at twelve o'clock! The younger men would sometimes stay later.

Madame Tellier's regulars are taken aback one night to find the house closed and dark. To their relief, it's only for a few days, and for the most respectable of reasons: Madame and the girls, all of them right-thinking Catholics, have gone to her niece's confirmation.

De Maupassant, an astonishing sexual athlete, was no stranger to brothels. When fellow writer Gustave Flaubert refused to believe his claim that he could ejaculate six times in an hour, de Maupassant took him to a whorehouse and proved his point, then impressed Flaubert even more by telling him he could continue almost indefinitely.

In Paris, everybody knew the most famous houses: Le Chabanais at 12 Rue Chabanais; Le Sphinx at 31 Boulevard Edgar Quinet, opposite Montparnasse cemetery; 6 Rue des Moulins, where Henri de Toulouse-Lautrec sketched many of his brothel pictures; and Le One-Two-Two at 122 Rue de Provence. Traditionally, they opened at 2 p.m. and closed around 2 a.m., when the girls' *mecs*, or pimps, came to collect them – and their takings. Every Monday, the Public Medical Inspector visited each house, checked the women for venereal disease and stamped their registration cards.

Le Sphinx opened in 1931 with a gala launch to which dignitaries brought their wives. It had a restaurant, a *bar américaine* with a black bartender to mix Stateside-style cocktails, and a four-piece band for dancing. Its art-deco décor, in the Egyptian style made fashionable by the discovery of Tutankhamun's tomb, included two life-size Pharaonic statues in the men's room. One awed patron said the Sphinx rivalled in sumptuousness the dining room on a transatlantic ship – except that none of the Cunard liners had forty nude girls gliding among the tables in a tireless parade.

Marlene Dietrich and the music-hall star Mistinguett, both bisexual, often visited the Sphinx, and were friendly with its *patronne*, Martoune. Journalist Waverley Root of the *International Herald Tribune* escorted visiting celebrities there so frequently that Martoune set aside one of the house's three telephone booths for his exclusive use. The bandleader Duke Ellington, taken along by friends, was hugely impressed:

> You can't imagine anyone going to a whorehouse with tails and evening dresses in a party of ten. Real class people ... Suddenly the wall opens up and there's fifty naked broads standing up on the stage, and this is the show, they just stand there ... At the end of the show, all these beautiful chicks come on to the floor with their evening gowns on, and they stand out there and they take their bows, and the Madame comes out and she says, 'All these lovely girls are here to entertain you, you can't buy a girl in this house since you have paid your cover charge, and you are cordially invited to have one of our young ladies.' ... 'Hey, Duke,' they say, 'here's your chance, why don't you get a girl?' ... So finally I

got up and waved to the Madame, I says, 'Madame? I'll take the three on the end.'

The magazine *La Vie parisienne* is like a time capsule of that period. A weekly of genteel titillation, it survived for almost a century on a ration of discreet nudes, naughty cartoons, and page after page of *petites annonces*. Through its advertisements, Norma Dixie sold *livres érotiques*, either from her premises at 34 Rue Godot de Mauroy, or by mail '*directe et rapide sous enveloppe fermée*'. *Préservatifs*, i.e., condoms, forbidden under American law, and in fact technically illegal even in France, could be bought by post from Maison Bellard in Montmartre, which also sold supposed remedies for impotence and even syphilis. Studios and pieds-à-terre were offered for rent, by the day, for 15 or 20 francs – about the price charged by a run-of-the-mill prostitute. There were also numerous ads for *sages-femmes* – strictly speaking, midwives, though actually in this case abortionists, or in the grisly argot of the time '*faiseuses d'ange*', angel-makers.

Around 1932, new advertisements began to appear. The Curious Bookshop of Mademoiselle Claude at 7 Rue de la Lune offered 'Realistic films ... Best models of MONTPARNASSE and MONTMARTRE. All films with two or four persons. SOMETHING YOU HAVE NEVER

SEEN BEFORE; films for the Pathé-Baby, Kodaks and other systems. Price from 1 pound and upwards. Beautiful collection of 6 REALISTIC-LOVE-ACTION FILMS for only six pounds. Rapid and VERY DISCREET SERVICE, letters sent out in ordinary plain envelopes, parcels in plain wrappers. SEND YOUR ORDER TO-DAY . . .' More intriguing still were the ads of Ginette for her bookstore at 4 Rue du Ponceau. 'FILMS CINÉMA *avec des personnages jeunes et beaux, filmés dans notre studio SECRET, donnant l'illusion de la VIE. Voici quelques séries uniques*: 1. VIERGES ET DEMI-VIERGES. 2. BRUTALITÉS FÉMININES. 3. MÉLANGES SAVANTS. 4. ÉTREINTES PASSIONNÉES. 5. LES 32 CARESSES. 6. SCÈNES D'ORGIE . . .'

The eagerness of the customers seems to be echoed in the breathless enthusiasm, sketchy syntax and notional punctuation of the ad copy. This was something new: pornographic films you could screen in your own home; that were small enough to fit in your pocket, and smuggle past customs. Not cheap, of course. A cassette for the 9.5 mm Pathé-Baby cost 100 FF and the 16 mm version 300 FF, at a time when 200 FF would buy a man's overcoat or a suit. But there was no shortage of customers.

These advertisements reflected a technological breakthrough. The first films had been on 35 mm stock, which amateurs could neither shoot nor process. But the arrival of 9.5 mm and then 8 mm film revolutionized the porn business as much as video was to do in the Eighties. Films could now be shot with light cameras. You didn't even need to duplicate them. By taping half a dozen 8 mm cameras together, with a single control, you could shoot six films at the same time. The resulting prints could be processed in any photographic darkroom and, most important, sent through the mail. As the bilingual advertising suggests, so many found their way to England that, until the 1960s, English pornographic films simply didn't exist. It was easier, cheaper and safer to buy them in France.

Some of this I picked up from reading, but for detail and the authentic tang of that forgotten age I had to thank Hugo. Marie-Do's sister introduced us. She'd already mentioned him a number of times: 'an American writer who lives in our building. *Très sympa.*' We met at last during a little family get-together in the spring. Whatever the term 'American writer' meant to me, Hugo failed to fit it. In his early forties, stooped, furtive, with an underslung jaw and a New York mumble, he resembled the illicit offspring of Bette Midler and Richard Nixon – until he grinned. Then his lopsided smile, revealing yellow, crooked teeth, made him a dead ringer for John Cassavetes in *The Dirty Dozen*.

The only puzzling element about him was his companion. Pretty, obviously intelligent, and very French, she clung to his arm, occasionally murmuring in his ear and surreptitiously insinuating her tongue. He shook her off, like a fly, which only seemed to encourage her.

'You're . . . uh, a . . . uh, writer?' he muttered when we met.

'Yes.'

'I . . . uh . . . write too.'

'What sort of things do you write?'

He looked offended, as if I'd asked for his inside-leg measurement. 'Oh. You know . . . stuff . . .' He waved a hand vaguely.

The conversation went no further and I wrote Hugo off as another lost soul, so it was a surprise when, the next day, he rang to suggest meeting for coffee.

This wasn't easy to arrange. The first café I nominated was too smoky; he had asthma. At another, 'They rip you off,' he said, never explaining why. A third was too far from his gym, his pretext for being in my area in the first place; Hugo always made you feel he was 'fitting you in'. We agreed on the Danton, at the foot of our street. ('Traditionally appealing to American students . . . worth a second look', *Cafés of Paris: A Guide*, by Christine Graf.)

I arrived first and took a table at the front. Hugo subsided opposite me five minutes later.

'You shouldn't sit here,' he said without preamble. Swivelling in his seat, he pointed to the framed *tarif des consommations* behind the metal-surfaced bar. 'If you stand at the bar, they can charge you only those prices. It's the law. If you're at a table, they add something for service.'

'How much?'

'About fifty per cent. If you sit out on the sidewalk – what they call *la terrasse* – it can be double.'

I tried to feel cheated, but if a dollar or two meant the difference between a comfortable, if tiny, table with a view of the most elegant street life in Europe, and jostling with the men at the bar drinking *doubles expressos* and puffing Gauloises, it seemed little enough to pay.

Over the next few months I built up a picture of Hugo's life, though seldom from him, since he was as close as an oyster. With the help of his father, a retired Wall Street broker, he'd amassed a small fortune before deciding in his late thirties to throw up everything, go to Paris, and write – which he'd been doing for five years, without commercial success.

Once a week, he taught at one of Paris's adult-education schools; I never understood why, since the pay was minimal. Like the professional expats who threw 'open houses' at so many euros a head, most men took these jobs to harvest lonely American women, but Hugo was the exception there as well, since, as long as I knew him, he had only French girlfriends, all young, all vivacious and intelligent, all sexy. He treated them like furniture, and they adored it, even after he broke it off. 'He *is* an *ordure*,' one of them said to me with a sigh afterwards, 'but you must admit, he is not bad-looking.' I stared at that barracuda profile and once again wondered what attracts some women to some men. 'You know,' a London publisher once hissed of a mutual friend, phenomenally successful with women, 'I believe he gives off some secret odour, like a goat, that draws them to him.' If such a scent did exist, Hugo clearly owned a Giant Economy Size bottle.

Though Hugo told me repeatedly that he was eager to marry, he perversely didn't want a French wife but an American one, Jewish for preference, who could offer him true love, be acceptable to his cantankerous parents and share his tiny, bare Paris apartment while he wrote; the sort of woman, in short, who had sustained Hemingway, Fitzgerald and other expat writers of the Twenties, but who were thin on the ground in the liberated Nineties.

I too had my place in his world scheme. What he wanted from me was an introduction to my agent.

'I'd have to see something you wrote,' I temporized. 'Agents are quite specialized; maybe my guy isn't right for you.' This was my standard line. It

216

prepared the way for me to say, after a decent interval, 'Your stuff is great, but he's got too much first-person fiction at the moment. Maybe next year.'

'OK,' Hugo said querulously. ' I thought of that. So I brought something.' He pushed a manila folder across the table.

I opened it. 'Just one page?'

He stared accusingly. 'That's not enough?'

'I don't know. Let me take it away and read it . . .'

'You can't take it away!'

'Why not?'

He glared, though there might have been a spark of panic there as well. 'Well, I'd rather . . . I mean, what if someone . . . Can't you read it here?'

As I prepared to tell him where he could shove his page, an attractive woman walked by the café window, on the arm of a much shorter and older man. He carried a small overnight bag.

Hugo shot them a glance. 'Cheating,' he said with a smirk.

'You know them?'

'No. But her . . . and the Baisenville . . .'

My face showed my bafflement.

His smirk deepened into a leer. 'You've never heard of a Baisenville?'

'It's a town,' I said, 'west of Paris.' Marie-Do's mother had her country house in the next village.

'Well, yeah. It is. But it's also what they call that

sort of bag.' When I looked blank, he said slowly, '*Baise . . . en . . . ville?*'

I picked at this etymological knot. Technically, *baiser* is the verb 'to kiss', but the French used *embrasser* for that. *Baiser* had only one meaning: to fuck.

'*Baise en ville* -- fuck in town?' I suggested.

'Right!' he said gleefully. 'You pack a shirt and a change of underwear in one of those bags, tell your wife you're working late at the office . . . but it's really *baise en ville*!'

The couple were crossing the street towards a small hotel. Did I imagine it, or were their steps more urgent, their demeanour more nervous? And didn't he, as they stepped inside, take a quick all-encompassing glance around the street?

I reassessed Hugo. His look of furtive knowledge. Those pale, slender, penetrative hands. The insinuating voice. His success with women, and their conviction that, all evidence to the contrary, he was somehow *gentil* . . . Until now, I'd never understood why prostitutes would work all day, then hand over their money to a lover who spent all day lounging in a café. Watching and listening to Hugo, I began to see. Here was a man born to be a vendor of dirty postcards, a gigolo, a pimp.

'Order us another coffee,' I said, 'and I'll read your stuff.'

18

Red Lights, Big City

Un gars: a young man/*Une garce*: a whore.

Un courtisan: someone close to a king/*Une courtisane*: a whore.

Un masseur: someone who gives massages/*Une masseuse*: a whore.

Un coureur: a runner/*Une coureuse*: a whore.

Un rouleur: a cyclist/*Une roulure*: a whore.

Un professionnel: a highly paid sportsman/*Une professionnelle*: a whore.

Un homme sans moralité: a politician/*Une femme sans moralité*: a whore.

Un entraîneur: a man who trains a sports team/*Une entraîneuse*: a whore.

Un homme à femmes: a ladies' man/*Une femme à hommes*: a whore.

Un homme publique: a public figure/*Une femme publique*: a whore.

Un homme facile: a man easy to get on with/*Une femme facile*: a whore.

Un homme qui fait le trottoir: someone who makes sidewalks/*Une femme qui fait le trottoir*: A whore.

Anonymous Internet posting, 2002

'HENRY MILLER USED TO WRITE COPY FOR THEIR brochures,' Hugo said. 'They paid him in girls.'

I scribbled a note, which was difficult, since we were walking up Rue Chabanais, a narrow street about equidistant – and not by accident – from France's national theatre, the Comédie-Française, its national library, the Bibliothèque Nationale, the Opéra, and the Bourse or stock exchange. Looking at the street's five-storey buildings, these days mostly divided into apartments, with boutiques at street level, one would never imagine that, from 1876 to 1946, Rue Chabanais, and one address in particular, was as renowned in the circles of power as the Champs-Élysées.

'Ya know Edward the Seventh?' Hugo asked from a few paces ahead.

'Queen Victoria's son?' Hugo had cast me in the role of Naïve Newcomer deferring to Old Hand, and I played up to it. 'The fat one? Prince of Wales for years? Because she wouldn't give up the throne?'

'Yeah,' said Hugo. 'He used to come here all the time. Too fat to fuck. They built him a special "armchair of love" so he could do it standing up.' He halted abruptly in the middle of the pavement, the better to describe it. 'It was like a little table, see. The girl lay on her back on top, with her knees up, and her feet on these two sort of stirrups at the corners. And Prince Eddie stood in front of her. The top part was on rollers, so it could move back and forward . . .'

He mimed an energetic hip motion, something like swinging a hula hoop. Women with shopping bags stopped to watch. *'C'est dégueulasse,'* one said. I knew that meant 'It's disgusting.'

'We're attracting attention here,' I said urgently. 'Where was it anyway?'

He nodded at the terrace building behind us, indistinguishable from the others on both sides of the street. 'Right there.'

This was the legendary 12 Rue Chabanais? Hard to believe that, in its day, it had been one of the world's most opulent whorehouses.

'It doesn't look like much.'

Hugo was aggrieved. 'What did you want – a neon sign? Everybody knew where it was. The restaurant across the road used to advertise: "We are just as good as the place opposite." Even the police knew – but that was the deal: you stayed in business as long as you didn't make waves, paid off the right people and nobody got the clap.'

From the reading I'd been doing, I knew he was right. The addresses of the larger whorehouses were common knowledge. Their owners belonged to the best clubs. Some were high government officials. A few had seats in parliament.

At certain cafés, owners or their agents regularly met pimps to discuss business and exchange gossip and girls. They also saw off any unwanted competition. In 1931, 'Texas' Guinan, sometime showgirl and movie actress, famous for running a series of wide-open New York speakeasies (and greeting clients with a genial 'Hello, suckers!'), arrived in Europe with a team of 'taxi girls', so called because they could be hired by the hour. When Britain refused them entry, she tried France, and never got off the pier at Le Havre.

Back home again, she resourcefully knocked together a quick revue called *Too Hot for Paris* and took it on tour, with considerable success. But the title was a misnomer: almost nothing was too hot for the French capital. A brothel visit was on the itinerary of every adventurous tourist, even if he did no more than gape. 'The ladies see no harm in you coming merely to inspect them,' wrote Bruce Reynolds in *Paris with the Lid Lifted*. 'They will parade for you in frankest nudity, and dance with one another in a mirror-walled room, so that of their charms you may miss nothing.' Le Sphinx and a few other houses encouraged tourism, but a visit to Le 122 and particularly Le Chabanais was only 'by appointment', if not 'By Appointment'; such establishments had a responsibility of discretion to the politicians, ambassadors and crowned heads who came there looking for a good time.

Not that anyone talked of a *bordel* or called a

whore *putain*. Euphemisms had long since replaced both words, leaving the originals free to take on totally different meanings. '*Putain!*' became, as it remains, the all-purpose French exclamatory swear word, equivalent to the appreciative 'Fuck me!' So what *did* you call a prostitute? In English, she could be a 'working girl' or a 'street-walker'. In France, she was a *coureuse* or *rouleuse* – a runner or roller, because she was always on the move – or an *entraîneuse* – a trainer – because the more select Edwardian hookers worked from horseback. Many gentlemen took their morning ride in the park mainly to encounter what the London press called 'these pretty little horsebreakers'.

At the *maisons de fantasie*, any flight of fancy could be realized – for a price. Their wardrobes contained costumes for nuns, brides, ladies in crinolines, and harem girls – or boys – which were as often worn by the clients as by the girls. At Le Chabanais, retired provincial administrators nostalgic for France's African colonies often requested the Moorish room, equipped with tropical plants and a swimming pool. If they liked, a canvas panorama of desert scenes could be unrolled discreetly in the background – the same one that provided a moving landscape outside the window of the simulated Orient Express sleeping car. One house even provided a mock igloo in which a girl could strip the chilled explorer and rub his limbs to restore circulation, but this was too obscure to attract a large clientele.

In those larger houses that maintained a restaurant, the chef had to be prepared for unusual orders. Eggs featured prominently. Some demands were wildly surrealist. A man might ask to have a fried egg pinned to his lapel and watch a naked girl squirt ink at it from a fountain pen. Even more popular was having a freshly cooked omelette slid, still hot, onto one's naked flesh.

Visiting a *bordel de premier ordre* was less like having sex than attending a reception at one of the best houses in Paris. Certainly the furnishings were no less elaborate. Ten years after a member of the exclusive Jockey Club started Le Chabanais, he bought the Japanese Chamber that won first prize at the 1896 Universal Exposition, and installed it at number 12. Shortly after, he added a suite in the opulent style of Louis XVI, with porcelain medallions painted with plump pink nudes *à la* François Boucher.

In an unheard-of refinement, water from the house's taps was filtered, to remove impurities which might give clients anything less than the smoothest ride. A special bathroom contained a gold-plated bath, decorated at both ends by large-breasted sphinxes whose heads reared up to give the impression of a Viking longboat. Edward VII liked to fill it with champagne, watch his favourite whore bathe in it, then sit around the tub with his friends and drink the wine.

Every new technological development quickly found an erotic use. Once electricity arrived, the brothels adopted it eagerly. During exhibitions, nudes revolved on electrically operated turntables. Vibrators were in use, half a century before the bedside torpedo of the Seventies. Some brothels employed mild electric shocks to stimulate failing erections. Others advertised 'Doctor Mondat's Suction Pump', which promised the same effect.

'They made movies too,' Hugo said.

'I've seen some.' It came as a shock to find how many distinguished pioneers of the cinema had dabbled in porn. Even Georges Méliès, creator of those 1890s trick-effect films about disappearing magicians and trips to the Moon, had made his share of movies such as *The Bridal Night* and *Paulette in the Bath*.

'Ever see the Graham Greene one?' Hugo asked.

'Graham Greene? The *writer*? In a porno movie?'

'No, not *in* it . . .' He glanced at his watch. 'Look, I gotta date. I'll bring it round. See ya.'

It took me ten days to track down the Graham Greene porn connection. On the way, I found even more evidence of the French intellectual enthusiasm for porn. Paul Éluard, a leading Surrealist, could scarcely contain his delight when he wrote to his wife Gala from Marseilles.

> Obscene cinema, what a marvel! It's exhilarating; a discovery. The incredible life of enormous and magnificent organs on the screen. The sperm that leaps. And the life of loving flesh, all the contortions. It's glorious. And very well made, a tremendous eroticism. How much I would like you to see it. And if you come to Marseilles, you will go – with Gaillard, who is an incarnation (truly) of decency, and who has already taken many very 'bourgeois' ladies.
>
> The movies turned me on in an exasperating way for an hour. It was a near thing that I didn't come simply from the show. If you had been here, I couldn't have stopped myself. It's a very pure show without theatrical effect. The actors don't move their lips, at least not to speak, it's a 'silent' art, a 'primitive' art; passion vs death and stupidity. They should show this in every theatre and in schools. It would result in workable marriages – the first; sacred unions, multi-faceted. Alas, that poetry is not born yet.

That Graham Greene also watched blue movies shouldn't have been a surprise. A lifelong client of prostitutes, he'd have seen plenty of them in brothels which, then as now, used them as 'warm-ups' for waiting clients. Greene collaborated on, or at least acted as technical adviser for, *To Beg I Am Ashamed*, the purported memoirs of a London whore published in 1938; but the closest link is provided by his 1954 short story 'The Blue Film'.

It's a typical Greene-ian vignette of lost hope and defiant desire. Carter, an ageing world traveller, is in Hong Kong on a rare holiday with his unloving wife. When she taunts him about the tameness of their visit, he takes her to see some pornographic films, projected on a tiny screen in a sordid shack.

The first film was peculiarly unattractive and showed the rejuvenation of an elderly man at the hands of two blonde masseuses. From the style of the women's hairdressing the film must have been made in the late twenties. Carter and his wife sat in mutual embarrassment as the film whirled and clicked to a stop.

'Not a very good one,' Carter said, as though he were a connoisseur . . .

The second film is more interesting. A girl picks up a young man in the street and takes him back to her room. With a shock, Carter recognizes the girl, the room – 'a doll over a telephone; a pin-up girl of the period over the double bed' – and, finally, the man. It's himself, thirty years before. As a student in

Paris, he'd made some money by performing in the film, but had entirely forgotten about it. This being Greeneland, Carter is filled with loneliness, guilt and a sense of loss. But his wife, after professing to be bored by the film and disgusted by his involvement, is so aroused that, when they return to their hotel and make love, she has her first orgasm in years.

Hugo turned up at Odéon with a video cassette which, though battered and nameless, bore a meticulously inked number. Part of an extensive collection? I didn't ask. In the world of sex, as in that of espionage, a respect for anonymity is simply good manners. As W. H. Auden wrote, 'In a brothel, both / The ladies and the gentlemen / Have nicknames only.'

What unreeled on the screen in jittering black and white was the film with the masseuses that Greene described.

Without preamble, it opens with a close-up of a gentleman in a smoking jacket and artificially greyed hair reading ads for patent sexual stimulants like Erector and Vigorax, or for 'Madame Irma', who promises to *rend la jeunesse aux vieilles cloches* – literally to put youth into old bells.

The scene changes to an apartment where two women wait expressionlessly, one reading a magazine, the other buffing her nails. They wear classic Twenties nurse regalia, complete with white surgical coats, white stockings and long Red Cross head-dresses. When monsieur arrives, he's quickly stripped and laid naked on a table. Madame Irma's methods do the trick, and after the film ends in traditional fashion the nurses, now wearing only their head-dresses, turn to the camera and mouth the invitation 'Your turn, ladies and gentlemen.'

'Well, Greene obviously saw the film,' I said. 'He got the details exactly right.'

'They were all mad for porn,' Hugo said sourly. Evidence of human weakness in the great gave him a bitter satisfaction. *So what if they can get their books published. They're no better than the rest of us.*

'The Surrealists too?' I suggested helpfully.

Hugo leaped on this like a dog on a bone. 'Not Breton. He didn't approve. His father was a policeman. But the rest of them, yeah. Buñuel, Dali ... Paul Éluard *loved* porn movies. He was a big *partouzer* too. He and and his wife Gala used to *partouze* with Max Ernst. Then he met Dali and tried to set up a *partouze* with him and Gala. But she left him instead and married Dali! So he started all over again with his new wife, Nusch.'

The thought of all this talent writhing in bed together induced a sort of glee.

'And then there was Man Ray,' he said breathlessly. A fleck of spit flew from his lips. 'And *1929.*'

'What happened in 1929?'

He looked at me again with that 'Don't you know *anything?*' expression. 'It's not a date. It's a book. Man Ray's porn book.' Before I could ask more, he snatched up his cassette.

'Let me guess,' I said. 'You've got a date.'

He looked at me suspiciously. 'Yeah. How did you know?'

'Stab in the dark, Hugo.'

Doubt played over his face, and a kind of fear. 'Did *she* tell you?'

'Who?'

'Doesn't matter,' he said hurriedly. 'Doesn't matter.'

Partway down the stairs, he paused. As if to make amends for a suspicion I hadn't understood, let alone deserved, he said, 'You want, I can take you to meet one of Man Ray's models. She'll tell you about *1929*.'

But that meeting had to wait, because very soon the real world caught up with me.

19

The Little Tenant

'The best of life, Passworthy, lies nearest to the edge of death.'

Raymond Massey in *Things to Come*; script by H. G. Wells
and Lajos Biro

MOST WEEKENDS THAT SPRING, MARIE-DOMINIQUE
and I made day trips outside Paris in her little Fiat.
We walked Swann's way along the canal at Illiers-
Combray, and, standing on the wooden bridge at
Monet's Giverny, watched the stream comb out the
long water weeds like a woman's hair.

In what was to be our final trip for some time,
though we didn't know it then, we went to Chartres,
approaching across the flat wheatlands, watching the
spires rising out of the horizon. Unlike more
domesticated British cathedrals, Chartres still has a
strong whiff of the medieval. There's a pronounced

hollow towards the back of the nave where pilgrims used to camp out, and which therefore had to be washed down regularly, like the elephant house at the zoo. Set in the floor nearby is an elaborate serpentine maze. Pilgrims ended their journey by crawling along this path, thinking devotional thoughts; a combination of the Stations of the Cross and Snakes and Ladders.

We were strolling along this path, trying to decipher the worn hieroglyphs, when Marie-Do said, 'I don't feel well.' She put her hand on her stomach. 'I have a pain.'

By the time we got back to Paris, it was obvious that this wasn't simply indigestion. Her gynaecologist said, 'Come right away.'

I navigated my way to the 7th *arrondissement* in an evening yellowed by the street-lamps. Dr Bougevoy had her office in a side street, next to a building ornamented in exaggerated art nouveau, its frontage tormented into a riot of plants, animals and insects. Beautiful but doomed-looking girls with swirling hair were swept up with snakes and other reptiles in whirlpools of stone. The door handle was a large lizard in black iron.

That whole area is dominated by the Eiffel Tower. Its pinnacle, festooned with TV and radio antennae, peeps over the top of the eight-storey apartment buildings like a giant mutant praying mantis from a

1950s science-fiction film, emphasizing the sense of Paris as a city with a ceiling. I could feel it looking over my shoulder as I slumped in the waiting room, read about the latest exploits of Princess Caroline of Monaco in *Paris Match*, and tried not to worry. After the first half-hour, that became increasingly difficult.

It was the first of many long waits in Dr Bougevoy's waiting room. I became intimate with her deep leather couches, her tattered magazines, her other patients: faded ladies past child-bearing age, and the occasional worried-looking girl, accompanied by harassed but elegant parents, or perhaps grandparents.

A small, dark woman in her early forties, with her hair twisted into a chignon, a taste for high heels and a gold ankle chain, Dr Bougevoy was, from the arrangement of north African vases and pots on her shelf, a *pied-noir*, a 'black foot', one of the French raised in Algeria who were dispossessed when it was made independent following a bloody civil war during which rebel generals made an attempt on De Gaulle's life — or, if you believe Frederick Forsyth's *The Day of the Jackal*, two. With her chattering, hand-fluttering manner and broken English, she was more like the proprietor of a boutique on the Faubourg Saint-Honoré than an obstetrician. In happier circumstances one would have enjoyed spending time in her company, but Marie-Do's drawn face when she emerged after an hour, and Bougevoy's relentlessly cheerful bedside manner, cast gloom over the waiting room.

Her explanations of the problem didn't dispel it.

Marie-Do, it transpired, had a fibroid. Probably this benign growth had been only the size of a cherrystone, but now, in pregnancy, it was growing apace with the foetus. The cherrystone was now as big as an orange, and getting larger. If it continued to grow, it would draw nutrients from the baby, and almost certainly cause a miscarriage.

'But there are medications . . .' I began.

No, apparently not. Any drug which reduced the fibroid would probably kill the baby. There was nothing to do but tough it out until the growth of the foetus outpaced that of the fibroid. Even painkillers were dangerous. The best Bougevoy could prescribe were ice packs for the abdomen, and lots of bed rest.

Our spirits were low during the ride back to Place Dauphine. Marie-Do fell into bed and I filled a rubber ice pack for her abdomen. Except for appointments with Bougevoy or the *échographiste*, a couple of visits to Europe 1 to tell them she was taking her maternity leave early, and the occasional painful walk around the park for some fresh air, she was hardly to leave it for two months.

20

Man Alive

It was as if he had embarked on a publicity campaign to prove that he was a three-ring circus unto himself, 'what with abstract and portrait photography, movies and now and then a painting ... But it's all one thing in the end,' he reported excitedly to his friend Katherine Dreier back in New York, 'giving restlessness a material form.'

Neil Baldwin, *Man Ray, American Artist*

A WEEK AFTER OUR FIRST VISIT TO THE OBSTETRICIAN, Hugo rang.

'You wanna meet Jacqueline?'

'Jacqueline who?'

'Jacqueline Goddard. I told you. Man Ray's model. She's in town.'

'It's not a good time, Hugo.' I explained why.

If he felt any sympathy, he hid it well. 'She lives in

England,' he whined. 'She's only here for a few days.'

From the couch, Marie-Do said, 'You should go, *chéri*. Mother comes anyway this afternoon.'

Maybe I had been in that apartment too long. Maybe I didn't want to watch the woman I loved in pain any longer. Maybe Hugo's self-absorption was catching.

'OK,' I told him.

'Meet me here.' He gave me an address.

'Isn't that in Pigalle?'

'Yeah. Just down the road from the Moulin Rouge.'

I knew that area. It was mostly sex shops, pornographic video outlets, and boutiques doing a nice line in manacles, whips and leather jockstraps.

'She's staying in a red-light district?'

'Did I say that?' he asked accusingly. 'I just said we can *meet* there.'

The Bistro du Curé turned out to be a modest café squeezed between a peep-show parlour with black-painted windows and a clothing shop beside which Frederick's of Hollywood was as staid as Brooks Brothers.

Hugo was waiting sullenly in the back. 'You're late,' he said.

'Good to see you too, Hugo.'

As I sat down, a pleasant middle-aged lady gave

me a menu and drew my attention to the day's specials chalked on a board.

'So what do you think?' Hugo asked, looking around.

'I think I'll have the *brandade de morue* and the *souris d'agneau*.'

'No. I mean the place.'

The floor was bare boards, the tables covered in checkered cloths. Nothing on the menu cost more than a few francs.

'What's to think? At these prices, it's never going to make a profit. Not in Pigalle at least. Whatever else gets eaten in this area, it isn't food.'

Hugo leaned forward. 'That's it. It doesn't need to make money. It runs at a loss. Always has.'

I looked around with new eyes, and noticed an unmarked door at the back.

'You don't mean to tell me *this* is a whoreho—?'

'No, no!' He nodded at the motherly waitresses. 'They look like hookers to you?'

'Then, what are they?'

'*Nuns!*'

'You're joking!'

'Cummon.' With a nod to the nearest waitress, he headed for the door at the back. A narrow staircase led upstairs. At the top, we entered a tiny chapel. The light burning in front of the tabernacle on the altar indicated that it held consecrated wafers.

'It's a *church*?' I said.

'Yeah. For hookers and pimps. Open day and night.' He nodded towards the curtain that cut off an alcove. 'Always a priest on call to hear confessions. That's why they call it the Bistro du Curé – the Priest's Café.'

'Is this where we're meeting your friend?'

'Jacqueline? No. Other side of town. We can get a cab. But I thought you should see it. You had enough?'

From behind the curtain, I thought I heard murmuring. Some weary *entraîneuse* begging forgiveness for her sins? The whole place made me acutely uncomfortable.

'More than enough, Hugo.'

As we left, I felt, for the first time since childhood, an impulse to genuflect and cross myself. If you could commit a mortal sin simply by visiting a place, we had just done so. Hugo had excelled himself.

In the taxi that took us across the city, I thought about Emmanuel Radnitzky, the persistent little guy with the low toneless voice and the humourless rat-trap of a mouth who rechristened himself Man Ray.

He and Hugo had a lot in common. Both were practical men who succeeded in New York before they came to Paris. And both decided in early middle age that America had no more to offer. But there their lives diverged. Hugo imported with him all the cargo of the businessman. It kept him anchored in a Manhattan past. Ray, who, for some time before he departed, had been writing to friends in France on a handmade letterhead with the repeated message '*De la merde d'Amérique*' – roughly, 'Shitty stuff from America' – made a definitive break by piling all his paintings in the middle of his studio and setting them on fire.

Arriving in 1921, Ray hit the road running. He'd already become friendly in New York with Marcel Duchamp and Francis Picabia, pioneers of the new art that, like Surrealism, sprang out of the war. It was Ray who found for Duchamp the shop-window sheets of glass he used to make his pioneering *The Bride Stripped Bare by Her Bachelors Even*. Duchamp persuaded Tristan Tzara, founder of the Dada movement, to give Ray a room, and, with Picabia and Tzara, 'launched' him with a show at Librairie 6, the Dadaist bookshop in Montparnasse.

Ray saw instantly that, with Parisians, style was everything. Later, he would write in an autobiographical poem:

> I'm ugly. I have an inexpressive face.
> I am small. I'm like all of you!
> I wanted to give myself
> A little publicity.

Spontaneously, he bought an ordinary flat iron, glued some nails to the surface, points outwards, called it *Cadeau* – Gift – and presented it to the composer Erik Satie, who provided the music for his show. It became one of the most familiar of Surrealist objects. Later, he'd paste a disc with the photograph of a woman's eye onto a metronome and call it *Object to be Destroyed*.

In New York, he'd photographed his own artwork and that of others, but now it became his speciality. He produced some of the most famous images of all time, almost always of women: a girl's face glinting with glass tears, or a naked back carved with the sound holes of a violin. The Dadaists and Surrealists hired him to document their shows, but Ray made more money with portraits, or fashion shots for designers like Paul Poiret. When money was short, he sold nudes and pin-ups to magazines like *Paris-Montparnasse* and *Allo*, the *Playboy*s of their time. He also shot pornography, often to order.

Ray picked up models and girlfriends in the cafés of Boulevard Montparnasse – where 'all languages were spoken, including French as terrible as my own'. One night, a girl came through selling copies of the magazine *Paris-Montparnasse*. She was greeted with loud good humour at every table, but finally sat down opposite him. Her name was Alice Prin, but everyone called her Kiki.

She was twenty-two, tall, wide-hipped, small-breasted, with narrow ankles and small feet. A prominent nose and receding chin were redeemed by electric eyes, which artists like Moise Kisling liked to elongate with mascara to give her the look of a startled faun. She'd posed for, and slept with, dozens of them, including some famous ones, like Foujita, Kisling and Pascin. 'I get a couple of *sous* for the magazine,' she told Ray airily, 'but the guys in the back room pay me ten francs to show my tits, so I don't do so bad.' She also confessed she never wore underwear.

Manny, inflamed, asked for a date. The next night, they went to the cinema. The film they saw, *Foolish Wives*, was set on the French Riviera, with Erich von Stroheim playing the archetypal seducer who preys on the neglected wives of American businessmen. As he lured his latest victim to the cottage of a confederate during a rainstorm, urged her to 'slip out of those wet things', courteously turned his back, then cooly appraised her over his shoulder in a pocket mirror, Ray clutched Kiki's hand and felt a matching excitement.

He invited her back to his room to photograph her. For the first session, Kiki stayed clothed. The next afternoon, she returned to see the results. 'Presently she undressed while I sat on the bed with the camera before me,' Ray recalled. 'When she came out from behind the screen, I motioned for her to come and sit beside me. I put my arms around her, and she did the same, our lips met and we both lay down. No pictures were taken that afternoon.'

Kiki moved in with Ray in December 1921. 'He photographs folks in the room where we live,' she wrote, 'and at night I lie stretched out on the bed while he works in the dark. I can see his face over the little red light, and he looks like the devil himself. I am so on pins and needles that I can't wait for him to get through.'

With Kiki in his bed, couturiers like Paul Poiret at his shoulder and some of the Surrealists at his back, Ray was set to conquer Paris. Gertrude Stein admitted him to her salon, and, quixotically, accorded him the exclusive right to take her picture. He also photographed Picasso, Matisse, Léger, Cocteau, even Breton and the rest of the Surrealists.

He continued to dabble in pornography. Kiki didn't mind. It aroused her to take part, and to see the reaction when he showed the pictures to prospective clients. When Henri-Pierre Roche, author of *Jules et Jim*, called to have his portrait taken, Ray, he wrote, showed him 'very moving pictures of lesbians, in eight most luscious poses. I know one of these beautiful girls. Then, two photos of love-making between a man and a woman.' Roche commissioned Ray to shoot some more. William Seabrook, as well as being a scholar of voodoo, author of *The Magic Island* (and sometime cannibal), was also an enthusiast for bondage, and would invite Ray to photograph the nude young women he kept bound or chained around his apartment.

But once Ray had made Kiki famous, she left him for one of her old lovers, Henri Broca, editor of *Paris-Montparnasse*, who convinced her they could become rich by publishing her memoirs. A furious Ray charged that Broca was 'a drinker and a drug addict, subject to hallucinations', but nobody took much notice; in Montparnasse, who wasn't? Broca did publish Kiki's skimpy memoirs, liberally illustrated with pictures of her nude body, including some shots by Ray. It sold well. Edward Titus at the Black Manikin Press commissioned an English version and persuaded Hemingway to write an introduction. Man Ray seethed.

Which brings us to Jacqueline Goddard and *1929* . . .

The taxi dropped us at a small hotel near Place de Furstemberg. Hugo led me fussily upstairs.

Jacqueline Goddard first posed for Man Ray in 1930, and worked for him until he left Paris in 1939 to wait out the war in Los Angeles. And though her mane of hair was now white, one could still see the leonine beauty that attracted him.

'My parents were Italian,' she told me. 'My father was a sculptor, so I started modelling for him.'

'And then for Man Ray.'

She smiled. 'For little Man, yes. He was *très sympa*. But if you ask if I was ever his lover, no. Not like Kiki. And I never posed for any of those pictures like she did.'

I glanced at Hugo. 'You mean pornography? The ones in *1929*?'

Jacqueline pursed her lips – both in disapproval, I thought, but also at the necessity of having to mar the reputation of a great artist.

'It is said', she conceded circumspectly, 'that Man Ray started with pornography. And I have seen recently a photograph of Kiki's mouth on Man Ray's private parts . . .'

The Surrealists of Paris in the late Twenties were less a movement than a gang, and an unruly one. 'We descend to the street with revolvers in our hands,' proclaimed André Breton. None of them ever *did* unholster a gun – they were respectable journalists and writers, after all – but if someone like Jean Cocteau, despised by Breton for his homosexuality, launched a new play, the Surrealists would be there in force to shout insults from the stalls and, occasionally, stampede onto the stage to scuffle with the cast. The next day, Breton usually sent a letter of apology to the theatre manager, often with a discreet splash of blood on one corner of the paper.

Given their penchant for direct action, the Surrealists were inspired when, in late 1929, after the American stock market collapsed and the tourists who were the life-blood of European capitals flooded back home, the Belgian chapter under Édouard Mesens announced it was broke. At the crowded lunchtime seances in the Café Radio on Place Blanche, one of the seedier Montmartre squares, the problem of how to help them was discussed.

'They could publish a special issue of *Variétés*,' suggested Louis Aragon, Breton's tall, soft-spoken lieutenant.

'They've just done that,' said Benjamin Péret. The Belgians were technically Dadaists, followers of the theories of random creation propounded by Tristan Tzara, but a Surrealist issue of their magazine *Variétés* published the previous year had been a huge success.

'Maybe a *Spécial* special issue . . .' mused Péret.

Péret was the most outrageous of the group. In the aftermath of the 1918 Armistice, with Paris still traumatized by the war, he arrived at his first Surrealist seance dressed as a German soldier. He was also the only one who took Surrealist anticlericalism to its logical conclusion and attacked nuns and priests in the street.

He and Aragon began talking quietly together in

the corner. That afternoon, Aragon headed across the Seine, to Montparnasse, the suburb that rose in a gentle swell above the Luxembourg Gardens, and along whose main thoroughfare, Boulevard Montparnasse, most of the great literary cafés of Paris were congregated: Le Select, Le Dôme, La Rotonde, La Coupole. But it was too early for the cafés, unless you were one of those Americans like Hemingway who spent his days there. Aragon knew he would find the man he wanted either at his apartment, on Rue Campagne Première, just beyond the Montparnasse cemetery, or in his studio at 8 Rue du Val-de-Grâce.

As he entered the little block of apartments in the shade of the huge seventeenth-century Val-de-Grâce church, with a distant view of the domed Observatory, built by Napoleon, Aragon heard the stomp of an American jazz band. It became louder as he mounted the stairs and rang a bell that whirred, he said later, 'like a desperate cicada'.

The music didn't stop, but the door was flung open. The man who stood there was short – only five feet two. With his big nose, glaring eyes, heavy brows and pronounced widow's peak, he reminded Aragon of a bird of prey, interrupted in tearing out the entrails of a hapless rabbit.

Man Ray didn't say anything – just stood aside to let Aragon enter. The studio was small, but meticulously neat. From the walls, Dogon and Senegalese masks glared down. They looked like the man who'd hung them.

'So, Louis,' Ray said in Brooklyn-accented French as he returned to his table, 'what's the news from Place Blanche?'

Pinned down to the table was a photograph of a woman in an evening dress – one of his portrait commissions. Ray's commercial success irritated Breton, one reason why he wasn't totally part of the group; technically, a true Surrealist scorned paid employment.

Aragon explained about the Belgians and the idea of a special issue of *Variétés*.

Ray stared at Aragon, a crooked smile on his face. '*How* special, exactly?'

Aragon told him what he and Péret planned: an issue of *Variétés* that would both attract attention to the movement and make a lot of money. An erotic issue. Perhaps with photographs by Ray?

Ray slid open the drawer under his worktable and took out a sheaf of prints. They spilled across the table, swamping the society matron in flesh. The faces were cropped out, but Aragon knew who'd posed for them. The male body, hairy and pale, was obviously Ray's. And everyone in Montparnasse knew who owned the wide hips being penetrated so vigorously.

'Could we really *publish* these?' Aragon asked.

'You can buy the same thing on Rue Saint-Denis any day of the week,' Ray said. 'Add some poems or something; do it in a limited edition. Sell it for five thousand francs a copy and it isn't dirty any more. It's fuckin' *literature*.'

Aragon saw why Ray was doing this. If Kiki wanted to be in print, he'd put her in print, and with a vengeance. He must, Aragon decided, really have loved her. 'Which ones do you prefer?' he asked.

Ray chose four. The first showed him sprawled on top of Kiki. In the second, her trademark lipsticked mouth was clamped around his penis. Another showed him penetrating her from the front, and in the fourth he was sodomizing her.

'The four seasons,' he said with a laugh. 'There's your theme: spring, summer, autumn and winter.'

Aragon did as Ray suggested. He and Péret composed some erotic poetry. An accommodating printer in Brussels produced 215 numbered copies. The book showed no publisher; neither were the poets nor the photographer named. It was simply called *1929*. A week later, a truck carrying the complete printing arrived at the French border, en route from Brussels to Paris. The driver expected to be waved through, but instead the *douanes* told him to pull off the road. Philosophically, he lit a cigarette, knowing what was coming.

The Surrealists predictably protested at the seizure and destruction of *1929*. A few surviving copies changed hands at sky-high prices.

Someone had slipped a word to the French customs. Was it Ray? Probably. By doing so, he would have revenged himself on Kiki. Now her body was for sale in clandestine copies all over Paris; a whore, like all the other whores who hung around Les Halles. And the Surrealists were happy; they had their cause célèbre.

And Ray? Soon there would be a new woman to replace Kiki. He would be more than ready to be tempted when Lee Miller, a beautiful and arrogant young American, appeared in Montparnasse and announced she had come to study with him. She modelled for him, slept with him, learned from him and in time outgrew him. Miller was the sort of woman all artists fear to meet: the Eurydice figure, the muse who is also lover and destroyer. She became Ray's obsession. For her, he painted his most famous work, *The Lovers: Observatory Time*, showing her lips, pursed, provocative, at the same time seductive and reserved, floating in the evening sky over Paris. *Soon*, they seemed to say. *Not just now, but soon . . .*

But then that finished too.

'I met Man in Le Dôme,' Jacqueline Goddard confided. 'I don't remember when. He was still with Lee, though it was ending. He was sure there were other men. (I *knew* there were, but I could not say that. None of us could.) He was angry, saying terrible things about Lee ... We had a drink. It was raining outside, and he wore a long *imperméable* ...'

'A raincoat,' I said.

'Yes. And as he moved, I heard something heavy bump against the leg of the chair. And I knew it was a gun.'

'He wanted to kill Lee Miller?'

'He was a passionate man. And he loved her. Perhaps he would not have shot her ... One never knows ...'

'But he didn't shoot her.'

Jacqueline smiled. 'I like to think I am responsible for that. He got up to leave, and I said I would walk with him. We left the Dôme, and walked down Edgar Quinet in the rain.'

Nothing had changed in that area in fifty years. I could imagine them moving slowly along the boulevard, with the wall of Montparnasse cemetery just across the street, and the soft, cold rain sifting down through the plane trees to bead on her magnificent head and the set, angry face of the little man with the pistol in his raincoat pocket.

'We walked past his studio on Rue Campagne Première. The light was on. Lee was there. But alone ...? Who could tell? But I feared that, if he went in and found her with someone, he would use the gun. So I said, "Man, walk with me. Walk with me in the rain." And he walked away, and Lee Miller and Man Ray were saved.'

'And Kiki. Did you ever see her again?'

Jacqueline shook her head. 'Not until after the war. Poor Kiki. She came to the cafés, always asking for money. She said it was to pay for her gas, her electricity ... But it was a lie. It all went ...' She sniffed melodramatically. In the last years of her life, which ended in 1953, Kiki became a slave to cocaine.

Kiki was the last vestige of a Montparnasse which, when Jacqueline re-encountered it after the war, had already lost its charm. 'After a day of work,' she said, 'the artists wanted to get away from their studios, and get away from what they were creating. They all met in the cafés to argue about this and that, to discuss their work, politics and philosophy ... We went to the bar of La Coupole. Bob, the barman, was terribly nice ... As there was no telephone in those days, everybody used him to leave messages. At the Dôme we also had a little place behind the door for messages.' She sighed. 'The telephone was the death of Montparnasse.'

'So now you know about *1929*,' Hugo said as we stepped out into the late-afternoon sunshine. 'Man Ray involved in a fuck book!'

Suddenly I felt I'd had enough of Hugo – certainly

for that day, but perhaps for good. 'You're all heart, Hugo.'

He shrugged off my evident dislike. 'Wanna grab a coffee?'

'I have to get back to Marie-Dominique.'

I left him under the big chestnut in the middle of Place de Furstemberg, below the windows of Delacroix's old studio, and walked back through the Rue de Buci market, heading home. From time to time, hovering on the other side of the Luxembourg Gardens, where Montparnasse begins, I might have glimpsed, peeping round a long terrace of beige stone, a corner of Lee Miller's hungry lips.

21

A White Paris

INTERVIEWER: 'What is your wish in life?'
MELVILLE: 'To become immortal – then to die.'

Interview with Jean-Pierre Melville, film-maker

THE WIDE-OPEN PARIS OF THE TWENTIES AND
Thirties didn't survive World War II. In 1946, Marthe
Richard, famous in World War I as a spy against the
Germans, launched her crackpot scheme to close down
all the brothels in France and allocate the buildings as
student housing, which was in short supply.

At any other time, the idea would have been
laughed away, but the fact that most French people
had, if not actively supported the Occupation and the
Vichy regime, at least been complicit in it, made them
eager to appear moral and patriotic. Women who'd
taken German lovers were being publicly humiliated

and having their heads shaved. Numerous public figures, including film stars like Arletty, were in jail awaiting trial for collaboration; a few would even be executed, including one well-known writer, Robert Brassilach. Others, like Robert Drieu la Rochelle, killed themselves. The Communists, who'd been the most active and best organized element of the Resistance, looked set to sweep the next election and turn France into a Socialist state.

Had Richard suggested closing the butchers and turning France vegetarian, they'd have ignored her. But whores and whorehouses . . . ? Who cared? Only the whores and their clients, and they were hardly likely to protest in public. The measure was passed, and prostitution and the keeping of a brothel became illegal.

With a show of regret, prostitutes and proprietors simply moved somewhere more discreet, where they continued to operate as before, though without the sensible public-health provision of mandatory weekly medical examinations. The famous houses and their furnishings were sold, mostly at public auction, which gave the owners a chance for revenge. In a glorious splurge, the *maisons closes* abandoned the discretion they'd maintained for a century. 'This armchair, suitable for three people,' announced the auctioneer, 'is the famous *Indiscret*, much favoured by our late valued client His Majesty Edward VII . . .

The couch on which that wonderful star X entertained her lesbian lovers . . . Item number 17 still has stains from the famous occasion when His Excellency Général de . . .' The equipment from the torture chamber at 6 Rue des Moulins, which included a stake, with simulated logs to re-enact burnings, attracted particular attention. The Establishment cringed, but could do nothing.

Any furniture remaining unsold at Le Chabanais was put on consignment to an antique dealer, who for convenience left it in the house, which became his shop. The telephone remained connected and, one day, rang.

'Rue Chabanais?' asked the caller tentatively.

'Yes,' said the dealer. 'How can I help you?'

'Well, I've just arrived back from Saigon . . . It's been a long time . . . the war, you know . . .'

'Welcome home, m'sieur. How can I help you?'

'Well, I wonder . . . do you have . . . a virgin?'

The antique dealer looked around. There were gilded statues from Renaissance churches, an icon with the same subject; in fact, numerous images of the Virgin Mary from a number of centuries. 'Can you be more specific? Sixteenth? Seventeenth? Eighteenth?'

'Frankly, monsieur,' said the puzzled client, 'the *arrondissement* is immaterial.'

*

Another element of the Parisian experience had also expired during the war. For intellectuals who needed some stronger stimulant than alcohol, there had been no shortage of drugs. Morphine and heroin, massively manufactured during World War I and still regarded as medicines, had been freely available from pharmacies in many countries, including the United States. (On the other hand, newfangled synthetics like aspirin could only be bought on prescription.) In some homes, a snort at the end of a meal was as routine a courtesy in Paris in the Twenties as in New York in the Nineties. It stimulated both sexual desire and the conversational urge, while extinguishing the need for sleep. Literary expatriates like Harry Crosby fuelled themselves on it.

Europe's real cocaine capital, however, was Berlin, where it fitted the febrile lifestyle. Fancying themselves more reflective, the French preferred something slower, more deliberate. Until 1912, the fashionable choice was absinthe, an anise-flavoured liqueur given a lethal kick by an alkaloid from the wormwood plant. The ritual of preparing absinthe, like that of clipping and lighting a cigar, was as much a part of the pleasure as the stupor it induced. One placed a little metal bridge across the glass, settled a cube of sugar in a hollow at its centre, poured water through the sugar, and watched the opalescent green of the liquor turn cloudy and white. Such was the charm of absinthe that, however far one was from Paris, one could squint one's eyes, stare at the sky and imagine you were back there. 'One cup of it', wrote Hemingway, 'took the place of the evening papers, of all the old evenings in cafés, of all chestnut trees that would be in bloom now in this month.'

Absinthe was outlawed in 1912 after hundreds of people had succumbed to wormwood poisoning. It continued to be drunk, but as the preferred addiction of Paris's smart set, opium took its place. France's colonies in Indochina offered unlimited supplies. Artists swore opium improved their creativity. 'Alcohol provokes stupidity,' claimed the doyen of France's addicts, Jean Cocteau. 'Opium provokes wisdom.' Cocaine accelerated the sense of time passing; opium suspended it. Its effect, said Cocteau dreamily, was like alighting from the moving train of existence, so that one no longer needed to think about life and death.

This sense wasn't entirely due to the drug. Opium users spent hours, even days, in a stupor, smoking five or six pipes in a night. The 'opium den' of legend was mostly dictated by the need for a place to doze between pipes. Such establishments, and the expensive equipment needed to smoke opium, were part of the drug's appeal, just like the ritual of preparing absinthe. 'It reassures by its luxury,' Cocteau wrote of the opium world, 'by its rites, by the anti-medical elegance of its lamps, its burners, pipes, by the ancient practice of this exquisite poisoning.'

When artist-photographer Brassaï visited a 'den', he was helped into a plush kimono and led into a low-lit apartment. 'A few male and female silhouettes gradually emerged from the shadows, as did divans, sofas covered with brocades and velvets, and low Chinese tables bearing trays loaded with pipes, lacquered boxes and ceramic bowls; oil lamps gave off a subdued light . . .'

Women in particular surrendered to opium's unique combination of relaxation and stimulation, and took it up with the same enthusiasm as they'd embraced laudanum, the tincture of opium in alcohol that had been 'mother's little helper' before the turn of the nineteenth century. One of the most evocative of Brassaï's photographs for his book *Secret Paris* shows a middle-class opium-user, fashionably dressed, lying on a bed, her cat beside her, a novel on the floor where it has fallen from her hands, and her pipe and smoking paraphernalia on a side table. She looks totally at peace.

In the same *fumerie*, Brassaï recognized a well-known actress and asked if he could take her picture. 'Of course!' she said. 'And you have my permission to print it. They say that after a while drugs, opium, will destroy you, make you thin, weaken you, ruin your mind, your memory, that it makes you stagger, gives you a yellow complexion, sunken eyes . . . all of that. Rot! Look at me. And tell me, frankly, am I not beautiful and desirable? Well, let me tell you, I've smoked opium for ten years, and I'm doing all right.'

Cocteau and his friends took their equipment with them when they went on holiday with hostesses like the Comtesse Marie-Laure de Noailles at her modern villa, designed by Robert Mallet-Stevens, overlooking the Mediterranean at Hyères. Some mornings, the stink in the tiny bedrooms was so strong it made other guests retch. Users, however, relished it. 'The smell of opium is the least stupid smell in the world,' wrote Picasso. 'Only the circus and the seaport come close.'

Cocteau, who began taking opium after the death of his young lover Raymond Radiguet in 1923, periodiocally gave it up, most notably in 1929, when he went through detox treatment in one of the discreet clinics of Saint-Cloud. His diary of the experience, *Opium*, became a classic of drug literature. An apologia for his addiction, it was also a tract for drugs, without which, he was convinced, many artists could not function. He looked forward to science producing a non-addictive opium. 'Certain organisms are born to become prey to drugs,' he wrote. 'They require a corrective, without which they are not able to make contact with the outside world. They float. They vegetate in the twilight. The world remains a ghost until some substance can give it body. It's a lucky thing when opium can steady them, and provide these souls of cork with a diver's suit.'

All the same, opium was demonized, particularly for its effect on women, who were shown in novels like Claude Farrère's *Fumée d'opium* as selling their bodies to sinister orientals in return for more dope. In 1930, the horror theatre of the Grand-Guignol presented René Berton's *La Drogue*. While the hero, Marsac, sleeps in a Saigon opium den, a jealous mistress pours acid on his face. Suspecting Madame Faverolle, a high-society woman, the investigating judge summons her to the *fumerie* for a confrontation with Marsac. He persuades her to try opium for the first time and, under its influence, she confesses. When the judge leaves, Faverolle, crazed by the poppy, tears her own eyes out.

As Paris came to life again after World War II, men and women all over the world felt the attraction that, even under the Occupation, had not been eradicated, merely suppressed. The grey, down-at-heel Paris wouldn't entirely disappear until the Sixties, when the threat of a socialist France was comprehensively neutralized and the country began to benefit from the emerging European Union. However, in the intervening two decades, Parisians cultivated their culture with customary vigour and imagination. A new generation of writers, mostly blacks and beats, gravitated there. So did jazz musicians from every country in the world. The medieval cellars of Saint-Germain-des-Près became laboratories of the new angular and dissonant music, bebop. Its greatest artist, Charlie Parker, spent much time in Paris, and would die in the apartment of an aristocratic French admirer, the Baroness Pannonica von Koenigswater.

Nowhere was innovation seen so vividly as in *haute couture*. The first fashion season after the war, in May 1947, expected to favour modest and discreet outfits, was electrified by Christian Dior's 'New Look'. Eric Newby, then running his family's London fashion house, remembered it hitting 'like a bomb'.

The Dior collection marked the re-birth of Women as they had always existed in the minds of Men – provocative, ostensibly helpless and made for love. He immobilised them in exquisite dresses which contained between fifteen and twenty-five yards of material; dresses with tiny sashed waists in black broadcloth, tussore and silk taffeta, each with a built-in corset which was itself a deeply disturbing work of art. By day, superb beneath huge hats that resembled elegant mushrooms, they were unable to run; by night they needed help when entering a taxi. As these divine visions moved, their underskirts gave out a rustling sound that was indescribably sweet to the ear.

Fashion pointed the way forward for France. To *look* right became everything. In the Sixties, André Malraux, as Minister of Culture, wrote a law requiring all Paris's buildings to be steam-cleaned every ten years. When he handed over his portfolio to Françoise Giroud in 1974, he could tell her with some satisfaction, 'Behold, I give you a white Paris.'

If I had to choose my favourite Frenchman, it would probably be Malraux. Politician, lover, soldier, novelist, art historian, grave robber – he was convicted in the Thirties of stealing statues from Angkor Wat – he could almost be the model for the crooked but flamboyant and romantic archaeologist Belloq played by Paul Freeman in Steven Spielberg's *Raiders of the Lost Ark*.

Malraux excelled in the *discours*. His masterpiece is the speech he gave when the ashes of Resistance leader Jean Moulin were installed in the Panthéon.

I knew of this event only by legend. Its full force didn't strike me until, a few years after I arrived in Paris, a friend from England persuaded me to spend a Saturday afternoon with his sister and her husband, showing them around. Clearly they loathed each other almost as much as they hated Paris. We parted with insincere expressions of mutual esteem, spoken through gritted teeth, and I walked back towards home in a spirit of black despair.

Passing the back of the Panthéon, I was struck by an impulse to go in. I'd visited it before, but always dutifully, staring around at the grandiose murals of Puvis de Chavannes celebrating France's military victories, watching Foucault's pendulum ponderously ticking its way around the circle marked out on the marble floor. This time, I felt like someone entering church, burdened by an unacknowledged guilt. As I'd never done before, I went downstairs, into the enormous crypt that runs under the entire building. Past the stone catafalques of Rousseau, Zola and the interred great of France, I came to the bare chamber at the end where two TV sets ran tapes of past interments: Émile Zola's – so huge, it's said, that more than the entire population of Paris watched the elephantine funeral wagon roll past; the installation of Marie and Pierre Curie, the columns of the enormous colonnade threaded with an even more gigantic *tricolor*; Malraux's own burial, his simple wooden coffin on trestles, flanked only by a life-size Giacometti statue of a tirelessly walking man.

And then a murky grey film of Malraux himself, in a heavy overcoat, mounting the steps before that same colonnade on an icy afternoon in December 1964 to speak of Jean Moulin.

Moulin was betrayed to Klaus Barbie, the Gestapo leader in Lyon, and tortured – among other things, all his fingers were crushed in the hinges of a door. He died on the train taking him to Germany. His body was burned. When his ashes were belatedly brought to the Panthéon for reburial, only Malraux could possibly have delivered the oration. After it, he led the crowd in the singing of the 'Song of the Partisans', the unofficial anthem of the Resistance.

The event was brilliantly stage-managed. The previous night, a tank bearing the urn had rumbled up Boulevard Saint-Michel to the Panthéon, followed on foot by members of the Resistance carrying burning torches. As they passed each building, the owners doused all its lights until the whole wide street was plunged into darkness.

Relays of generals stood guard through the night, until the following afternoon, when Malraux spoke. Nobody there has ever forgotten his speech. It managed to be at the same time brilliantly manipulative and completely sincere; flattering to De Gaulle and General Leclerc, who led the Allied troops into Paris in 1944; ingenious in the way it recruited the great dissident figures of the past – Victor Hugo, Jean Jaurès, assassinated for his anti-war sentiments, Carnot, who held the country together after the Revolution; subtly self-aggrandizing for Malraux himself – 'I was out there too, fellows' – but diplomatic in its attitude to those who collaborated; sliding, too, around the inconsistencies in the stories about Moulin, the identity of those who betrayed him and whether, in fact, he did die when he was supposed to have. And yet, with all this, a moving piece of literature – the *discours* and the French writer at his contradictory best.

As General Leclerc entered the Invalides, trailing his glories won in the sun of Africa and the battles of Alsace, so you will enter here, Jean Moulin, at the head of your terrible retinue.

With those who, like yourself, died in cellars, silent to the end.

And as well – which is perhaps more atrocious – with those who gave up their secrets, and were murdered just the same.

With all the shaved, striped victims of the concentration camps.

With the eight thousand French women who did not return from prison.

With the last woman to die in Ravensbruck for having given shelter to one of ours.

Enter, with all those people who lived in the shadows and who died in them – our brothers in the army of the night . . .

Today, youth of France, look, if you can, on this man as he was on his last day, with his ruined hands and his poor face, and his lips that had not talked: on that day, this was the face of France.

I sat in that icy chamber, weeping like a fool for a man I never met, for a war in which I'd never fought, for a country that wasn't mine.

22

Aussie dans le Métro

The first time in my life I rode the Métro, from Montmartre to the main boulevards, the noise was horrible. Otherwise it hasn't been so bad, even intensifies the calm, pleasant sense of speed. Métro system does away with speech; you don't have to speak either when you pay, or when you get in and out. Because it is so easy to understand, the Métro is a frail and hopeful stranger's best chance to think he has quickly and correctly, at the first attempt, penetrated the essence of Paris.

Franz Kafka, *Diaries*, 1911

WITHOUT SOCIALIZED MEDICINE, MARIE-DO AND I would never have got through the spring and early summer. But years of handing a slice of her salary to the Sécurité Sociale purchased a gold-plated claim on its attention, and the state paid off handsomely. Medical support wasn't simply available; it was obligatory. Six months' leave on full salary and a further optional year after the birth were guaranteed by law. Everything was covered, including a weekly massage at home, and, during one terrible weekend, twice-daily visits by a nurse to give pain-killing injections – reluctantly authorized by Dr Bougevoy as the lesser of two risks.

As if in sympathy with our problem, the weather changed to something more like autumn. Dribbling rain lacquered the roofs into a sea of gleaming grey stretching away towards Notre Dame. I spent mornings at home, writing, and afternoons sitting with Marie-Do as she watched TV, read or fitfully slept. When a friend or a member of the family relieved me, I caught a movie – avoiding those with even a passing mention of poor health or babies.

By comparison with other cities, large parts of central Paris are underground, and I came to know most of them. In my state of mind, subterranean Paris felt as seductive as it does to Parisians, who flock to anything that reverences their taste for warm, dark places.

Once a decade, somebody reincarnates, on stage or in film, Gaston Leroux's *The Phantom of the Opera*, set in the flooded sewer tunnels that supposedly give access to the backstage areas of the rococo Opéra Garnier. You can tour these sewers, or at least a cleaned-up and deodorized section of them, and glimpse the less accessible branches used by the anti-Nazi Resistance. And no tour of Paris is complete without someone pointing out a hump in the lawn next door to the Air France terminal in the gardens of Les Invalides. Known as '*La Piscine*', the swimming pool, it hides the government's wire-tapping operation. In its sub-sub-basement, the *salles des auditeurs* – 'the halls of the listeners' – 360 agents of the Groupement Interministériel de Contrôle transcribe conversations from 75,000 wiretaps annually. And that doesn't include the legal ones, mandated by court order.

Most popular of all are the catacombs. Every year tens of thousands of people descend sixty metres under Place Denfert Rochereau, where, at the end of a labyrinth of narrow tunnels and beyond a portal with the carved welcome '*Ici commence l'empire de la mort*' – Here commences the empire of death – they confront the skeletons of medieval Paris. Eleven kilometres of tobacco-brown bones, barely visible in the dark, they've been neatly stacked head-high on both sides of the tunnels by businesslike bricklayers who, with a vestigial respect for these ancient remains, built them up like walls; a course of skulls, ten courses of femurs and tibias, then another course of skulls. Stone tablets tell from which cemeteries and plague pits the eighteenth-century masons, rebuilding the centre of the city, excavated these relics. Nearby are meditations in French and Latin on the transitoriness of life, and the sarcophagi – whitewashed, spectral – of people who chose to be buried in this dripping dark. Geology students hold end-of-term parties here, baptizing new graduates by lowering them head-first into silent subterranean pools, the water of which, filtered through metres of rock, becomes a spectral essence, still and colourless as air, and so clear that the men who built the tunnels feared to drink anything so insubstantial.

Though cities that are frozen part of the year, like Montreal or Moscow, have more tunnels, only those of Paris wind so sinuously, like intestines – a reminder of the national preoccupation with what takes place below the belt. And naturally the most elaborate complex lies under the now-vanished Les Halles, the wholesale food, vegetable and meat market which Émile Zola christened 'the guts of Paris'. Established in 1183, Les Halles was at its height in the nineteenth century, a sprawl of cavernous wooden sheds on which the culinary *patrimoine* of the world converged daily. When a bell, *une cloche*, signalled the end of trading, the homeless surged in to grab bruised fruit, mashed sausages and crushed baguettes. Paris's bums are still called *clochards*.

Les Halles aimed to satisfy every appetite. Along one end, restaurants stayed open all night to serve hot onion soup, ladled over a slab of bread and toasted cheese, to hungry workers and home-heading party-goers. At the other end, whores and hot-sheet *hôtels de passe* clustered along Rue Saint-Denis – the setting for Marguerite Monnot's *Irma La Douce*. (On location in Paris to film it, Billy Wilder promised to send his secretary a real French bidet. When it didn't appear, she wired him a reminder. 'BIDET UNAVAILABLE,' Wilder wired back. 'SUGGEST HANDSTAND IN SHOWER.')

But Les Halles was unsanitary, inefficient, immoral. In the 1970s, the markets moved to Rungis, on the periphery of Paris, and Les Halles was demolished to make way for a labyrinthine traffic underpass, a giant park and an underground shopping mall, l'Espace les Halles.

The designers hoped that the park, a maze of bowers, nooks and hedged walks, would become a haven of Proustian calm, like the gardens at the foot of the Champs-Élysées where Marcel played as a child with Gilberte. They must be disappointed by the result, which quickly became a hangout for drunks and a crapping paradise for dogs. But, perhaps to their surprise, and certainly to that of Paris, the nearby Centre Pompidou, christened 'the Beaubourg', the ancient name for that end of the *quartier*, quickly made itself indispensable to the city.

The decision of Renzo Piano and Richard Rodgers to put its *tripes* on the outside, not only exposing the tubes of gas, water and electricity lines, but highlighting them in colour, preserved the area's traditional association with digestion. Emphasizing the anatomical metaphor, gaudy mechanical sculptures by Jean Tinguely and Nikki de Saint Phalle, including a set of crimson lips, squirt and jiggle in a nearby pool, while the laboratory of experimental music, IRCAM, gurgles, blurts and farts in the basement. Edmund White describes how a modern-music-hating friend, passing the gratings that feed air to IRCAM, never fails to pause to allow his dog to crap into them.

The head of this supine corpse – spread out before us like Eliot's 'patient etherized upon a table' – lies half a kilometre away, in the park that blankets the site of the old market buildings. Intended as a plaything for children, the head, three metres long and with a hand to scale, rests on its ear in a shallow declivity, like St John the Baptist's on Salome's dish. Below it, in varying degrees of fetidness, lies L'Espace les Halles, four levels of shopping malls where pizza and hamburger joints, cinemas, record shops, Métro stations, a concert hall and a swimming pool compete for the attention mostly of black teenagers cruising the corridors, or German tourists convinced that, somewhere in this lost world, a good time must be hiding.

Commercial white elephants creep down here to die. In Captain Jacques Cousteau's crackpot waterless underwater museum, you can prowl the rusted catwalks of a once-sunken ship and creep through a life-sized model of a whale. Hologram boutiques, sellers of antique newspapers and magazines, and the crankier health-food outlets – what more hopeless activity than selling bran and molasses to a city of gourmets? – cluster around it.

On the lowest level, the jewel in the head of the toad, lurks the Orient Express cinema complex. No stranger to cinematic squalor, I've watched rats scampering among the discarded beer cans in Virginia drive-ins, survived the kamikaze plumbing of Sydney's crumbling Capitol cinema, declined blow jobs from whores working the stalls of cinemas in downtown Los Angeles, fended off cruising gays in London's Waterloo station, where the door to the men's toilet never stopped swinging, and ducked dope dealers strolling the aisles of 42nd Street theatres in New York murmuring, 'Coke or smoke; check it out.' I'd even been forced to see a film at gunpoint when Marshal Tito's bodyguards at the Pula Film Festival in the former Yugoslavia refused to let us walk out on a screening of *The Battle of the River Neretva*, an epic celebrating his World War II partisan triumphs. But the Orient Express, a rat's nest of cardboard-walled mini-theatres, with a wheezing ventilation system, crumbling Spraycrete walls, and sewer pipes gurgling above the heads of us abject punters, was uniquely sordid. Whoever named it didn't range far enough in his search for an exotic title. It should have been called The Black Hole of Calcutta.

Les Halles does have its treasures, however. Surrealistically sited next to Cousteau's marine museum is the Olympic-sized Piscine Municipale de Paris Ière. Its panoramic windows turn the steamy chlorinated space into a wide-screen documentary. Each time I passed, a shifting population of voyeurs stood in silent admiration of the teenagers on lunch break who, dressed in tiny triangles of shiny synthetic, giggled and posed along the tiled margin, while classes of schoolkids chased one another, and veterans in round black rubber goggles ploughed their daily laps.

At least twice each week, I briefly joined them on my way to the Videothèque de Paris, where, slumped in a deep black wing armchair with stereo speakers built into the headrest, I browsed its collection of films, chosen and maintained by the city government solely because they'd been shot in Paris. A robotized filing system, proudly displayed behind glass, grabbed cassettes from the shelves and fed my choices to twin TV screens hovering a metre away in the half-dark. For me alone, Jean Vilar dispassionately tracked traitor Yves Montand through the Métro in *Les Portes de la nuit*, an innocent Gerald Blain arrived in Paris in *Les Cousins* to fall instantly for Juliette Mayniel, sunning herself half-naked on the balcony of Jean-Claude Brialy's apartment, and Charles Denner as the serial killer Landru charmed elderly widows in the Luxembourg Gardens before taking them off for a weekend at his country place and a rendezvous with a carving knife and the kitchen range. Lyon, Nice and Nantes can complain all they like; the French cinema is a cinema of Paris.

On other days, I rode the Métro, travelling out to the end of the line, then coming back, all on a single ticket. No matter how far one travels from Paris, one can never escape the rumble of the Métro's solid rubber wheels, which, as they round curves, emit an unforgettable grating squeal. It is integral to the myth of Paris the Seducer, Paris the Lover who can satisfy you as no other can, Paris the Adored, without which life has no meaning. No other city possesses such a mythology. Chekhov's three sisters may pine for Moscow but they wouldn't die for it, and, much as Rick Blane yearns to get out of Casablanca, he'd just as soon not go back to New York. ('Can't return to his own country,' muses Colonel Strasser. 'Reasons are a little vague.') Yet sacrifices to the love of Paris are scattered throughout fact and fiction.

I'd seen one of them at first hand. On that day in November 1979 which I'd recalled so vividly under hypnosis, Marie-Do and I had been in the crowd near Clignancourt flea market who pressed against the police barriers surrounding the bullet-riddled BMW of Jacques Mesrine. It was still guarded proudly by the policemen who'd killed him a few hours before, ambushing him at a red light and pouring Uzi fire into the car from a camouflaged van. Paris had lured France's Public Enemy Number 1 out of hiding, and he died for it. But the city made him immortal. The papers published his letter to his mistress in which he affectionately warned her that he was doomed, but that he loved her for staying with him at the risk of sharing his fate. (She lost an eye, but otherwise survived the ambush.) Fifteen years later, the Biennale of Contemporary Art in Lyon devoted an entire room to an *'Hommage à Jacques Mesrine'* – an identical car, bodywork punctured with 9 mm slugs, windscreen shattered, upholstery blood-stained, the dangling speaker of its radio rattling a tinny tape by The Clash.

Inevitably, people compared Mesrine to Pépé le moko – Pépé the pimp – the Parisian criminal of Julien Duvivier's 1937 film who takes refuge in the Kasbah quarter of Algiers but yearns for Paris and is lured to his death by a woman who reminds him of the city. Pépé is one of those mythological figures, like

Mesrine, whom the French love: half hero, half crook. However distant their flight or extreme their crime, such men are redeemed by their love of Paris, for which they yearn, and to which they must return, or die in the attempt.

In Duvivier's *Pépé le moko*, Jean Gabin played Pépé. Mireille Balin was Gaby, the Parisienne who, briefly trapped in the Kasbah during a police raid, fatally reignites his love of Paris. They sit in the Ali Baba café and reminisce. For Pépé, the line to Paris ends at the gate of the Kasbah – literally, in his case, since that's where he stabs himself to death rather than continue to live in exile. Nostalgically they list the Métro stations on the way to Place Blanche, the stop nearest the Moulin Rouge (but also, by coincidence, to the meeting place of the Surrealists). That each nominates a different route, only to arrive at the same destination, adds to the sense of inevitability.

Sex and mass transit have a long and intimate history, from the Orient Express to the Boeing 767. Photographer Diane Arbus would ride Greyhounds out of New York, taking the rear-facing back seat, a signal of readiness for anonymous sex. The Mile High Club won official recognition in the book and film *Emmanuelle*, though how Sylvia Kristel found room to spread her celery-stalk legs, even in first class, remains one of aviation's great mysteries.

Maurice Dekobra, the John Grisham of France in the Twenties, first struck it rich in 1924 with *La Madone des sleepings* (*The Madonna of the Sleeping Cars*) about a temptress who rode the Orient Express, a character François Truffaut updated in *Love on the Run*, in which Jean-Pierre Léaud, meeting his old love Marie-France Pisier on a long-distance train, discovers that, though a lawyer by profession, she boosts her income by whoring on the TGV. And in Michel Houellebecq's *Platform*, on a train en route to a Channel coast health spa, a girl masturbates her lover under the flimsy cover of his coat, watched conspiratorially by a woman who, also staying at the spa, later joins them for a threesome in its steam room.

Tube trains, however, remain the eroticist's transport of choice. During World War II, when the Underground became London's air-raid shelter, orgies were commonplace, strangers reaching for strangers in the dark. In Paul Brickman's film *Risky Business*, Tom Cruise and Rebecca de Mornay fuck on a late-night train to the echoing drums of Phil Collins's 'Comin' in the Air', a sequence terminated brilliantly as their car bullets into the dark with a *zspit!* of orgasmic electricity.

Luc Besson set his film *Subway* in the Paris Métro. Appropriate to a film about people who live always underground, it starred the fabulous white lily of French cinema, Isabelle Adjani – ideal casting too should anyone decide to film *Heloise* by Québecois writer Anne Hebart, about a Métro passenger enchanted by a beautiful young vampire who endlessly rides the trains and never sees the sun. The real-life Paris Métro, less glamorously, has become the late-night hangout of lonely masturbators who haul out their dicks to jerk off as students on their way home disdainfully turn their backs. Houellebecq perversely celebrates them in *Atomised*. A middle-aged schoolteacher uses a geography textbook as a partial screen, catching his emission – but hopefully only his emission – by slamming it shut at the crucial moment.

All the same, the Métro remains a setting of erotic mystery. As the critic and long-time Paris resident Paul Jansi writes:

For many, Paris is a museum of museums, but she is actually an art gallery herself, populated with the most beautiful ladies in the world. Taking the Métro is like visiting an exhibition of treasures where the oeuvres are alive, where art breathes, where each piece is unique and irreplaceable. In the Underground waits a fine arts museum where Levi's is my favorite sculptor and the eyes of the masterpieces follow me wherever I go, or not, depending on how lucky I am. Yet, as with traditional art, the intrigue is in the secrets guarded behind the façade, for most of the women are like symbols too deep for me to understand.

23

A House in the South

'... sizzling down the long black liquid reaches of *Nationale Sept*, the plane trees going sha-sha-sha through the open window, she with the *Michelin* beside me, a handkerchief binding her hair ...'

Cyril Connolly, *The Unquiet Grave*

JUNE AND JULY CRAWLED. THE BUMP UNDER THE bedclothes was now more than visible, and Marie-Do's pains, if no better, at least no worse. We read stories to the *petit locataire*, our 'little tenant', as we'd started calling Louise, and directed Mozart and Rossini at her in the hope that something might percolate through the wall of flesh. Maybe literature and music really do have a healing effect because, by the end of the month, the pains were receding and Marie-Do could get up for hours at a time. The visits to Dr Bougevoy didn't become any shorter, but when she and Marie-Do emerged from her surgery, both were usually smiling. By the last week in July, it seemed we would be parents towards the end of October.

One morning, we woke to a reiterated thud that reverberated through the walls, throbbing like a sick headache. From the terrace, I could see scaffolding spidering up half a dozen buildings. Skips were filling with rubble. Marie-Do took in the chaos without surprise. 'August,' she said, as if that explained everything.

In midsummer, French schools, businesses, government offices and the smaller shops all close. Department stores cut staff and stock. Museums and galleries offer stopgap shows, or go onto a three-day week. Cinemas programme the sort of revivals that almost guarantee empty houses. Restaurants and cafés start renovations. Then, in a ponderous game of musical chairs, millions of Lyonnais pack up their cars and drive to Normandy, while just as many Normands travel to Provence, and the equivalent number of Provençaux head for Brittany, while the total population of Paris hits the road for almost everywhere. Once each person reaches his or her destination, the country, with an almost audible squeal of brakes, stops dead. It's *les vacances*.

August isn't so much a holiday as a reaffirmation of one's heritage, a chance to refresh oneself with air that hasn't been breathed by a million others, to stand on soil that retains some of its spiritual nutrients, to eat food not handled by fifty pairs of hands. Only Thanksgiving in the United States really compares.

Everyone has a *maison secondaire* – a second home, spiritual or physical, whether a château that's been in the family since Charlemagne or a campsite they visited as students in 1954. And there are plenty of stories – metaphors, really – about the French attitude to *les vacances*. One of the best tells of M. Croisset who, on the first of August, arrives at the Hôtel du Commerce as he has every year for the past fifteen. Greeted by M. and Mme Beaumont, the owners, as an old friend, he's shown to his usual room. Unpacking, he realizes he's forgotten to bring his flip-flops. He'll need to buy another pair.

That evening, he dines in the Café de la Gare across the square, returns to share a cognac and coffee with the Beaumonts, and settles down to the fat paperback he's been saving since spring. In the morning, he comes down late, takes breakfast at the pavement tables with a few other guests, reads the local paper he never sees except on holiday, strolls to the shoe shop for another pair of flip-flops . . .

And so the holiday of M. Croisset continues, refreshing his soul, clearing his mind. After ten days, he packs, finding his old flip-flops in the process – they were in a side pocket of his bag all the time!

– says goodbye to the Beaumonts and the proprietor of the Café de la Gare, boards the train – and gets off three stops down the line, where he lives.

On the last day of July, we strolled through what had become a Paris of the dead. The parking spaces for which people normally skirmished were empty, the air hot, and heavy with the smell of burned dust. M. Daninos, who owned the secondhand bookshop opposite, was using a long rod to crank down a metal shield over his window, while Mme Daninos loaded what looked like the contents of their apartment into a little Peugeot.

'*Bonnes vacances*,' we said.

'*À vous aussi, 'sieur'dame.*' Daninos rubbed his hands and looked at the blue sky. '*C'est un beau jour, n'est-ce pas?*'

In his mind at least, he was already browsing through a street market in Provence or sunning himself by the Gironde as he sampled a particularly mellow Pessac-Léognan.

We strolled down to Boulevard Saint-Germain. Every second pedestrian was a tourist. Germans with backpacks the size of small refrigerators and Americans in pastel polyester paused on the same street corner to consult the same folded maps. English couples ambled by in shorts, legs mushroom-pale. Most shops displayed the same sign inside their windows: *Fermeture annuelle*, annual closing. Interiors were shadowed and empty. Others were being gutted; bars ripped out to be rewired; tables upended to replace the terrace tiles. Over the whole city, like the soundtrack of a film about the Liberation, hung the rat-tat of pneumatic drills and the growl of heavy machinery.

The cafés themselves looked dingy. It wasn't only the yellow summer light reflected from dust-white pavements. The regulars had taken their fug of cigarette smoke with them, and, without it, the gravy-brown varnish and mock marble surfaces revealed themselves in all their tawdriness. Nobody stood at the *zinc*. At the tables, American teenagers filled spiral-bound notebooks or stared into space, chewing their pens over blank postcards. You could tell they were American because no French person, least of all a professional, would be seen writing in a café. Literature wasn't something you carried on in public, any more than dentistry. 'The other day,' wrote the Canadian author Mavis Gallant, a long-time Parisienne, 'I was asked, in all seriousness, where one can see authors at work in cafés. It sounded for all the world like watching chimpanzees riding tricycles: both are unnatural occupations. I have only one friend who still writes her novels in notebooks, in cafés. She chooses cafés that are ordinary and charmless, favouring one for a time,

285

then another, as one does with restaurants. Some are near home, many involve a long bus trip. If anyone she knows discovers the café, she changes at once for another, more obscure, hard to get to. About café writing, in general, old legends and ancient myths die hard.'

Dr Bougevoy wasn't enthusiastic about Marie-Do leaving Paris so far into the pregnancy, but since she herself would be in the Lubéron for most of August she could hardly present a strong argument. By nine the next day, the car was packed, and we drove down a shuttered Rue de l'Odéon, heading, like the rest of France, to our *maison secondaire*.

24

The Rich

Let me tell you about the very rich. They are different from you and me. They possess and enjoy early, and it does something to them, makes them soft where we are hard, and cynical where we are trustful.

F. Scott Fitzgerald, *The Rich Boy*

Poor Scott said, 'The rich are very different from you and me, Ernest,' and I said, 'Yes, they have more money.'

Ernest Hemingway

TO SOMEONE RAISED IN A SMALL AUSTRALIAN country town, the notion that a family might have more than one home seemed almost farcical. A house of your own was rare enough; almost every unmarried person I knew, not to mention many couples, still lived with their parents. To own a house indicated the sort of wealth not available to most working-class Australians. Renting was far more common, with the landlord a stock figure, usually malign, of fiction and mythology, wreathed in tales of foreclosure, eviction, and families 'put out on the streets' or 'shooting the moon' – that curiously poetic phrase for sneaking away at night with the rent unpaid.

Teaching at a college in Virginia in the Seventies, I found myself on the same flight to New York as one of my students, the stepdaughter of Governor Nelson Rockefeller.

'Hi, Mr Baxter,' she said. 'You going to New York too?'

'Yes. I'm doing some interviews for a book.'

'Do you keep an apartment there?' she asked casually.

I must have looked as bemused as I felt. *Me? An apartment in New York?*

'No,' I improvised. 'I like to stay at the Algonquin. For the literary associations.'

'Oh, right,' she said. 'Cool.'

But her comment, with its casual evocation of a world where one's being was not uniquely invested in a single arrangement of walls, floor and furniture, tickled my mind, as an unexpected sexual signal will stir erotic fantasies. Throughout the flight, I imagined myself entering my Upper West Side pied-à-terre, working my key into the stiff lock, pushing open the door against the accumulated mail, sniffing the stuffy air of the long-unventilated space, and, putting down my bag in the living room, looking around at . . . what?

My treasured possessions? But why would I keep such things here, not in my real home? Did one divide: this book in the apartment, its companion volume in one's house? One painting here, separated by a continent, or a world, from its twin? Or did one duplicate, creating identical libraries, décors – and even lives?

A wife in one place, a mistress in the other?

The French find this idea attractive; the *petite amie* in her little apartment, lounging in a flimsy peignoir, a chilled kir already poured, the bed turned down. They even have a phrase for it, *le cinq à sept*: that period between five and seven in the evening when the executive, ostensibly delayed at the office, visits his mistress, before heading home for dinner with his accommodating wife, who, of course, knows and understands – like Diana Cooper, wife of the philandering Duff Cooper, Britain's ambassador to France after World War II. 'I don't know which is worse,' said one of his lovers. 'Being dumped by Duff, or having Diana come round to comfort you.'

Now I began to understand the appeal of the *cinq*

à sept. To glide from one woman to another, one home to another, one life to another: wasn't this, in effect, to live twice? To experience a kind of immortality . . . ?

Though the jolt of landing at Kennedy put these thoughts out of my mind, watching pretty Ms Rockefeller being met by two stoical bodyguards and her presumed boyfriend – his tweed topcoat worth, from the looks of it, a semester's salary – ensured that I never quite forgot them.

And now, living in France, I was, though not rich myself, the owner, by alliance anyway, of a second house. In my mind, I tried it out for size. *'We live in our country place but keep an apartment in Paris . . . We'll open up the summer place in August . . . John Baxter and Marie-Dominique Montel advise their many friends that they will be out of town . . .'*

Each sounded more ludicrous than the last. Clearly my sense of place would never survive such radical division. 'Any old place I can hang my hat is home', said the old blues, but that didn't apply to me. Yes, the rich *are* very different. They have more than one hat.

Fouras is on the western coast of France, about two-thirds of the way down to Spain. It straddles a narrow promontory jutting out to sea at the point where the *café-au-lait* Charente pours into the Atlantic. In a languid attempt at promotion, the *syndicat d'initiative* has erected a sign at the turn-off from the coast road between La Rochelle and Rochefort, indicating the route to 'La Presque Île', the Almost Island.

Fouras does have something of the island about it. Low, sandy, built up over millennia by Charentais silt, it breathes detachment and isolation. Its narrow streets follow paths worn by fishermen while Louis XIV was still on the throne. The fishmarket, an ageless stone barn, predates him. No building in town is taller than three storeys. Even the Napoleonic fort that stares out across the estuary is decently in scale.

To invaders and smugglers, the wide river mouth and the sheltering offshore islands have always suggested an invitingly open door, so antique stone abutments and gun emplacements protect every cape and point, and many of the villas that face the sea, mostly built by retired military men, are crowned by stubby towers like look-outs or lighthouses. To fortify Île d'Aix, the nearest offshore island, Louis XVI sent Choderlos de Laclos to design and build an elegant network of walls, docks and forts. In the long nights, fuelled by limitless aphrodisiac oysters, and with nothing but memories to sustain him, he composed an erotic novel in the form of letters between a manipulative countess and her immoral suitor. Without Fouras and its shellfish, we wouldn't have *Les Liaisons dangereuses*.

Napoleon sequestered himself here after Waterloo. He was accommodated on Île d'Aix, in the house of the garrison commander. An obelisk on the river beach at Fouras marks the point where, in 1815, the failed master of the world, rather than wet the imperial feet, was carried through the shallows to the ship's boat on the back of a sailor, en route to exile on St Helena.

Marie-Do inherited her house from her paternal great-grandparents, who sold shoes in Saujon, an hour further south. On retiring there in 1910, they built a two-storey, four-bedroom home in a walled garden, conveniently close to the beach and the railway station; a house which, with a fashionable use of English, then *très snob*, they called 'Remember'.

The station's gone now, along with the railway, but little else has changed. In the garden, an ancient gnarled pear tree discards tiny inedible fruit into the ankle-deep grass. Sand grates underfoot on the black and white chequered tiles of the kitchen. Several generations of children pounding back from the beach have worn the wooden stairs concave. In the bedrooms, mosquito nets are gathered like cocoons above big beds plump with feather duvets, which in turn disguise heavy linen sheets almost as old as the house. Each time we arrive, I dump our bags in the kitchen with the sense that this isn't holidays but time travel.

I still had no right to hang my hat here – but can you lend me one, just for the summer . . . ?

It is no big thing to be an aristocrat in France. The country overflows with counts and countesses, dukes and duchesses, princes and princesses, even a king and queen or two. One would have thought that France's nobility was terminated definitively when the mob decapitated most of its members during the revolution of 1789, including Louis XVI and his queen Marie Antoinette, but it proved a hardy weed. Napoleon reinstituted the monarchy with himself as emperor, and even after his defeat at Waterloo the lavish lifestyle under his nephew, Napoleon III, and the empress Eugénie, conjured most of the old noble lines back into life. The so-called Second Empire put the fun back into being an aristo. When Eugénie, gaping at the city's lavish new opera house, with its gilded cupolas and marble staircases, its frescoed ceilings and sculpted goddesses with the bodies of showgirls, asked the architect, 'But Monsieur Garnier, what style is it?' he suavely replied, 'It is *your* style, Your Imperial Highness.'

French became the official second tongue of Europe. In particular, it was the language of diplomacy, not only because of its capacity for nuance, but because, even if Hungarians were haggling with Romanians over a border in Hercegovina, the negotiators, aristocrats all, would have learned it in childhood and probably used it at home; Vladimir Nabokov's family spoke French, German and English for two days each week, and Russian on Sunday. No wonder then, that, when war and revolution once again split Europe open between 1914 and 1918, dispossessed aristocrats from every principality and dukedom between Moscow and Vienna headed for their spiritual home, Paris.

It must have been a wonderful time to be in Europe, particularly if you were young, even better if you were rich, and best of all if you were a noble. James Thurber, at that time one of the US servicemen who stayed behind after World War I, wrote nostalgically in *Memoirs of a Drudge* about an idyllic time working on the Riviera edition of the *Chicago Tribune* during the winter of 1925–6.

Nice, in that indolent winter, was full of knaves and rascals, adventurers and imposters, *pochard*s and *indiscret*s, whose ingenious exploits, sometimes in full masquerade costume, sometimes in the nude, were easy and pleasant to record . . . The late Frank Harris would often drop in at the *Tribune* office, and we would listen to stories of Oscar Wilde, Walt Whitman, Bernard Shaw, Emma Goldman, and Frank Harris. Thus ran the harsh and exacting tenor of those days of slavery.

Had Thurber been writing there today, he'd undoubtedly have devoted a few paragraphs to The Count.

Marie-Do met him while researching a film. A distinguished if vague Englishman in his eighties, he lived part of the time in Italy, but the rest in France, usually in his eighteenth-century townhouse, deep in the old Jewish quarter, the Marais.

For their first meeting, Marie-Do asked where he'd like to meet.

'I'm in Berlin,' he said, 'but I'll shortly be in Paris. What about somewhere in between? Cannes, say? The Hôtel des Anglais. You can park right in front...' He paused. '... At least I assume so. I haven't been there since '19.'

He also, he said vaguely, 'had a country place', and, when he heard we'd be summering in our 'place', invited us to lunch.

Driving there, Marie-Do and I discussed the Count's pedigree. His title was German, with a plethora of 'vons' and 'zu's, which beckoned one into the shadowy world of Debrett's *Peerage* and the *Almanach de Gotha*. In France in particular, where so many noble lines were literally cut short in 1789, it didn't do to delve too deeply. The conceit behind one of my favourite movies, Ernst Lubitsch's *Love Me Tonight*, in which a family of aristocrats accept Maurice Chevalier, a tailor, as one of them, simply because he dresses well, always seemed absurd. Now I wasn't so sure.

'Just take the road to Montmerand,' he said when I asked for directions.

'What's the address?'

'Just Montmerand is enough. About noon, then?'

Even ten kilometres out of Montmerand, we could see why no other address was needed. The village clung to the base and slopes of a conical hill as if cowering from the château, as big as a resort hotel, that sprawled across the summit. No prizes for guessing who lived where.

We wound through the village's narrow streets to a gate of seventeenth-century wrought iron, dragged open for us by a tottering oldster. Before us stretched the hilltop, comprehensively levelled about the time of Henry VIII, and crossed by a wide gravelled avenue flanked with weathered stone lions, with, at the end, the castle – there was no other word for it – which reared up like the De Winter mansion in *Rebecca*.

In fact, our visit was less in the spirit of Manderley than Blandings Castle, and proceeded in a spirit of Wodehousean dottiness. The front door, a giant of gnarled chestnut, strapped and studded with rusted iron, swung open easily and silently when we rang, to reveal the Count's Julie Andrews-ish 'companion', Miss Waverley.

Always impeccably conservative in a silk dress and 'sensible' heels, Miss Waverley never betrayed, by act or word, that her duties went beyond being the Count's dispassionate if dedicated helper, secretary and chatelaine. No Jeeves could have been more aware of her 'place' – nor more capable, one sensed, of offering far more, if she cared to, and if the price was right.

'Ah, you found us, then?' said the Count when she showed us into the cavernous dining room. 'Jolly good, jolly good. Let me show you round.'

The hour-long tour took in every shrub and tree ('Planted by the Queen Mother, that one'), his private library and chapel, both of them eighteenth-century buildings standing alone in the splendidly landscaped grounds, and finally the archaeological excavations which honeycombed the hill.

'Now here', said the Count, striding across the swaying wooden walkway that arched over the massive stone foundations of the first castle on the site, a leg-breaking drop below our feet, 'are our crusader tombs.'

We looked through a door and down into a large underground chamber, where some stone sarcophagi lay half-covered in rubble. Evidently the room on our level had fallen in. All that remained was a ledge of shattered floorboards clinging precariously to the walls.

'Came down here one day to poke about on my own,' said the Count, 'and the whole thing collapsed under me. Shook me up, I can tell you. Come on!'

Waving his stick, he led us around the surviving ledge to the door on the other side. Followed by the imperturbable Miss Waverley, we inched after him like characters in *King Solomon's Mines*. The room on the other side contained nothing but a couple of dusty glass-fronted cabinets, age indeterminate. Scattered across a ledge in front of one were some yellowed fragments of bone.

'Finger bones,' said the Count, poking them with his own skinny digit. 'From the tombs. Should put 'em back where they came from, I suppose.'

Inside the cabinets lurked what appeared to be ancient chalices and drinking vessels.

'And these?' I asked. 'From the tombs as well?'

He peered through the dusty glass. 'Ah, no. Some of my golf trophies, actually.'

We surfaced amid the hectares of woodland that occupied the rest of the hilltop. It was interesting to see that even the grounds of the nobility were littered with the relics of dead enthusiasms. Where we have old barbecues and rusted bicycles, he had Renaissance statuary and a tumbledown chapel or two.

He pointed his cane in the direction of an imposing stone monument, half visible through the trees.

'Grave of my wife. Thought she'd be happier here.'

We tried to assume an expression combining condolence and architectural enthusiasm.

'Our guests might like to see the ice house,' Miss Waverley said, steering him, and us, down a wide path cut in the woods.

'Yes! Indeed. The ice house.' He waved his cane like a sabre, stepped out down the avenue, and farted.

No discreet escape of gas this, but a thunderous report. Crows perched in some nearby beeches flapped into the grey sky, squawking.

I remembered a story told by a journalist who went to interview ageing silent movie star Mary Pickford. The secretary asked him to wait in the living room, where he was watched carefully by two large dogs. When she was safely out of earshot, he allowed himself the luxury of a fart – at which the dogs leaped up, yelping, and bolted into the garden.

The secretary returned at a run. 'You didn't fart, did you?'

'Well, er, yes . . . But I don't understand . . .'

'It's Mary,' explained the secretary. 'She does it all the time, without realizing it. We blame the dogs, and beat them.'

None of us made any comment, least of all Miss Waverley. As the echoes diminished, she said imperturbably, 'I think it might be easier if we went this way.'

'You think so?' he said, changing direction abruptly, and let fly again.

It continued in this style. 'Our Egyptian obelisk. Eighteenth-century.' (*Brack!*). 'Nice stand of oaks.' (*Blurt!*). 'West front, restored by Violet-le-Duc.' (*Froop!*).

I felt like a blind man at a fireworks display. Who would have thought the old man had so much gas in him? It was a wonder he didn't float off like a dirigible.

Throughout, Miss Waverley remained the soul of discretion, good manners and quiet dignity. For each wide-eyed young Anglo-Saxon who arrived in France determined to defeat the country, and perished in the attempt, a few Miss Waverleys coolly took on the French, and, through intelligence, persistence and charm, beat them at their own game.

25

On the Golden Slope

Côte d'Or, literally the Golden Slope or Escarpment; the area of Burgundy between Dijon and Santenay where some of the greatest Burgundies are made.

Don and Petie Kladstrup, *Wine and War*

LIFE IN FOURAS SETTLED INTO A WARM BATH OF laziness.

Most days, Marie-Do was content to sun herself – and our *petit locataire* – in a deckchair, reading, and only rising from time to time for a careful stroll or a snack. I'd stocked up with books myself, but by lunchtime most days I was itching to do something. Anything.

Eating took care of a few hours a day. Oysters usually featured somewhere in the meal. Fouras and Oléron were the national crustacean capitals, and the estuary a maze of oyster farms, often marked with no more than a few twigs jutting out of the alluvial mud. The local speciality is the *fine de claire*, a small oyster that's kept in freshwater ponds after harvesting to clear out the salt. A microbe in the water leaves the flesh a faint translucent green. The road to La Fumée, the little dock where ferries head out to Île de Ré and Île d'Aix, was lined with stalls selling a dozen varieties. We got to know the *ostréculteurs* and heard the local gossip – mostly about oyster rustlers, who looted the more isolated farms. One owner, infuriated by them, set a trap by planting a few empty shells sealed with wax among his stock. Inside was a note saying 'Congratulations. You have won a hundred oysters. Just ring . . .' When the winners phoned, he asked casually, 'Who sold you these, by the way?' The culprit turned out to be his next-door neighbour.

If we wearied of oysters, there were mussels, for which the locals have developed two recipes that provide a change from the wine-stewed *moules marinières*. *Mouclade* bathes them in cream with a touch of curry powder, a reminder that most of the spices for France used to flow through La Rochelle. The other, *l'éclade de moule*, definitely falls into the 'Don't try this at home' category. Dozens of mussels are balanced upright on a heavy slab of natural cork bark, then covered with 300 cm of dry pine needles, and the whole thing set alight. The needles burn furiously for a few seconds. If you've done it correctly, when you brush away the carpet of fine white ash the mussels will have burst open and their flesh will be deliciously flavoured with pine resin. If you've got it wrong, the kitchen is in flames and there's an omelette for dinner.

After lunch, most of Fouras went to sleep. All the shops closed at 1.30 and reopened at 4.00. Puzzlingly, however, the siesta seemed only to be a Monday-to-Friday ritual. On weekends, the average holidaymaker burst out of bed at 8 a.m. and by 9 o'clock was eager for diversion.

Fortunately there were plenty of antique markets and *brocantes* to justify long excursions. Charente is the national attic, from which Paris *antiquaires* load up for the rest of the year. Accustomed to tatty overpriced post-World War II 'collectables', I wasn't prepared for shops filled with ancient rusted farm implements, trunks of legal documents from a century ago, helmets and water bottles abandoned in the Great War, and bits of wormy panelling torn from private chapels during the Revolution. One street-market dealer sold only old linen. We fingered petticoats and knickers that once clothed the servants of some great estate, napkins stained with meals eaten when aborigines were still spearing people in Australia, and shook out linen sheets so heavy – the seams hand-sewn, the hand-embroidered family monograms of entwined initials welted like scar tissue – they might have been sodden wet.

Another dealer, a dour old boy with a Clemenceau moustache, grey except where his pipe stained it yellow, had filled a barn with the detritus of the surrounding villages, most of it from the time of World War I. We found a military bicycle made of bent wood, its frame moulded like a kitchen chair, the tyres solid red rubber. And there were artificial limbs. Dozens of them; arms, legs, hands, accumulated with a Frankensteinian obsessiveness.

'Now these', he said, pointing to a mismatched pair of legs jutting from an ancient barrel, 'I could let you have quite cheap.'

'But what would we use them for, monsieur?'

He lifted out a leg, all cracking leather straps, rusting buckles and crazed proto-plastic, and rested it foot-down on the floor. 'Maybe . . . a lamp?' he said.

'We can't keep buying antiques for ever,' I said to Marie-Do after yet another flea market. 'There won't be room in the flat.' I also visualized myself hauling all these armchairs and lamps up six flights of stairs. 'What else is there to do around here?'

Marie-Do, lying as usual under the pear tree with a book, looked up at me over the hump that was Louise. 'We could take a thalasso,' she said thoughtfully.

Not content with giving the impression that they invented and patented oral sex, the French also have their own parallel system of healthcare, and even their own private disease: *spasmophilie*, a chronic lethargy ascribed to a deficiency of magnesium. It has never been diagnosed outside France, but that doesn't hinder its popularity within. And despite the fact that *thalassothérapie* – healthcare from the sea – hasn't caught on world-wide either, the coasts of France are thick with clinics offering the notional benefits of immersion, inundation and ingestion of products related to sea water.

Having found one on Île de Ré that could fit us in that morning, we took the ferry across. The low, ominously silent one-storey modern building lurked in the dunes on the seaward side of the island, flanked by Edwardian guesthouses that catered to weary matrons and captains of industry who, worn out with a year of *foie gras* and *Bordeaux*, lined up to be revived by the healing power of the sea.

At the entrance, I was relieved of everything but swimming trunks and given a bathrobe, flip-flops and a towel.

When I came out, Marie-Do was nowhere in sight. 'Where's my wife?' I asked the burly attendant in the white housecoat.

'We don't recommend the full *thalassothérapie* for pregnant women,' she said. 'It's too strenuous. She will meet you in the main pool afterwards.' She pointed down a long corridor. 'Room 17, please.'

Room 17 was white, as narrow as a railway carriage, but half the length. Just inside, a woman with arms like hams, leaning on a plain counter, motioned for me to take off my robe and stand against the far wall. I'd encountered ladies like her in the saunas of Finland. Grabbing customers as they staggered from the steam room, they flung them down on plastic-covered kitchen tables and scrubbed them raw with the sort of brushes usually reserved for tiled floors.

'Ready?' she demanded.

I nodded.

A stream of water hit me with fire-hose ferocity, slamming me hard against the wall. What I'd taken for a counter actually enclosed a sort of hydrant, with a heavy-duty canvas hose and a swivelling brass nozzle attached. Mouth and nose filled with sea water, I tried to fend off the blast. No hope. For three minutes, every inch of my body was battered by an inexorable torrent. If you could drown standing up, this was the way to do it.

Finally it ended. Reeling, my ears ringing, I let myself be led, half conscious, into a smaller room. In the centre sat a galvanized tank the size of a skip. A new attendant helped me up a set of steel steps. Too numbed to resist, I sank into the warm, slightly slimy water. It was just about neck-deep, but by grabbing a set of woven straps attached to the edge one could float half-submerged.

Somewhere out of sight, a motor started up, and the water began to roil. At the same time, the attendant decanted a coffee-can full of ash-like powder into the bath.

'Hey! What's that?'

She shrugged. '*Algue*, m'sieur.'

Seaweed? I bobbed like a cork as the dust settled into a scum, then dissolved in the sluggishly churning water. It carried a faint odour both medicinal and culinary, somewhere between bronchial inhalation and fish stock.

As a kid, I'd been fed Bonnington's Irish Moss, with 'Perpetual Oxymel of Carragheen'. The label, with an Edwardian engraving of a colleen lugging a basket overflowing with wet black glop, explained that carragheen was seaweed scraped from the rocks of Ireland. What was Bonnington's supposed to cure? Colds? Constipation? Leprosy? I'd forgotten, if indeed I ever knew. Maybe it didn't matter. If it tasted nasty and came in a brown glass bottle, it was sure to help. 'You can feel it doing you good', murmured its advertising slogan encouragingly. (This was often the literal truth, since many patent medicines contained a jolt of alcohol, codeine or even opium, which, while not curing your complaint, certainly made you worry about it much less.)

I dozed off, and only half remember being led down the hall to another room with a shower. Rinsing off the residue of the seaweed broth, I discarded my sodden trunks and, since my robe had been confiscated, wrapped myself in a towel. Just as I did this, the door opened and a pretty girl in an entirely inadequate white coverall looked in.

'*Nous sommes prêt*, m'sieur?'

Ready for what? I looked past her. The room contained only a floor mattress and a low table with some squeeze bottles.

She was a very skilful, very gentle *masseuse*. But, with nothing between us but a thin towel, the experience was hardly relaxing. One tries to think calming thoughts in these situations – waves lapping the sea-shore, grain swaying in the breeze – but it's not easy. Peter Finch was once asked how a man like him, so hetero it hurt, could show conviction while kissing Murray Head in *Sunday, Bloody Sunday*. 'I closed my eyes,' he said, 'and thought of England.'

I too found refuge in patriotism. '*Je suis*, um . . .' (waving pines, trickling streams) '. . . *australien*.'

'Oh, I 'ave been in Australia,' she said. 'I live zere for one year.'

'Really. Where?'

'Bendigo.'

That did the trick. I defy anyone to be sexually aroused while thinking of Bendigo.

All but boneless, I was decanted into a room where low couches looked out through a faintly tinted picture window at the dunes and the Atlantic. With the rest of the recently thalassothérapied, I lay there, drowsing to the faint sounds of muzak. For the French clients, being soaked in the sea and its products is another affirmation of the Gallic soul. They would return home reassured that, inside and out, they were suffused with the spirit of France. All I took with me was a pleasurable fantasy of what might have ensued had the masseuse not been to Bendigo.

The fashionable novelist Michel Houellebecq had the same idea. Both his novels *Atomised* and *Platform* suggest that French 'health resorts' are really pick-up spots for the ageing rich, who, having formed a taste for casual sex in the Sixties, can afford to keep enjoying it as fitness and potency decline. Some people may read Houellebecq for his resonances with Louis-Ferdinand Celine and Jean Genet, but most are there for the fucking. 'I'm better than the others in sex scenes,' Houellebecq says with gloomy satisfaction. 'Mine are more realistic. I think that's because I describe the sensations and emotions, whereas the others just name different acts. Among my colleagues, it's more a fantasy. In my case, one has the impression of reality.'

If 'reality' means showing survivors of the student

rebellion of 1968, the so-called *soixante-huitards*, now rich, middle-aged and out-of-shape, libidos as baggy as their genitals, shagging themselves silly with a sense that every coupling could be their last, then the claim holds water. Some, like Bruno, the hero of *Atomised*, find passing gratification in the nudist colonies-cum-sex resorts that dot the Mediterranean coast, or the *échangiste* clubs of Paris, but most spend their time masturbating furiously, noses pressed to the steamed-up window that separates them from the hard-bodied young.

Houellebecq incorporated a thalasso sex scene into *Platform*, his typically bitter look at sexual tourism. His main characters, a man and woman who run sex trips to Thailand and other Third World countries, enjoy a threesome with a woman in the hammam or steam room of a thalasso centre at Dinard on the Channel coast, a scene that angered genuine eroticists. One of them told British author Julian Barnes, who helped award *Platform* the prestigious Prix Novembre, 'I've been there and it's *just not possible.*'

Our August ended, unexpectedly but not uncharacteristically, with a glorious blow-out. Two old friends of Marie-Do's, Frédéric and Marguerite, passed through Fouras for a few days. Some antiques they bought at a local shop weren't ready by the time they left, so we agreed to collect them and stop off at their house in Burgundy on our way back to Paris.

'If you like,' Frédéric said, 'we could visit a few vineyards. My father can arrange that.'

Everyone knew about Frédéric's father, Claude, a member of the Grand Association of Tastevins, France's premier association of wine fanciers. A distinguished man in his sixties who – talk about style! – raised wild boar for a living, he was the sort of authority the French really respected.

Shortly after, Frédéric rang back. Claude had arranged a three-day visit to six or seven of the main winemakers. The names of the vineyards flowed off his tongue: Puligny-Montrachet, Gevrey-Chambertin, Pommard, Meursault. All four of us could stay at a small hotel in the area, and spend a leisurely time sampling by day and checking out the restaurants at night.

'Sounds like fun,' I said, after Marie-Do got off the phone.

So it did – for me at least. In a cruel twist of metabolism, pregnancy had turned Marie-Do, normally an enthusiast for red wines, off all alcohol. The very idea of drinking revolted her. But she was happy to go along for the ride.

Unfortunately Claude's name drew interest like flies. For the French, being an industrialist or a politician was fine, but a *grand tastevin* ... From hundreds of kilometres around, friends as bored as I was after two weeks of inactivity were calling up, just to pass the time of day – and to mention that they'd heard something about a wine trip . . . What started as a little tour with Frédéric, Marguerite and Claude snowballed. By the time we reached Burgundy, the group filled a small hotel, and when we set out the next morning it was in six cars with eighteen people.

The rest of the trip is a blur; sunlit valleys, every hill topped with a castle or an abbey, and the slopes below covered in vines; country restaurants where the regulars, exiled to the café opposite, glumly munched ham and cheese baguettes as we devoured their snails and *boeuf bourguignon*.

Unlike Charente, Burgundy was hot and humid. From eight in the morning until well after dark, the air hung on your back like an overcoat. But just as the heat started to stifle you, there was another vineyard, another chilly *cave*, another refreshing glass.

Until that trip, I'd always felt uncomfortable visiting vineyards. If you weren't an expert, able unerringly to tell Merlot from Pinot, you were by default a pisspot looking for cheap plonk. With Claude as our host, however, we were treated not as connoisseurs or drunks but honoured guests. Sweeping through the gates of the tiny vineyards, he led us into the main house, kissing the cook and embracing the owner like a member of the family. In the *caves* themselves, however, moist dark cellars packed with thousands of bottles, he was as devout as a bishop in church. By noon of the first day, our group had divided. The serious drinkers – about half – gathered around Claude, eavesdropping on his conversation with the owner, sniffing, sipping, nodding, spitting. The rest of us tried this but, at the first really delicious glass, drank rather than expectorated, fell to chatting, and quickly lost interest, if not consciousness.

Dieter, an old boyfriend of Marie-Do's friend Sophie, turned out to be a fan of modern sculpture and architecture, and knew intimately the world of Beuys and Christo. He had even visited Walter de Maria's *Lightning Field* in New Mexico's high desert. Maybe it was our conversations, but as we sped down the valley from vineyard to vineyard I became more conscious of the cellars than the wine. In the older ones, the range of slime on the bottles is astonishing. At Meursault, almost every bottle was covered in shaggy green moss, while the walls displayed three distinct varieties of mould: the first, soft, grey and spongy; the second, translucent and clear, like snot; and the third, slug-like, black and glistening. These coexisted in layers, so you stared through the shiny outer layers at formations that, if you drank enough, could resemble a skull in one of Roger Corman's cheesier film adaptations of Edgar Allan Poe.

The end of the first day found Marie-Do in the car, intently listening to the well-lubricated wife of a friend explain how her brother had probably murdered their ageing mother, while Dieter and I lay under a chestnut tree as he described how the four hundred polished stainless-steel poles of *Lightning Field*, arranged in a grid one mile by one kilometre, suck down electricity during a storm, when blue flame pirouettes in a diabolic gavotte over the invisible dance floor furnished by the plane of points. The hard cases lingered in the chilly cellar, trying to decide if the '82 tasted better from the vines grown on the chalkier slope rather than the clay. Occasionally, someone would climb unsteadily out of the dark, bottle in hand, and slur, 'Listen, ya *gotta* try this.'

How would Bert and Marlene have liked this trip, with gallons of high-priced wine, shaming confessions, often strongly psychosexual, meals heavy on paté, underdone beef and cream tarts, and not a scrap of Vegemite in sight? I was a long way from home, and that suited me just fine.

26

The Doctor Will See You Now

The old system of having a baby was much better than the new system, the old system being characterized by the fact that the man didn't have to watch.

Dave Barry

IN BILLY WILDER'S *ONE TWO THREE*, SET IN THE Berlin home of James Cagney, the local Coca-Cola branch manager, a German doctor arrives in evening dress, humming 'The Ride of the Valkyries' under his breath. He takes the patient's wrist, looks at his watch and shakes his head.

'It's bad?' asks Cagney's wife.

'*Ja*,' says the doctor. 'I'm missing the first act of *Die Walküre*.'

I used to think exchanges like this were a joke until

we started dealing with the French medical system over the birth of Louise.

With only weeks to go, Marie-Do was enormous. Louise seemed ready to emerge at the slightest encouragement. There were more and even longer consultations with Dr Bougevoy. The fibroma had shrunk as Louise grew, but it was still a factor. Maybe Marie-Do would need a Caesarean. Nothing could be decided, however, until D-day. Meanwhile, we shuttled between Bougevoy, the midwife and the obligatory pre-natal classes.

In films, the midwife is always a plump no-nonsense type in late middle age who rolls up her sleeves, orders the men out of the room, calling after them, 'Boil water; lots of it!' Mme Clément didn't fit this image. A chic woman in her late thirties, she clearly enjoyed a lively romantic life which placed considerable pressure on her time. Though she aspired to being well-organized, lugging about a ledger-sized diary as jammed with crossed-out and altered entries as one of Proust's proof sheets, she was forever ringing us up breathlessly to change appointments. We visualized her reaching for her mobile as her lover rolled a condom on, and murmuring, 'I must just reschedule my three-thirty.'

She could afford to be casual, because her classes, spelling out the basics of birth in almost kindergarten language, told the wives nothing they hadn't known since the age of five. Sex is freely and frankly discussed in every French home from the time a child can toddle. Well, at least it is by mothers and daughters. One could see, however, from the intent, not to say horrified, looks on the faces of the husbands that much of it was news to them, and alarming news at that. When Mme Clément asked how many prospective fathers wanted to be present at the birth, only a few nervous hands were raised. Mine was one of them.

We'd had detailed consultations with Bougevoy about the clinic where Louise was to be born. We mentioned a few, close to the centre of Paris.

'They are quite good,' she said. 'I have nothing against them . . .'

'But?'

'Well, there is only one where I feel entirely at home.'

Which was how we came to the Trianon.

Driving along the Seine on the road to Versailles, you arrive in Saint-Cloud. Cosying up to the gardens of a long-since-destroyed palace, the suburb is the most elegant of Parisian satellites, with a long tradition of discreet, expensive medical treatment (though it was also, during World War II, the place to which the Nazis brought the condemned to be executed). Jean Cocteau dried out from opium addiction in a clinic there, and, since French doctors are often both wealthy and cultured, the streets are filled with houses by Le Corbusier, Mallet-Stevens and Mies van der Rohe, most of them in the height of 1920s *art moderne*, with façades out of Mondrian.

In the nineteenth century, however, this was open woodland, and a prime spot for hunting. Which is why, in the midst of these cool monuments to the Bauhaus, one encountered the Clinique Trianon, a rococo hunting lodge in the style of Napoleon III that had become a maternity hospital. As we crunched up the gravel drive and mounted the wide steps, we could imagine the clomp of cavalry boots and the jingle of spurs.

The foyer was baronial, heavily panelled, with vast mirrors, their speckled silvering showing their age. A high-ceilinged waiting room was furnished with armchairs in pale-green brocade. Beyond was a garden with a fountain.

'One desires . . . ?' enquired the lady in black silk and pearls behind a *directoire* table. If Mrs Danvers, the sinister housekeeper of *Rebecca*, had a French niece, this was her.

Marie-Do, however, was not awed. 'M'sieur and Madame Baxter,' she said. 'We are expected.'

Not being married hadn't discouraged us from using this form. It wasn't out of any discomfort at being expectant unmarrieds – France had no shortage – but because of the effect of my surname. No less a writer than Marguerite Duras had adopted it for one of her plays, *Baxter, Vera Baxter*, and it also had some notoriety as the name of a film about a malign and super-intelligent dog, the ad line of which, '*Méfiez-vous du chien qui pense*' – 'Beware the dog that thinks' – followed me for years. Being a Baxter in France was regarded as *très snob*.

'But of course,' said mademoiselle. 'You wish to see our little *établissement*. I will call someone to show you round. Please wait in the salon.'

The salon was even more opulent close up. It looked like the set of a Stewart Granger cape-and-épée movie. On the wall, framed testimonials, all on heavily embossed letterheads, lauded the clinic's service. 'His Majesty wishes me to say...', 'The Princess has asked me to convey...', 'His Serene Highness is pleased to advise...' Framed next to some of these were photos of various ecstatic kings, sheiks, margravines and royal pretenders, all cuddling cross-looking babies wrapped in yards of shawl.

'Are you sure...' I started, but just then another of the ladies in Chanel and pearls arrived to give us the tour. After glancing in on various dispensaries and examination rooms, we were led to a set of baroque double doors at the end of a long corridor.

'And this', she said, flinging them open, 'is the most beautiful delivery room in France.'

She did not exaggerate. The fan-shaped chamber had once obviously housed a throne. Now there was only a bed, though a gigantic one, its head and foot boards elaborately inlaid with marquetry. Three armchairs, upholstered, like the walls, in green silk, faced it in a semicircle. This still left enough empty space for, if not a full orchestra, then at least a string quartet.

Later, neither of us could remember her actually saying that Louise would be born in this chamber, and that it would be our family and friends who sat in those armchairs while we displayed our child. But it was with memories of its splendour still in our minds that we were led into the office of the director to sign the papers.

The first time we really woke up was ten minutes later, when we faced the anaesthetist.

'Wong,' he said, shaking our hands. A young and cheerful East Asian, he seemed as improbable in these surroundings as he would have been at Versailles in the days of Marie Antoinette.

'So . . . when's the happy day?' he asked.

'Well, we don't exactly know . . .'

'Fine, fine,' he said briskly, grabbing a form. 'We can deal with that later. It's not this week, though, is it? Ha ha.'

He rapidly ticked off half a dozen boxes. 'Weight . . . Age . . . Not allergic to . . . No? Problem with anaesthesia . . . ? No? Fine. Fine.' He looked at me. 'You'll be there, Monsieur Baxter?'

'Oh, yes. Wouldn't miss it.'

'Well, the big question, then. You shooting video or just stills?'

I blanked for a moment. Was it a joke? But he wasn't laughing.

'You're allowed to have a camera in the delivery room?'

'Naturally. It would be a pity not to have a record of the birth of your . . .' he checked the forms, '. . . daughter.'

'Only stills, then. If that's OK.'

'Oh, yes. No problem,' he said. 'If you like, I can take them for you. Just give me your camera before you go in. Sometimes, you know, fathers . . .'

I wasn't sure whether he meant that they got too involved to take pictures, or fainted dead away, but it seemed just as well to cover both contingencies. 'Sounds fine,' I said.

'What sort of camera do you have?'

'An Olympus.'

'Yes.' He was decidedly unimpressed. 'Good little camera, of course.' He laid down his pen and slid open a drawer in his desk. Inside was a 35 mm Nikon with three sorts of flash and a battery of extra lenses and filters. Next to it was a semi-pro Sony video outfit, complete with lights. I'd seen TV stations with less gear. 'Nothing like a Nikon, though,' he said. 'Especially when the pressure's on.'

321

Before we left, we agreed that he would shoot the birth of Louise on both video and stills. Dr Wong clearly had the bucket in his hand and was headed for the well.

With the clinic sorted out, we went back to Bougevoy to talk about dates. She turned to her diary and indicated a swath of blank space towards the end of the month. 'You could have your daughter any time. Except the twenty-third. On that day I won't be available, nor will most of my colleagues.'

'Is there a congress somewhere?' Marie-Do asked.

She shrugged. 'What congress? It's Yom Kippur. And I don't recommend the first of November either.'

That was what they call in France '*Toussaint*' – All Saints' Day.

'Why?' I said. 'Are you superstitious?'

'Not at all. But it's the first weekend of the ski-ing season.'

Again, as with Wong, I thought she was joking. 'And that matters?'

'I wouldn't choose it,' she said, 'unless you want your baby delivered by the gardener.'

Registering at a clinic convinced everyone that the birth of Louise was imminent, and not just a notion we would get over in time. Heirlooms – an antique cradle, a pram, a cane carry-cot – were unearthed and ceremonially presented to us. Jean-Paul, my gruff uncle-in-law-to-be, offered us a painting as a birth gift – a considerable honour, given that his works sold for thousands of francs and President Mitterrand had just selected one of them for his personal Christmas card.

One sunny day, we drove to Richebourg to make our choice. Marie-Do's aunt Françoise opened the door of his studio. One end was filled with bulging portfolios of watercolours. 'I'd forgotten there were so many,' she said, gnawing her lip.

We hauled the portfolios out into the shade under a big cherry tree and started going through them, putting aside those that caught our eye, until the lawn was littered with fragments of colour. Jean-Paul is an artist of the old school. For him, Impressionism had come but not yet gone. There were no assaults on the eye; just a succession of reminders of what, to him, and to millions of other French people, the country is all about. Châteaux under snow, clematis spilling down a sun-drenched wall, piles of melons and flowers, villages like puddles of brown roofs amid the vineyards. We reduced our choices to ten, three, then one: an olive grove baking in Provençal sun, the sense of heat so vivid that one could smell the hot stone and wild thyme.

The trickle of gifts swelled to a flood. Just as

over-eager gardeners in my Australian country childhood would arrive in high summer with groaning baskets of tomatoes and chokos, abandoning them on our doorstep like orphans, French friends unloaded their baby clothes and equipment. Some days, we got home to find the doormat piled with bags and bundles like a Saint-Vincent-de-Paul shop.

There was just as much gratuitous health advice. For a country that places so much importance on what it puts into its stomach, the French are astonishingly prone to alternative medicine. Homeopathy and herbalism share space with modern medications on chemists' shelves. Herbal teas – *tisanes* – are offered as normally as coffee after meals, sometimes because the drinker likes the taste but just as often because many infusions, especially the mildly soporific camomile, have a medicinal effect.

This can backfire. A friend bought some tea that was supposed to be good for sore feet, and drank a cup before going to bed.

'The dreams I had!' he said. 'A blue rhinoceros stampeded through the bedroom. I saw rainbows.'

Next morning, his wife read the packet and pointed to the directions. You were supposed to soak your feet in it, not drink it.

One believer in homeopathy urged us to preserve the placenta after Louise's birth. It could be used for making medication for her in later life. Sceptically, we asked around, and found that this had been common practice for decades, but was now out of vogue in the era of Aids. We used this as an excuse for declining, though Wong's video coverage included a lingering close-up of the bloody mass lying in a dish. 'Bad sight of the week', as Clive James used to say in his TV reviews.

And then, suddenly, it was time.

After another of the interminable appointments with Bougevoy, she and Marie-Do emerged, chattering like finches. Marie-Do looked radiant and nervous at the same time.

'Is Thursday,' Bougevoy said. Tired of waiting, and presumably worried that a natural arrival might cut into her holiday plans, she'd decided to induce the birth.

But that was less than forty-eight hours away! We went home and I had a large cognac. Now that it was a *fait accompli*, the whole idea seemed both preposterous and alien. And I was actually to *see* it. What if a Caesarean was necessary? Could I stand to watch them slice open the abdomen of the woman I loved? Would I embarrass everyone by throwing myself across her body like the hero of a vampire movie as the hunters of the undead advanced with hammer and stake? I poured another cognac.

Marie-Do came out of the bedroom, the clinic's list of requirements in one hand, a bundle of clothes in the other. 'You look terrible,' she said, patting my head. 'It won't be so bad.'

Her calm made it worse. Only Valium got me to sleep, and by the time we drove out to Saint-Cloud on Thursday morning I was the classic expectant father, vibrating like a tuning fork.

'It will be some time yet,' the receptionist said kindly. 'Perhaps monsieur would care to take a walk?'

Obviously she'd given this advice before. The silent, empty streets of Saint-Cloud and the complacent façades of the villas were as calming as a warm bath. For the rest of the morning I walked, returned to the clinic, walked, returned ...

On the fourth occasion the receptionist looked up as I came in and said urgently, 'Monsieur, please see the nurse in room 17.'

Mouth dry, I hurried along the lofty corridor. What had gone wrong?

The nurse handed me a green hospital gown. 'Come with me.'

'It's started?'

She looked at her watch. 'Monsieur, it is almost finished. We thought perhaps you had changed your mind and gone home.'

In the corridor, I turned automatically towards 'the

326

most beautiful delivery room in France', but she steered me in the opposite direction. The wing we entered had no green silk upholstery or gilt armchairs. The ceilings were lower, the floor white vinyl, not clacking parquet, the lighting halogen. After turning half a dozen corners, we arrived at a door with a glass square let into it. She checked, then pushed it open.

Marie-Do was on the table, under a green sheet. She smiled weakly and I took her hand. Bougevoy was there too, in a green gown and a mask. Wong stood by Marie-Do, giving her a shot in the arm. I realized I'd forgotten my camera. I had time to kick myself mentally before I glanced at the table at my elbow. Sitting beside the stainless-steel surgical dishes were his Nikon and Sony video outfit. We were in good hands.

The rest was a kaleidoscope of impressions: sweat, strain, blood, tubes, needles, grunts, a moment when I was sent out of the room as Bougevoy used forceps to position the baby's head – apparently the point at which many fathers faint. Then more blood, more pain, and a sudden slick wet emergence, and a little naked creature choking and coughing on the green sheet while Marie-Do and I stared at one another in a delirium of delight.

27

The Long Conversation

Marriage is the triumph of imagination over intelligence. Second marriage is the triumph of hope over experience.

Oscar Wilde

THE PRIEST WHO WAS TO MARRY US STOOD IN THE doorway, a bit winded from the stairs. 'Hi,' he said. 'Call me Bruno.'

When you call up a man of the cloth, you don't expect the cloth to be denim. Though Father Bruno wore an antique wooden cross on a chain round his neck, his style was belligerently secular. The lumberjack shirt needed an iron, and his leather jacket looked like it had spent the last six months wedging the spare tyre in the boot of a clapped-out Datsun. But if you have to hire a priest, you take what you can get.

We showed him into an apartment that, for the first time in almost a year, was quiet. The last of the foreign visitors had left. My brother and sister, who'd come to view the family's only grandchild, were back in Australia, after an extended stay and some side trips, including a visit to the châteaux of the Loire. They'd booked into an aristocratic B&B, where my sister, trying to explain that she'd come to France to be a godmother, instead informed their baffled hosts that she was the Mother of God.

Half Paris had been round to view Louise. For weeks after her birth, the place reeked of roses and chocolates, and was strewn with stuffed animals like a battlefield after the Nursery War. Most of these were now heaped in the corner of her nursery, a bank of friendship to be drawn on in the years to come. Over her cot we'd hung the major Australian contribution, a mobile of brightly coloured felt koalas, kangaroos, platypuses and emus, our shot at instilling a sense of her shared heritage. Sadly for any innate Australian-ness, however, she preferred a distraught-looking rabbit in a flowered dress, ears standing straight up, and pinprick eyes like a speed freak's. If Norman Bates, the hero/villain of *Psycho*, had a doll as a child, this was it.

So far, Louise showed no signs of future genius, though she did quieten down when we played string quartets, giving us hope that she was musical. Still, one remembered that scene in *Humoresque* where J. Carroll Naish says to his wife of the infant who will grow into John Garfield, 'You thought he was musical when he followed the organ grinder, but it was the monkey he was interested in.'

We were more than ever delighted that Wong had taken coverage of the birth out of my hands. Not for the first time, movies organized human experience into a form in which it could be digested. Instead of a few blurred snapshots, we possessed a lavish coverage, discreetly edited to emphasize the joys of the day. The morning after, Wong shot reels of mother and child surrounded by bouquets – some of it through a hand-cut mask in the shape of a heart. With masses of flower beds for cutaways, a tinkly music track, and the nastier moments disguised by shooting through a fly's-eye filter that multiplied the image, obscuring the blood, the whole thing was reminiscent of a sanitary-towel commercial, but for our own daughter we were more than happy to suspend our critical faculties.

Bruno took a seat and, without hesitation, a Scotch too. He made the right goo-goo noises at Louise, now almost eight months old and gurgling contentedly in her crib. She was a charmer, well on the way to becoming so actinically blonde and blue-eyed that people would goggle at her in the street and little boys bend down shyly to kiss her.

'Now,' he said, opening his battered briefcase. 'I understand you want to get married.'

'And have Louise christened at the same time,' I reminded him.

'Baptized,' he corrected me. 'Yes.' He checked some notes. 'But . . . perhaps I've got this wrong. You don't want me to perform the marriage service? Only the baptism?'

We both nodded.

'Well, I could do both, you know,' he said. 'And as long as you have the church . . .'

It was the church – not the Church – that was at the root of our problem. An imposing fourteenth-century building with conical towers like something in Disneyland, it sat at the edge of Richebourg, the Montel family village where we'd decided we wanted to be married. If Louise was to be christened, that was obviously the place to do it.

But with numbers declining, the church had amalgamated Richebourg with two other parishes under a single priest who only said mass there one week in three. The Sunday we needed him wasn't one of them.

As with everything else in France, the family solved this problem. A cousin was a *grand fromage* in the Catholic hierarchy. A call produced a list of priests-for-hire, from which we chose Bruno.

'We really don't want to be married in church,'

Marie-Do said. 'We would prefer a civil ceremony at the *mairie*.'

'And then we thought we could go on to the church . . .' I said.

'Maybe in a procession . . .'

'. . . perhaps with a fiddler leading the way. Like in *Madame Bovary* . . .'

'. . . and have the christening . . . er, baptism there,' Marie-Do concluded.

Marie-Do had her mind set on an event that would somehow celebrate two important moments in her life with appropriate gravity. It was *her* wedding and *her* christening as much as mine or Louise's. Her family would be attending both, and these ceremonies would take place in the village where she had spent her holidays since childhood. The reception would be held in the garden of the house which her mother had inherited from her parents, and which they had in turn inherited from theirs. This was *pour le patrimoine, la gloire, la France*.

Everyone to whom we'd described this plan had greeted it with wholehearted enthusiasm. Of course it was a little unusual for the happy couple to be carrying their new-born child, but this was the 1990s after all.

Father Bruno, however, wasn't about to give up without a fight. 'I do an excellent wedding,' he said. He sounded like Marryin' Sam in Al Capp's comic strip *L'il Abner*, who offered a five-dollar wedding in which he stripped off and wrestled a bear.

He took a folder from his case, started to open it, then saw from the look on our faces that it was pointless.

'. . . But I also have a fine baptism service.' He chose another folder. 'I begin by greeting the parents at the door of the church. I ask them why they are there, and they reply with a statement of their belief in God and the divine order.' He looked at us. 'You *do* believe in God and the divine order?'

'Um . . . well . . .' we temporized.

'But . . . if you don't believe . . .' Bruno said hesitantly.

I felt sorry for him. 'It's not a question of not believing,' I said. 'It's a question of *what* one believes. C. S. Lewis says . . . or maybe it's Graham Greene . . .'

Graham Greene! Bruno's eyes glazed. He slumped a little, then dug in his bag again and came up with a book. 'This is a catalogue of . . . well, prayers, I suppose you could call them . . .' He paused. 'Prayers are all right?'

'Yeeessss . . .' we said cautiously.

He didn't even bother with the first five or six pages. After that, he started reading out snatches. For one reason or another, none of them sounded right. Towards the back, he found one we both felt worked for us. Essentially it said that, if you happened to believe there was a God, then you might conceivably, all other things being equal ... It combined pious sentiment with evasive detail as effectively as the best political campaign promises.

'That sounds fine,' I said.

'Yes.' He sighed, and closed the book. 'It's Protestant, actually.'

'So,' I said hurriedly, 'what happens after you meet us at the door?'

'Well, there are some more ... er, prayers. Then someone will read the lessons. Perhaps you have some friends who'd like ...'

News of our marriage reached every corner of the world, or so it seemed. Charles, an Englishman married to a Frenchwoman, sent an acceptance from Kathmandu, where he was deciphering ancient Nepalese inscriptions. Kelvin and Barbara, my friends from Los Angeles, announced they wouldn't miss it.

'Kelvin could read the first part of Genesis,' I said. '"In the beginning was the Word ..."'

'In *English*?' Bruno said.

'Naturally. The King James version.'

Listlessly he made a note. 'And then,' he continued, 'the actual immersion ...'

'*Immersion*?'

'Now, I know it sounds a bit alarming,' he said, 'but these days it's generally thought that trickling a little water on the baby's head is . . . well, perfunctory. It suggests none of the importance of the ritual. I prefer to immerse the baby completely.'

'In her clothes?'

'Naked, naturally.'

Marie-Do didn't quite fling herself defensively between Bruno and the cradle, but the effect was similar. 'A trickle of water will be fine,' she said.

Thinking of the icy Richebourg church, I agreed with her, though I was sorry in a way to have missed total nude immersion for Louise. Faced with that sort of affront, she was inclined to pee furiously. It would have been a memorable christening.

If finding a priest and a service was difficult, assembling the rest of the package was even more daunting.

Richebourg had a few amateur pianists and piano-accordeonists, but a strolling accordeonist called up memories of Place Dauphine and the grizzled old player who arrived under our window every day in summer, favouring the lunch crowd at the café with 'Kiss of Fire' until they paid him to go away. Nor did either of us care to be followed to the church by an open-sided lorry on which a piano player thumped out 'Roll Out the Barrel'. We tried Houdan, the larger town a few miles away. Nobody was registered in the phone book under 'Musicians', but fortunately the town's one-woman music school had a student skilful enough to play and walk at the same time – no mean feat for a violinist, apparently. The teacher agreed to coach her in an appropriate gavotte, and we crossed off that problem. Food, wine and the guest list followed.

Then, suddenly, it was July, and Marie-Do was gingerly putting on the wedding dress she'd found in Beaune on our jaunt to Burgundy, a 1920s creation in fragile lace that threatened to evaporate if she made a sudden movement.

The *mairie* was jammed. Cousins had appeared from every corner of France. Dozens of children sat in a square of sunlight streaming through the window of the building, a converted farmhouse that had been old when white men discovered Australia. Across the narrow courtyard, an open barn was kept as a sort of museum. Inside were ancient ploughs and harrows, and a huge cart, every part made by hand.

The mayor's *adjoint*, a pleasant woman in her forties, who was to perform the ceremony, stood up behind the table on which the register and other documents were arranged. Louise sat on my lap, a comfortingly solid presence, taking some interest in what was going on, but essentially involved in her own concerns. From time to time, she lifted a foot to her mouth and sucked her toes reflectively. Already, in some indefinable way, she looked, even sounded, French.

Marriage, said the *adjoint* during the ceremony, has been described as a long conversation. And between two writers, there should never be any lack of things to say.

The long conversation has been going on for more than fourteen years now, as much between myself and France as between myself and Marie-Dominique, and we haven't found ourselves lost for words yet. Occasionally, our voices – France's and mine – rise above a discreet murmur. When President Chirac elected to test his atomic weapons at Mururoa in 1996, for instance, my adoptive country and I had a bitter domestic row. But on the whole, I feel myself at home in France, and in the New Europe. There's nothing like marrying and having a child to instil a sense of belonging. Watching Louise grow has been like watching my own roots penetrating the French soil in a way they never quite managed to do in the hard-baked earth of Australia.

A few weeks after the wedding, I received a letter from Richard, an old friend in Australia. His daughter had come home from the National Film and TV School, where she was a student, and told him, 'You know John Baxter, don't you?'

'Of course,' Richard said.

'Well, Brian . . .' (an old antagonist who was teaching there) 'says to tell you that he's dead.'

Shocked, Richard phoned Brian, who said, without preamble, 'I suppose you heard about Baxter?'

'Yes,' said Richard. 'I'm devastated.'

'Oh, I don't know,' said Brian. 'It could happen to anyone.'

Taken aback, Richard said, 'I know you two had your differences, but frankly I'm surprised at how offhand you're sounding.'

'Well, it will change his life-style a bit.'

'You could put it that way,' said Richard.

Brian continued, 'Anyway Baxter has obviously fallen on his feet as usual.'

'How can you be so flippant about someone who's just died?' said a puzzled Richard.

'What do you mean "died"?' Brian laughed. 'I didn't say he was dead. I said he was a *dad*!'

And so I was.

Sources of Quotations

The author and publishers have made every reasonable effort to contact the copyright owners of the quotations reproduced in this book. In the few cases where they have been unsuccessful they invite copyright holders to contact them direct.

Algren, Nelson. Interview, 8 May 1981.

Aragon, Louis. *Paris Peasant*. Translated by Simon Watson Taylor. Jonathan Cape, London, 1971.

Baldwin, Neil. *Man Ray, American Artist*. Crown, New York, 1988.

Brassai. *The Secret Paris of the '30s*, Thames and Hudson, London, 2001.

Buchwald, Art. *Art Buchwald's Paris*. Little, Brown, Boston, Massachusetts, 1952.

Citizen Kane. Screenplay by Orson Welles and Herman J. Mankiewicz. RKO Pictures, 1941.

Cocteau, Jean. *Opium. The Diary of a Cure*. Translated by

Margaret Crosland and Sinclair Road. Peter Owen, London, 1957.

Coffee, Lenore. *Storyline. Recollections of a Hollywood Screenwriter*. Cassell, London, 1973.

Coward, Noël. *Private Lives*. Heinemann, London, 1930. Extract reproduced by kind permission of Methuen Publishing Ltd.

Dowse, Sara. *West Block*. Penguin Books, Melbourne, 1983.

Ellington, Edward Kennedy 'Duke', quoted in Nicholson, Stuart. *A Portrait of Duke Ellington. Reminiscing in Tempo*. Pan, London, 2000. Extract reproduced by kind permission of Macmillan UK.

Eluard, Paul. *Letters to Gala*. Paraon House, New York, 1989.

Fitzgerald, F. Scott. *The Great Gatsby*, Scribners, New York, 1925, and 'The Rich Boy', in *The Collected Short Stories*, Penguin, 1986. Fitzgerald / 22.10.04, reproduced by permission of David Higham Associates.

Flanner, Janet. *Paris Was Yesterday 1925–1929*. Popular Library, New York, 1968.

Gallant, Mavis. *Diaries*, on the web magazine *Slate* (Microsoft), 13 August 1997.

Greene, Graham. *Collected Short Stories*. Penguin, London, 1987. Greene / 24.09.04, reproduced by permission of David Higham Associates.

Hemingway, Ernest. *A Moveable Feast*. Jonathan Cape, London, 1964.

Holmes, John Clellon. *Displaced Person. The Travel Essays*.

University of Arkansas Press, 1987.

Kafka, Franz. *The Diaries of Franz Kafka 1910–1923*. Schocken, New York, 1968.

Kladstrup, Don and Petie. *Wine and War*. Broadway Books, New York, 2001.

Malraux, André. *Anti-memoirs*. Bantam, New York, 1970.

Maupassant, Guy de. *The House of Madame Tellier and Other Stories*. Everyman's Library, London, 1991.

Millet, Catherine. *La Vie Sexuelle de Catherine M*. Translated by Adriana Hunter. Serpent's Tail, London, 2002.

Molinier, Pierre, and Arsan, Emmanuelle. All quotes from both are taken from Petit, Pierre. *Molinier: Une Vie d'enfer*. Ramsay/Jean-Jacques Pauvert, Paris, 1992.

Monnier, Adrienne. *Rue de l'Odéon. Souvenirs de la Maison des Amis des Livres*. Albin Michel, Paris, 1960.

Moore, Marianne. *Collected Poems*. Macmillan, London, 1955.

Newby, Eric. *Something Wholesale. My Life and Times in the Rag Trade*. Picador, London, 1985. Reproduced by permission of HarperCollins UK.

Nin, Anaïs. *The Early Diaries of Anaïs Nin: 1927–1931. Volume 4*. Harcourt Brace Jovanovich, New York, 1985.

Ninotchka. Screenplay by Charles Brackett, Billy Wilder and Walter Reisch, based on an original story by Melchior Lengyel. Paramount Pictures, 1939.

Pascal, Blaise. *Pensées*. Published in 1660.

Paterson, Andrew Barton 'Banjo'. *The Man from Snowy*

River and Other Verses. Angus and Robertson, London, 1969.

Porter, Hal. *The Watcher on the Cast-iron Balcony*. Faber, London, 1963.

Proust, Marcel. *Remembrance of Things Past*. Translated by H. K. Scott Moncrieff. Thomas Seltzer, New York, 1925.

Ray, Man. *Self-portrait*. Little, Brown, Boston, Massachusetts, 1999.

Renoir, Jean, and Koch, Karl. *Rules of the Game. A Screenplay*. Simon and Schuster, New York, 1970.

Reynolds, Bruce. *Paris with the Lid Lifted*. George Sully and Co., New York, 1927.

Routh, Jonathan. *The Loos of Paris. Le Guide porcelaine*. Wolfe Books, London, 1966.

Sartre, Jean Paul. *Words*. Translated by Irene Clephane. Hamish Hamilton, London, 1964.

Stein, Gertrude. All quotes from *Gertrude Stein: Writings Vol. 1* (1903–1932). Library of America, New York, 1998.

Thurber, James. 'Memoirs of a Drudge' in *The Thurber Carnival*. Hamish Hamilton, London, 1945.

Toklas, Alice B. *The Alice B. Toklas Cookbook*. Michael Joseph, London, 1954. Reproduced by permission of Penguin UK.

Tynan, Kenneth. *Curtains*. Longmans, London, 1961.

Wells, H. G. *Things to Come. The Screenplay*. Cresset Press, London, 1935.